Test, Measurement and Evaluation in Physical Educaiton

Edited & Compiled by
Dr. P.L. Karad

KHEL SAHITYA KENDRA
7/26, Ansari Road, Daryaganj,
New Delhi-110002

Published by:
KHEL SAHITYA KENDRA
7/26, Ansari Road, Darya Ganj, New Delhi-110002
Ph.: (O) 011-65190343, 43551324, 42564726
(M) 9811088729, (Fax) 011-42564726
(Res.) 47091605
E-mail: khelsahitya1@rediffmail.com
Web: www.khelsahitya.com, www.kskpublisher.com

ISBN : 978-81-7524-601-0

PRINTED IN INDIA 2026

Printed by:
ASIAN OFFSET PRINTERS,
Delhi

Laser Typeset by :
Jain Media Graphics, Delhi

Price: Rs. 1,400/-

CONTENTS

1

TEST AND MEASUREMENT— AN INTRODUCTION

History reveals that as humans became more civilized they also become more scientific, and subsequently sought more exact ways to measure. The history of measurement in physical education and sport has paralleled the growth and development of research and the rise of the field to a more respected position in the educational spectrum. For many decades knowledge and skills in the area of measurement have been considered important for graduate study in the field of physical education and sport. But today measurement skills and knowledge are also deemed a necessary part of the professional preparation of sport management professionals. Employers assume that candidates for positions of leadership in the field of physical education and sport understand the potential value of accurate measurement, are familiar with a variety of measurement tools, know how to administer tests and inventories, and can evaluate the results of such measurements.

The Language of Measurement

There are several key terms that often cause confusion among students beginning their study of measurement. Already in the two paragraph that you have just read, you came across the words, "tests", "inventories", "measurement", and "evaluation". We suspect that you have some idea of what is meant by of these terms, but you may need some clarification to understand exactly how these terms are used in this area of study.

Laboratory and Field Tests

There are many highly sophisticated and precise tests, e.g., treadmill tests and reaction time tests, that can only be given in exercise physiology or motor learning laboratories. Laboratory tests typically require specialized equipment and specialized training on the part of test administrator. Another distinguishing feature of laboratory tests is that they are usually administered to only one person at a time. These features make laboratory tests impractical for use by most physical education and sport practitioners. The alternative to laboratory tests is field tests.

Additionally, they are time-effective, in that they can often be administered to a group of individuals simultaneously. Field tests must, of course, be accurate measures of the characteristic under investigation, but often these measures are less precise than laboratory tests of the same characteristic. Depending upon the intended use of the measurement, however, this lack of precision is often deemed acceptable or even preferable due to the gained advantages in practically. This text is devoted to the presentations and discussion of field tests appropriate for use by the physical education and sport practitioner in setting such as schools, camps, YMCAs, YWCAs, private clubs, and gymnasiums.

Norm-Referenced and Criterion-Referenced Tests

There are two broad classifications of measurement instruments that are referred to as norm-referenced and criterion-referenced. These are also important terms for the beginner in measurement. Norm-referenced tests are designed by the test developer to measure individual differences so one person's score on such a test can be compared to the scores of other similar persons who have taken the same test. These scores are known as norms. From tables of norms, one's score is interpreted in terms of how it compares to the scores of other similar person's scores. The standardized tests that you have taken through your years of schooling were norm-referenced tests. Perhaps you remember being told that you scored, for example, at the 85th percentile; this meant that you scored equal to or better than 85% of the similar students. The majority of physical education and sport tests that have been developed to date are norm-referenced. In recent years, however, more and more criterion-referenced tests have been developed. In this type of testing test scores are compared, not to each other; but to a standard that is referenced to a criterion behaviour.

The criterion behaviour is a satisfactory level of performance, so performers whose scores meet or exceed the standard are claimed to be masters and those whose scores fall below the standard are nonmasters. There are no limits to the number of persons who may achieve mastery on the test. In fact, a teacher may be proud indeed if all of his/her students meet or exceed the standard on a criterion-referenced test in which the standard is keyed to a meaningful criterion behaviour. American Red Cross certification tests and refereeing certification tests are examples of criterion-referenced tests.

Why Test and Measurement

For every student the word "test" surely conjures up a vivid picture of writing answers to questions presented on a page of paper. However, in the study of measurement in physical education and sport, "test" is applied in a broader sense. Test refers to any specific instrument, procedure, or technique used by a test administrator to elicit a response from the test taker. Tests, always specify a particular protocol, but vary greatly in their form. In physical education and sport contexts, some tests are paper-and-pencil instruments that require a written response directly from the student, athlete, or client.

Many of our tests, however, employ physical devices such as stop-watches, tape measures, skinfold callipers, or even treadmills. Some tests restructure the normal sport environment with cones, ropes and targets with associated point values. Many of our tests yield objective estimates of the characteristic of interest; others, known as rating scales yield subjective estimates. Most physical education and sport tests and rating scales attempt to assess a characteristic of an individual student, athlete, coach, or administrator, but some tests and rating scales are designed to assess characteristics of groups, teams, and programs. "Test" generally is used to describe instruments, procedures, and techniques that result in responses that can be evaluated in terms of their correctness.

Instruments, procedures, and techniques that assess affective qualities of one's interests, attitudes, beliefs or personal values can be included within the general definition of "test". They are however, more commonly referred to as inventories to emphasize that they do not have clearly defined right and wrong answers. In this text, measure is used to connote tests, rating scales, and inventories. When speaking collectively about different tests, scales, and inventories, "measurement instruments" and "assessment tools" are used synonymously. The term battery is used to refer to a group of several tests, scales or inventories intended to be administered in succession to the same subject or subjects. The group of measures is usually designed to accomplish a closely related set of measurement objectives. Measurement refer to the process of administering a test or inventory. The usual result of measurement is quantitative data that are characteristically expressed in numerical form. These data are referred to as scores.

Qualitative assessments usually result in assignment of words or phrases such as "excellent" or "is characteristic of the student". Evaluation refers to the process of interpreting the results of measurement. Test scores and qualitative assessments are evaluated by making comparisons with preconceived criteria in order to make judgments about people or appropriate courses of action. In other words, evaluation is the process of making qualitative judgments based upon measurement evidence. But then, these judgments are usually subjected to careful examination that often require another round of measurement and re-evaluation.

Brief History of Measurement in Physical Education and Sport

Testing and measurement in physical education and sport in America is only a little over a century old. Its history can be divided roughly into periods extending from about 1860 to the present. These periods can be loosely categorized by the prevailing interests of the times. It should be realized, however, that there are no clear-cut lines of demarcation separating them. These periods merely indicate the times when the specific measurement types came into prominence. The first three periods clearly reflected an emphasis on the physical capacity of humans, while the latter periods indicate emphases on efficiency and performance abilities, and on the "wholeness" of the physical performers.

Strength Measurement

Around 1880, interest in anthropometry began to wane as interest in strength testing waxed. Although Hitchcock had included some strength testing in his program at Amherst, the real pioneer in this area was Sargent. Sargent, along with an anthropologist named William T. Brigham, experimented with the newly invented dynamometer, and devised a strength test battery comprised of measures of the legs, back, hand grip, and arms. His strength test battery also included a measure of lung vital capacity, made possible by the invention of the spirometer. Strength testing has never truly gone out of vogue in the measurement area, although it never again received the attention that it did in the period of 1880 to 1910. In the 1920s interest in strength testing was revived to some extent and several new tests were developed. The best known of these was one by Frederick Rand Rogers. His scheme of testing differed from others in the manner of test construction. His test was devised in a scientific manner and was shown to have high relationship with general athletic ability.

Roger's ingenious use of the Strength Index and the Physical Fitness Index made his test one of the true classics in the field. Strength testing today occurs both in the exercise physiology laboratory and in the gymnasium and weight training room. In the laboratory, this testing employs dynamometers, cable tensiometers, and various electronic machinery such as the Cybex. Field tests of strength require the performer to lift maximal loads of free weights or plates on Universal or Nautilus machinery.

Sports Skills Testing

The initial use of sports skills tests was the Athletic Badge Test in 1913. However, great interest i this testing area did not develop until the 1920s. Brace presented one of the earliest skills tests for basketball. Skills test to measure achievement in specific sports were devised by statistically determining a few simple test items that could effectively measure the total activity of that sport.

During the decades of the 1920s, 1930s and 1940s, tests were devised for nearly every sport, and norms were established for appropriate age and gender. However, sports skills test construction continues today because these early tests were designed to reflect the rules and techniques of their day. Many sports have undergone major rule and technique changes, so many older tests are no longer appropriate. Furthermore, the norms of decades ago often no longer match the performance skills of modern sport participants. Today's sports skills tests are being developed against even more stringent standards and by using even more sophisticated measurement techniques. AAHPERD-sponsored committees have gotten together experts from across the nation to develop quality sports skills tests. These new tests are characterized by conscientious presentation of validity and reliability evidence and by updated performance norms.

Anthropometric Measurements

The oldest form of measurement, known as anthropometry, is the measurement of human body parts. Anthropometry was of interest in ancient India and later in Egypt where study was undertaken to find one part or component of the body that could be used as a common measure for all body parts. Egyptians, for example, believed that the length of the middle finger could be used as a common measure; the knee should be 5 finger lengths from the ground and one's arm reach should be 8 finger lengths. The early Greeks also practised anthropometry in their studies of body proportions.

Hippocrates, the "father of modern medicine" believed that body symmetry and proportion were related to health. Greek artists studied body symmetry and proportion for aesthetic reasons. The Greek athlete alone revived the gods as subjects for sculpturing. Interest in anthropometry is also responsible for the beginning of the testing and measurement movement in physical education in the United States. In 1861 Edward Hitchcock, a medical doctor, was hired at Amherst at the director of student health. He initiated yearly measurements of all students. His detailed records included such factors as height, weight, age, reach, girth, vital capacity, and selected strength measures. The ultimate purpose of Hitchcock's measurement was to define the ideal physical proportions of man. To the work of Hitchcock was added the significant efforts of Dudley Allen Sargent.

Sargent was hired in 1878 to oversee the health of students at Harvard University, Delhi his tenure there, Sargent devised more than 40 different measurements of anthropometric types and used them to prescribe a program of exercise for each student. His system was subsequently adapted for use in both public schools and colleges and in YMCAs across the nation. Sargent actively promoted testing and measurement by publishing the first manual on measurement and by writing numerous articles for professional journals. Anthropometric measurement is still practised today. There are, however, few physical educators who identify themselves as specialists in this area of measurement. The anthropometric researchers of today usually focus their attention on elite athletes and dancers. These researchers have added body fat measures to the traditional measures of height, weight and girth.

Physical Fitness Testing

In a sense, a form of fitness testing has always been done. Individuals have been assessed for their ability to meet the requirements of their environment. This was true in World War II, which followed in the wake of two decades of scientific test-making in physical education. Great stress was placed on fitness, and this emphasis brought about a rush to develop fitness tests. These tests were geared to the needs of the war era. They could be mass administered and easily scored and interpreted. All branches of the armed forces devised fitness tests with appropriate norms for both genders. A number of such tests were also developed for school and college groups. Among the latter were Cureton's 14-Item Motor Fitness Test at Illnois and Bookwalter's Indiana Motor Fitness Index. After World War II, President Eisenhower became an advocate for the development of the physical fitness of school-aged American children. His advocacy was largely in response to the shocking results of the Kraus-Webber Test, which suggested that most American children were less than minimally fit, and significantly less fit than European children.

AAHPER got into the act in 1958 with publication of the Youth Fitness Test for school-aged children. This test has undergone revisions through the years, but in general it has always attempted to measure physical characteristics related to effective athletic performance. In the 1970s a major philosophical influence drastically changed the focus of fitness testing. It changed from the assessment of qualities of athletic performance to that of health-related performance. In 1980, AAHPERD developed the Health-Related Physical Fitness Test. This test include only components believed to be related to health and functional capacity.

In 1988, AAHPERD revised this test and titled it

Physical Best. The emphasis on health-related physical fitness remained the same; however, it cut new ground by setting criterion standards below which one's health or functional capacity would likely be negatively affected.

Program Evaluation

As school programs in physical education grew in number and quality, there was a corresponding need to evaluate them to answer the calls for accountability of tax dollars. In the 1930s the subjective elements that go into program evaluation began to be quantified. The first such quantitative device to receive wide recognition was devised by LaPorte and his committee. Since that time program evaluation instruments have been developed for nearly all school and non-school physical education and sport programs. These include program evaluation instruments for all levels of school physical education, intramurals, athletics, and youth sport. One recent aspect of this area of measurement is a focus on the processes of effective teaching and coaching. Instruments have been developed that require observation of these physical activity leaders as they perform their leadership roles.

Cardiovascular Measurement

At the turn of the century, measurement interests again began to shift. The new interests were concerned with the efficiency of heart and vessel function. Just as strength testing had taken on new meaning with the invention of the dynamometer, cardiovascular testing changed as a result of Mosso's invention of the ergograph in 1884. Physiologists studied the effects of fatigue and the relationship of muscular work to the circulatory system, while physical educators sought methods of testing the cardiovascular efficiency of the body. The first test of cardiac function, the Blood Ptosis Test, was published by C.W. Crampton in 1905. Crampton's seminal test was based upon changes in heart rate and blood pressure as one assumes a standing position from a starting supine position. E.C. Schneider designed a similar but a more sophisticated test that was used during World War I to assess the fitness of military aviators. This test included a measure of one's ability to recover to normal after a measured exercise bout.

In 1931, W.W. Tuttle presented his Pulse-Ratio Test that specified a block stepping protocol to standardize exercise bouts. Tuttle's test influenced L. Brouha and his co-workers in their 1943 development of the Harvard Step Test. This test subsequently inspired the development of less strenuous field tests of cardiovascular function such as the Tecumseh Step Test and the Queen's College Step Test. The Balke Treadmill Test was developed in 1952. This development led the way to increased sophistication in the laboratory measurement of cardiovascular function related to exercise stress. Despite strong validity and reliability evidence, sophisticated laboratory tests that specialized training and expensive equipment are clearly not feasible for the practitioner.

The need for a valid and reliable field test of cardiovascular fitness was, perhaps, best met through the effects of Dr. Kenneth Cooper. In 1968 he published Aerobics in which he proposed a practical field test of cardiovascular fitness that he had originally developed for the United States Air Force. His test required a simple-to-administer, 12-minute walk/run during which performers tried to cover as much distance on a measured track as possible. It seemed too good to be true, but Cooper's 12-Minute Walk/Run Test was validated against treadmill performances in the laboratory. Since that time, numerous other walk/run field tests have been developed. Cooper himself even developed alternate versions of his test, including a 1.5-Mile Run Test, a 3-Mile Walk Test, a 12-Minute Swim Test, and a 12-Minute Cycle Test.

Social Values Measurement

During the 1920s attention was first directed toward some of the intangibles that had been attributed to well-directed physical education programs. Since character, personality and other social values had been considered outcomes of the new sports and games program and where stated as objectives, it seemed logical that status and improvement in them should be measured in some way. McCloy again made a major contribution to testing by developing one of the first character inventories. B.E. Blanchard devised a Behaviour Rating Scale for the measurement of character and personality in physical education classes. In more recent years, affective measurement has focused on the interests and motivations of performers and on the self-concept and body image of participants in physical activity programs. As researchers in the sub-discipline of sport psychology identified psychological constructs that they wished to study, they typically had to figure out ways to measure these abstract phenomena. Sport psychology researchers have been responsible for the development of many new affective measurement instruments.

Athletic Ability Testing

Interest in athletic ability testing was largely a result of the "new physical education" movement inspired by the philosophies of Wood, Gulick, and Hetherington. As sports and games became an important part of the school physical education curriculum, concomitant interest in the measurement of athletic ability developed.

However, this movement was not restricted to the public schools. Even before the turn of the century of the YMCA and the Turners had developed pentathlon tests of athletic achievement. The Athletic Badge Tests were developed in 1913 by the American Playground Association with standards for both boys and girls. Test items were heavily weighted with track and field events along with a few items like the rope climb and vault. Colleges began to follow the lead of other organizations because even leaders in the strength testing movement such as Sargent had begun to realize that strength per se was not as important as the way strength was used for effective performance. The 1920s were particularly significant for the field of measurement. Before this period much of the work done in measurement was unscientific and based on empiricism.

Standards were arbitrarily established by the test maker in most instances and were not clearly identified. No provision was made for increments in scoring tables as performance reached the more difficult levels of attainment, nor were there ways to equate scores on different tests. During this era, however, new statistical techniques became available and more scientifically constructed tests were developed. Validity and reliability of tests were improved and better means of developing scoring tables were used. Pioneer work in the field of scientific test construction was done by C.H. McCloy of the University of Iowa. He developed achievement scales for boys in track and field, gymnastics, games and swimming. Some new luminaries appeared on the scene with tests in the areas of motor ability and performance.

David K. Brace of Texas developed a motor ability test that was later revised by McCloy and became known as the Iowa Revision of the Brace Test. This revised test was termed a motor educability test, claiming to measure one's potential to learn new motor skills. Frederick Cozens devised a test of general athletic ability for college men. All of these were developed in accordance with the newest scientific approaches in research and statistics. These early tests served as models for modern test construction. In the late 1920s and early 1930s, the concept of measuring general qualities was explored further and well-constructed tests were developed in general motor ability, motor capacity and motor educability.

McCloy again revised a test developed by Brace, and published the General Motor Capacity Test. This test presumably was a test of innate performance; it yielded a Motor Quotient that is the motor analogue of the Intelligence Quotient. In the same era, Humiston developed a motor ability test for women. The popularity of the notions of general motor ability, motor capacity and motor educability continued into the late 1950s. A widely used motor ability test for college men and junior and senior high school boys was designed by Barrow in 1953. Subsequent motor learning research evidence began to suggest the high task specificity of motor skills. As a result, the use of generalized motor measurements is today questioned by many measurement of experts.

Knowledge Testing

Knowledge testing has probably always been a part of school physical education programs; however, most attempts to measure knowledge have been done through the use of teacher-made tests. Although these tests serve an important function, they have not been scientifically constructed and devised. Standardized tests are certainly a rarity in physical education and sport, though a few notable exceptions exist. The first knowledge test reported in the literature was a test of knowledge related to basketball, developed by J.C. Bliss. In 1969 AAHPER published Knowledge and Understanding in Physical Education, presenting the body of knowledge for elementary and secondary schools. The Education Testing Service of Princeton, New Jersey, developed standardized tests from this publication. These tests became known as the Cooperative Physical Education Tests. Unfortunately these tests never gained much popularity. AAHPERD now boasts a series entitled Basic Stuff that identifies the essential body of knowledge in six sub-discipline areas of physical education and sport. As yet, no standardized tests have been developed from these materials.

Who Uses Measurement?

Measurement is a universal practice, something that all persons engage in either informally or formally. Professionals in the field of physical education and sport are no exception. Instructors, administrators, coaches, sport performers, and researchers use measurement for a variety of purposes and in a variety of settings. They perform measurement in both school and non-school settings such as YMCAs, YWCAs, private health clubs, employee fitness centres, and summer camps.

What Sorts of Things are Measured?

When an individual is the object of measurement in a physical education or sport setting, the purpose is usually to assess learning or achievement of the individual in one of the three educational domains. Tests in the psychomotor domain measure motor skill, motor development, and physical fitness. Psycho-motor tests are generally of two kinds—those that test the product of a motor performance (like the speed, accuracy, or consistency of a tennis serve) and those that test the process that is employed in the performance (e.g., determining the pattern that is used in p.. forming the tennis serve). Cognitive tests measure acquired knowledge relating to techniques, rules and strategies of sports, and concepts relating to the development and maintenance of physical fitness and the prevention of injuries. Tests in the affective domain assess interests, attitudes, feelings, and values in relationship to purposeful physical activity. Some of these tests also assess psychological constructs such as aggressiveness, exercise addiction, and pre-competitive anxiety. Individuals can also be the object of measurement when job effectiveness is assessed.

Paper-and-pencil instruments have been developed to measure the effectiveness of physical education teachers, coaches, and athletic administrators. Groups are sometimes the object of measurement in physical education and sport. A group that we find most interesting is, of course, the athletic team. Qualities of the team, such as team cohesiveness, are assessed with the ultimate purpose of determining ways to optimize team performance. Measurement is also applied to athletic, instructional, and recreational programs as part of an overall evaluation process. A program may be evaluated in one of two ways. First, it may be evaluated when measurement techniques are applied directly to components of the program; second, it may be evaluated indirectly by measuring the status and progress of the products of the program, i.e., the participants or graduates.

Why Measure?

Since measurement is a universal practice engaged in by humans in many aspects of their lives, there are many possible answers to the questions, "Why measure?". In general, however, most intentional human behaviour consists of a process that involves establishing of some value or criterion, the exercising of a judgment, and a follow-up involving a choice. Most of the time this process is informal. For instance, in all sports, evaluations occur whenever a player or a coach must make a choice—when a golfer selects a 5-iron rather than a 6-iron, when a basketball player shoots rather than passes to a team-mate, when a football coach decides to go for the fourth down yardage rather than punting. Physical education and sport professionals face a myriad of choices as they go about performing their jobs. Most of the time the evaluations of their choices will be informal.

Information evaluations can sometimes, however, be inaccurate and even biased because of their highly, subjective nature. Formal measurement is a perquisite to evaluations that are more likely to be honest and accurate. So perhaps a general answer to the question of "Why measure?" is "to formalize the evaluation process". It must be realized, though, that tests are merely the tools of measurement. The test itself never make decisions; the test user does. There are, however, more specific answer to the question of "Why measure?" that are width discussing. These answers are based upon the ways in which test results are used by physical education and sport professionals.

Grading

Test scores are used more often for grading purposes than for any other reason. In one way this appears sound because it assures at least some objectivity in the assignment of grades. In another way it may be questionable if this is the sole application of test scores. Grades probably should not be based exclusively on test scores, nor should test scores be relegated to this one narrow purpose. Grades can reflect attainment, improvement, and a standard of achievement. They are educational indices to help students understand levels of competency.

Grades are relative, however, because they must be interpreted in relation to the tests used, the group tested, and the standards that the teacher believes to be appropriate for a particular group.

Guidance

Guidance concerns are so interwoven throughout the whole realm of test scores and their uses that it is difficult to delineate them. A series of test scores can provide a cumulative record to provide a complete picture of the physical, social and academic status of an individual. The more complete the information, the better the counselling can be for that individual. Of particular value to instructional counselling in physical education and sport are diagnostic tests, prognostic tests, and proficiency tests. Diagnostic tests are designed to identify weaknesses. On the basis of diagnostic test results, fitness instructors, PE teachers, and coaches can prescribe exercises, learning activities, or skill drills that are needed to remedied the identified weakness.

Prognostic tests are designed for determining levels of potential skill development. Such tests are concerned with capacity and ultimate skill attainment. As predictors of skilful players, they could be especially valuable to coaches. Unfortunately, there are only a few good prognostic tests available at the present time. The area of test development needs much work. Proficiency tests are beginning to receive considerable attention. They are being used to determine placement at appropriate skill levels and to justify exemption from required coursework. For example, on the basis of his or her score on a tennis proficiency test a student could be placed in an intermediate tennis class or be excused from a required beginning tennis course. Proficiency tests are criterion-referenced, based on the concept of mastery learning.

Research

The research uses of the test results in physical education and sport are many and varied. Practitioners and theoreticians in all of our sub-disciplines conduct research. The variables under investigation are often operationally defined in terms of scores generated by a particular measurement instrument. Thus, test results generally provide the data that are analysed in order to answer the problem under investigation. Researchers realize that the quality of their research hinges on the quality of the data they collect. They are, therefore, concerned that the measurement tools are good and that they are administered accurately.

Psychomotor Learning

Motor learning specialists have determined that performance feedback is essential for learning to occur. Through the use of lines, ropes, cones and targets, sport skill tests often provide greater performance feedback than is available in the natural sport environment. Therefore, sport skill tests can be used by instructors and coaches to create an effective and interesting practice situation for learners. The scores, per se, do not even have to be tallied or recorded. This is also true for fitness tests. Most fitness tests require a maximum effort on the part of the test taker. As such, the tests themselves can be used by fitness leaders to provide a good workout for the participants.

Motivation

The use of test results for motivational purposes is

somewhat nebulous, but nevertheless significant. Students and players often can be motivated to perform at their maximum because of their inherent competitive spirit, because they are anxious to make the best possible showing, and because the activity itself is important to them. This is true for performers of all ages. They should, however, be encouraged to perform, well as they compete against themselves and not always against other members of the group. Self-improvement and self-realization are the keys to effective motivation through the use of testing.

Classification

Classification implies a grouping of individuals for instruction or activity. At times, performers of similar skill or fitness levels are grouped to enhance instruction, practice or competition. This is done with the belief that such a grouping better meets the needs of the participants than would a grouping in which participants have a heterogeneous mix of skill and/or fitness levels. There are times, however, when a heteogeneous grouping is desired, for example, to form teams of near-equal abilities or to enhance interpersonal relationships. Classification is accomplished by using, either alone or in combination, basic ability tests, fitness tests, sport skill tests, social scales, and attitude scales. Unfortunately, classification is one application of test scores that is not used to its fullest by physical education instructors and coaches because of the perceived inconvenience of testing. Many times, a quickly administered observational screening test is all that is required to make sound grouping judgments. The instructional or competitive benefits derived from better groupings are usually worth the time and effort.

Vocational Suitability

Physical performance tests are increasingly being

used by employers to determine applicant's suitability for particular jobs. Military fire, and police personnel are now commonly subjected to such testing, though performance testing also occurs in the private business sector. Knowledge tests are also used to ensure qualified practitioners and professionals in some areas of physical education and sport. Certification tests are now regularly being used by the aerobics industry. And, the American College of Sports Medicine has developed certification tests for many areas of sports medicine.

Affective and Cognitive Learning

There are other uses of tests that are especially appropriate for physical education teachers. Tests can be used to stimulate class discussions about issues related to personal health, sportsmanship, or attitudes toward competition. Similarly, tests can be used by a teacher to illustrate bodily functions and stimulate cognitive understanding of exercise physiology.

When is Measurement Done?

You can surely guess that the answer to this question is, "Anytime". Testing can be done daily, monthly, yearly, or over even longer time periods. Testing should be done when it can contribute positively to instructional, recreational, or athletic objectives. It should not be done when it detracts from more important learning or performance goals. In general it is believed that testing should take no more than 10% of the allotted time for a program. This is, however, only a rough guideline. An important distinction is made between summative and formative evaluations. These terms have to do with the timing of testing. Summative evaluations are the result of testing that is conducted at the end of an identified class or program. This is the commonly used pattern of test administration when tests are used for grading purposes or for evaluating programs of instruction. Formative evaluations rely on testing at a variety of times during the ongoing program, i.e., while skills, knowledge, and/or attitudes are still developing. Both measurement and learning specialists strongly endorse the use of formative evaluations. And, believe it or not, students actually appreciate tests that give them important feedback about their performance in a class while there is still time for them to work on any problems before the unit ends.

How is Measurement Done?

Measurement data derive from a variety of testing techniques. Some of these techniques yield data that are numerical, i.e., quantitative in nature and can be tabulated and statistically summarized. Other techniques yield data that are generally in the form of written words and phrases, i.e., qualitative. No one technique will be best for use in all situations. A person knowledgeable and skilled in measurement will have the ability to discern which of the many available techniques will best meet the needs of a particular measurement and evaluation situation. Following are brief descriptions of several types of data collection tools that the measurement specialist in physical education and sport has at his or her disposal.

Physical Performance Tests

In general, these types of tests have a structured protocol under which the test taker is required to perform a physical task within strictly specified conditions. The resulting product of the performance is measured. This measurement is then compared to the preconceived definition of a "good" performance upon which the test was designed in order to evaluate the quality of the physical performance.

Sociometric Inventories

Sociometric inventories allow for measurement of the amount and nature of organization within a social group in order to identify patterns of relationships among the group members. The sociometric inventory starts by asking group members to indicate their feelings about each other. Its results simply and graphically show who would like to be grouped with whom for a particular activity. It can be carried a step further to permit the group members not only to choose those with whom they want to be grouped, but also to reject those with whom they do not want to be grouped. In the final analysis, sociometric instruments indicate which individuals are accepted and which are not. These findings can provide the basis for classification of group members into cooperative and productive units, location of group leaders and social "outcasts" or "loners", and identification of gangs or cliques that might resist integration into the total group. Sociometry, the process of using and interpreting sociometry inventories, might be used for a variety of social groups in physical education and sport settings. Examples of such groups include athletic teams, athletic coaching staffs, physical education classes, physical education department faculty members, pre-professional clubs or professional organizations, and employee fitness workout groups.

Anecdotal Records

The anecdotal record is a means of recording the actual behaviour of a student, athlete, or client. Perhaps its techniques apply best in the area of affective learnings, although its use is certainly not limited strictly to this area. The anecdotal record may be defined as a written objective record of an incident in the life of a student/athlete/client as observed by a teacher/coach/leader. Anecdotal information becomes much more meaningful when a number of observations are made because it is always dangerous to draw a conclusion from too few samples. When a number of observations are made, patterns of conduct emerge and behaviour trends become quite evident, thus giving greater insight into the problems and social adjustments of the person being observed. The anecdotal record should never be a time-consuming task for the report is a short, concise description of significant incidents. This technique in physical education and athletic settings should probably not be applied to an entire class or team, but should be used in special cases in order to better understand certain students with special problems.

Written Tests and Self-Report Scales

These measurement techniques require a written response on the part of the examinee. After a dozen or so years of schooling we are sure that you are intimately familiar with written tests and realize that the many different types of written tests vary greatly in the response requirements for the examinee. Objective tests typically require the examinee to indicate the true or best choice from among two or more alternatives. Subjective tests require the respondent to provide a word, phrase, or entire essay in response to a particular query. Written tests are used to measure one's achieved knowledge or aptitude for cognitive learning, so responses are evaluated in terms of their correctness. Self-report scales differ from written tests in that they are used to measure attitudes, beliefs, feelings, and opinions of the respondent.

Although, preconceived desirable responses are generally identified, such affective responses cannot be evaluated strictly in terms of correctness. In fact, great care must be taken by the administrator of a self-report scale to communicate the importance of an honest response on the part of the examinees. Examinees must be thoroughly convinced that no harm will come to them should their responses be deemed undesirable. If this is not achieved, the self-report scale becomes useless as a measurement instrument.

Autobiographies

Teachers and coaches use various means to understand their charges. If educators are to make the fullest use of their opportunities for guidance, they should understand more about each individual's needs, problems, and ambitions. A technique designed to obtain some of this information is the autobiography. It is similar to the anecdote except that it is written by the student/athlete instead of the teacher/coach. An autobiography is a self-written story about some phase of the writer's own life and experience. If stories are done well, they give a good picuure of attitudes, feelings, and actions concerning the indicated phase or topic addressed. For instance, the teacher may want to learn something about Jerry's past experience in fitness activities and his attitude toward fitness. Jerry's autobiography will reveal much insight into what he has done to become fit and the importance he attaches to fitness.

Questionnaires and Interviews

These measurement tools can obtain information directly from individuals regarding the present status of their behaviour, beliefs, attitudes, or interests. Questions are asked directly of the respondent. In the case of questionnaire the questions and answers are in a written form; the interview might be rightfully termed an "oral questionnaire", for the questions and answers are exchanged orally either in a personal face-to-face interview or over the telephone. These measurement techniques have been used extensively in physical education and sport research, for they can be designed to answer nearly any research question. They are also a favourite measurement technique of administrators.

However, there is a major concern associated with their use, for questionnaires and interviews are seldom subjected to testing to determine whether or not the questions actually yield consistent and honest answers that can be interpreted in an unbiased fashion. It is recommended that if an alternate method for obtaining the same measurement data exists that has been subjected to such quality testing, that one refrain from use of home-made questionnaires and interviews. Or, if an acceptable measurement alternative does not exist, enrol in a course in which you learn the intricacies of questionnaire and interview design and analysis before you blindly attempt to use these valuable measurement techniques.

2

TEST AND MEASUREMENT IN PHYSICAL EDUCATION AND SPORTS

The proper selection of tests if of little value unless testing programs are conducted in an efficient manner. Efficient test administration provides maximum accuracy for valid and reliable results and insures that time has been used to the best advantage. In addition, if the collected data are to have significance and value, the teacher must be able to interpret to the appropriate people the meaning of those data. Efficiency and management in testing are the result of careful step-by-step planning and preparation. There must be an understanding of the techniques to be used and a competence in the actual administrative procedures along with proper utilization of space and time, effective use of leadership, and an adequate follow-up process. It is essential that the teacher have an appreciation for the effective utilization of time.

Physical performance tests are generally more involved than mental tests, and the actual time allotted to the physical education class generally is shorter than for other subjects because of the time invested in uniform changes, showering and other administrative procedures. Unless special precautions are given to conserving time, testing might consume more than its proportional share of the total time allotment and result in excessive loss of instruction. However, time should not be saved at the expense of accurate scores. The program of measurement should be organized as an integral part of the instructional program, and with certain definite purposes in mind. When it is organized in this manner, the time devoted to testing is not wasted. Testing becomes a part of teaching and is thereby an education activity in itself as is any other procedure.

Although there is no arbitrary rule in the matter of time allotment, it is generally accepted principle that testing should take no more than 10% of instruction time. If tests are used as teaching devices, however, and if they are made to serve a number of purposes, this percentage of time may be greater. In reality, most good teaching involves testing in one form or another and, in a like manner most testing is teaching. The very nature of testing requires supervision by highly qualified personnel. Test results are only as valid as the basic data that have been collected through testing techniques. Tests carelessly administered, or tests administered to a group of students who are not motivated, provide results that may have little significance or value. Students have not been tested until they have given maximum effort, nor are their scores accurate if the test has been improperly administered, judged, or scored. Since tests vary according to objectives, purposes, and type, no arbitrary rules may be established to cover all administrative procedures. More specific suggestions are made for particular tests in the chapters where those tests are presented in full. However, for purposes of simplicity, some general suggestions can be made. These suggestions are listed in 3 categories: (1) advanced preparation; (2) duties during testing; and (3) duties after testing.

Advanced Preparation

Testing, like any other educational procedure, requires careful and sometimes precise planning ahead of time. In some cases such planning may begin weeks or even months in advance of the actual testing.

Following is a list of suggested considerations for making preplanning more efficient:

i. Selection of the Appropriate Test—The selection of the appropriate measurement techniques is the first consideration in test administration. Selection of the exact test depends upon the type of information that is sought by the teacher. Tests should be selected with certain considerations in mind. First, it is necessary to identify whether the product or the process of education is to be measured. If the process is to be evaluated, it is also necessary to know what facet of educational procedures is being considered and for what purpose the results will be used. It is possible to evaluate the teacher and staff, the methodology, the curriculum, or the total program. If the product is to be measured, the administrator of the tests should know the purpose for which the results will be used, such as classification, grading, diagnosis, or evaluation of the process itself.

In addition, tests must be selected in the light of certain administrative procedures that are especially important. Tests should be chosen with a view to the time available, the size and age of the group, the number of qualified leaders, the difficulty of test administration, the financial cost, and the amount of equipment and facilities on hand. One or more of these considerations might eliminate an otherwise highly desirable and valid test from use. Finally, the test should have high standards, in the selective criteria of validity, reliability, objectivity and norms. Furthermore, these criteria should be accompanied by good physiologic and psychologic reactions on the part of the student.

ii. Knowledge of the Test—The director of testing

should have a thorough knowledge of the test to be used and a prècise understanding of its administrative procedures. All procedures and techniques should be studied carefully. The inexperienced teacher profit by writing out all the necessary details. Frequently this can be done on 3×5- or 5×8-inch card. The cards can then be shuffled at the convenience of the instructor. A good plan is to provided a diagram of the complete layout, including a traffic flow pattern. This diagram or chart can be displayed at a convenient location for the benefit of the students.

iii. Equipment and Facilities—A study can be made of the space needs, special equipment, courses, courts, special markings, and supplies. The proper use of space, equipment, and materials reduces the amount of time needed for conducting tests. Proper space planning also reduces confusion and minimizes crowding and congestion around stations or along the flow of traffic. The following suggestions should be helpful:

Course and Markings. Most tests provide sufficient directions for the layout of testing stations. All directions regarding courses, courts, special designs, and markings should be observed carefully. If the accompanying test norms are to be used for conversion of scores, test directions should never be modified by the inexperienced tester. The veteran tester should modify directions only when it is assured that the proposed change or changes will in no way affect the scores or use of these scores. The field or floor should be laid out properly and marked for rapid scoring in such events as throws, jumps, and kicks for distances. A football field that has been marked into 5-yard zone provides an excellent layout for throwing and kicking events for distance. A mat with parallel lines marked at 1-, 2- and 3-inch intervals can be used for the standing broad jump. Perhaps the simplest way to set up the standing broad jump station is to use an already established line on the floor for the takeoff line and secure a tape measure to the floor at right angles to this line.

Scoring can be done by observing across the tape measure where the best jump was indicated. Lines on walls or floors can be painted with rapid-drying washable paint, or can be constructed with making tape or adhesive tape. Targets can be made in the same manner or they may be painted on canvas, oil cloth, plastic, mats, or plywood. Movable equipment provides more flexibility in its use.

Equipment. All necessary equipment such as horizontal bars, parallel bars, chinning bars, targets, ropes, poles, jumping standards, and special devices should be available and put in place before testing begins. Student safety is an important consideration in the placement and use of equipment. Common sense should prevail in the design of testing stations. Some logical order should be selected. Overlapping of areas and overcrowding are dangerous and are not conducive to best results. However, testing is expedited when as many testing stations are set up as leadership, space and equipment permit.

Materials. Some tests require a great many supplies and materials. Most test directions indicate the type and amount. If they are not indicated, the director of testing should determine the kind and amount needed and secure them prior to the testing period. These materials might include such items as hand dynamometers, stop watches, balls, tape measures, signs, string, cord, chalk, pencils, score cards, and tongue depressors for markers.

If students are to do their own recording or if partners are to score, pencils in quantity should be provided. The novice should make out a list of the needed supplies and check them off as they are provided. The important thing is to have them on hand and ready for use. Test administrative procedures should follow the directions explicitly as indicated in the test manual if the test administrator intends to use the test norms accompanying the manual or if comparisons are to be made with either state or national norms. However, if such comparisons are not indicated, the test administrator may modify the test in any manner consistent with common sense in order to measure the expressed objectives. If modifications are to be made, the test administrator should be consistent in the modified procedures for all students being tested.

iv. Preparation of Score Cards—Scoring forms should be designed and prepared in advance of the testing period. Sometimes students may even prepare their own from models made available to them. There are several kinds of score cards and various methods for recording scores. The particular situation dictates the kind of card to be used. Each kind described below has its strong points:

Class Roll Sheet. This score sheet has names of all class members in alphabetical order with spaces for their scores and other pertinent data that may be needed. This type of score card can be used more readily when one examiner administers and scores all test items, or when the station-to-station method is used and each station has class roll sheets. Sometimes such score cards are used as cumulative records for the group when scores from individual score cards are transferred to them. In any event this method expedites the conversion of raw scores to scale scores and presents an overview of class performance.

Squad Cards. The squad card is used sometimes when the squads rotate from station to station and the squad leaders carry the squad cards with them. It is a smaller version of the class roll sheet and has the same characteristics. It is more flexible, however, and permits the squads to score themselves under the direction of squad leaders or a trained tester.

Individual Score Card. Perhaps the best method for recording scores is the individual score card which permits the students to move from one station to another independently of their group. All students carry a card with them and assume responsibility for its care. This card usually is designed for specific tests and generally provides space for such information as the student's name, class, date, age, weight, height, raw score, and converted score. If the scores can be summed, as is the case with all standard scores, there should be a place for a composite score.

Generally a 3×5 card serves the purpose for most score cards, but in some cases the 5×8 card is better. This individual card, or "carry type" as it is sometimes called, is generally used when the students score for each other or when they rotate from station to station independently of their group and are scored by a trained assistant. Since students must assume responsibility for their card and also share in the rotational procedures, they share to a greater extent in the testing process and at the same time learn some self-direction. In addition, they can see their scores and they have a better idea of their achievement status. If the score cards are cumulative, the students may easily see their progress and achievement. Two disadvantages of the "carry type" card are that students frequently lose it, and if the card is used more than once, it tends to become mutilated. When individual score cards are employed, scale scores conversion tables with scale scores for all possible raw scores can be posted at some convenient place for the benefit of the students who want to convert their raw scores.

With a minimum of training the students are then able to convert their raw scores by using the prominently posted norms. These norms answer many questions for the students such as "How good was my throw?" or "Which was my best or weakest event?" Scale scores may even be printed on the obverse side of the individual card, a practice that expedites considerably the student's conversion of their own scores. Conversion tables are more practical when they are constructed so they can be easily read at a glance by the instructor who may have to convert all raw scores for all students on all test items. Scale scores for each item on the battery sometimes are placed directly on the individual score card along with the corresponding raw scores.

This permits the students to convert their own raw scores immediately to scale scores by merely encircling their raw scores or indicating it in some manner. They may then connect the circles with lines and construct a profile directly on the card. This enables the students to see in a graphic way their status in the various test items. When a second administration of the same test is plotted along with the first, progress may also be noted.

Preparation of Standardized Directions. In the administration of most tests 2 kinds of directions are necessary. One set should be prepared for the trained test administrators so that they will know exactly how to explain, demonstrate, administer, and score particular test items. The second set of directions concerns the instructions to be given to the students who are taking the test. These 2 sets of directions may differ somewhat. The directions should be standardized for consistency and prepared in written form. They should create interest and stimulate maximum performance. If possible, they should be memorized by the examiner. If they are not memorized, they should be written on cards that can be easily shuffled as the tester gives directions. They should be read exactly as they are written.

The following suggestions are made with reference to test directions for students: (1) They should be as brief and concise as possible. (2) They should accompany or precede the demonstration. (3) They should be adapted to the age level of the subjects by using language appropriate to age. (4) They should emphasize the correct procedure rather than the incorrect one. Sometimes it is possible to combine into 1 set the direction to both the students and the test administrator. The directions for the student might be placed in italics or bold type on the instructor's cards. In this way the directions will stand out and can be more easily read by the examiner.

v. Preparation of Score Cards—Scoring forms should be designed and prepared in advance of the testing period. Sometimes students may even prepare their own from models made available to them. There are several kinds of score cards and various methods for recording scores. The particular situation dictates the kind of card to be used. Each kind described below has its strong points.

Class Roll Sheet. This score sheet has names of all class members in alphabetical order with spaces for their scores and other pertinent data that may be needed. This type of score card can be used more readily when one examiner administers and scores all test items, or when the station-to-station method is used and each station has class roll sheets. Sometimes such score cards are used as cumulative records for the group when scores from individual score cards are transferred to them. In any event this method expedites the conversion of raw scores to scale scores and presents an overview of class performance.

Squad Cards. The squad card is used sometimes when the squads rotate from station to station and the squad leaders carry the squad cards with them. It is a smaller version of the class roll sheet and has the same characteristics. It is more flexible, however, and permits the squads to score themselves under the direction of squad leaders or a trained tester.

Individual Score Card. Perhaps the best method for recording scores is the individual score card which permits the students to move from one station to another independently of their group. All students carry a card with them and assume responsibility for its care. This card usually is designed for specific tests and generally provides space for such information as the student's name, class, date, age, weight, height, raw score, and converted score. If the scores can be summed, as is the case with all standard scores, there should be place for a composite score. Generally a 3×5 card serves the purpose for most score cards, but in some cases the 5×8 card is better. This individual card, or carry type as it is sometimes called, is generally used when the students score for each other or when they rotate from station to station independently of their group and are scored by a trained assistant.

Since students must assume responsibility for their card and also share in the rotational procedures, they share to a greater extent in the testing process and at the same time learn some self-direction. In addition, they can see their scores and they have a better idea of their achievement status. If the score cards are cumulative, the students may easily see their progress and achievement. Two disadvantages of the carry type card that students frequently lose it, and if the card is used more than once, it tends to become mutilated

When individual score cards are employed, scale score conversion tables with scale scores for all possible raw scores can be posted at some convenient place for the benefit of the students who want to convert their raw scores. With a minimum of training the students are then able to convert their raw scores by using the prominently posted norms. These norms answer many questions for the students such as “How good was my throw?” or “Which was my best or weakest event?” Scale scores may even be printed on the obverse side of the individual card, a practice that expedites considerably the student’s conversion of their own scores.

Conversion tables are more practical when they are constructed so they can be easily read at a glace by the instructor who may have to convert all raw scores for all students on all test items. Scale scores for each item on the battery sometimes are placed directly on the individual score card along with the corresponding raw scores. This permits the students to convert their own raw scores immediately to scale scores by merely encircling their raw score or indicating it in some manner. They may then connect the circles with lines and construct a profile directly on the card. This enables the students to see in a graphic way their status in the various test items. When a second administration of the same test is plotted along with the first, progress may also be noted.

Preparation of Standardized Directions. In the administration of most tests 2 kinds of directions are necessary. One set should be prepared for the trained test administrators so that they will know exactly how to explain, demonstrate, administer and score particular test items. The second set of directions concerns the instructions to be given to the students who are taking the test. These 2 sets of directions may differ somewhat. The directions should be standardized for consistency and prepared in written form. They should create interest and stimulate maximum performance. If possible, they should be memorized by the examiner. If they are not memorized, they should be written on cards that can be easily shuffled as the tester gives directions. They should be read exactly as they are written.

The following suggestions are made with reference to test directions for students: (1) They should be as brief and concise as possible. (2) They should accompany or precede the demonstration. (3) They should be adapted to the age level of the subjects by using language appropriate to age. (4) They should emphasize the correct procedure rather than the incorrect one. Sometimes it is possible to combine into 1 set the directions to both the students and the test administrator. The directions for the student might be placed in italics or bold type on the instructor's cards. In this way the directions will stand out and can be more easily read by the examiner.

vi. Preparation of the Testing Area—Careful planning in setting up the testing area is important. If the test instructions call for a specific arrangement, that pattern should be followed explicitly. If not, the instructors can establish an order and make their own arrangement with certain principles in mind:

(1) The stations and all traffic patterns should be arranged to accommodate the flow of student traffic. A diagram of the area can be drawn indicating the floor plan and space requirements.

(2) The station should be arranged to offset student fatigue and should be placed from the least strenuous to the most strenuous. Or they should be spaced so that alternate sets of muscles are tested.

(3) The stations should be clearly identified by name or number so that rotational procedures will be clear to

the students.

(4) Safety should be considered in the placement of events that might be dangerous if they are permitted to overlap. It is particularly important that in events involving an all-out spring sufficient space be provided for deceleration of the runner at the finish.

vii. Selection of Organization and Administration Procedures—Nothing should be left to chance. In advance of the time for testing the test administrator should carefully plan all procedures for organizing the students. Where, when, and how the demonstrations will be done are important questions. When the order for rotation of the test items for a battery is not suggested by the test author, an order must be established by the test director. Ways and means for economical administration of tests should be studied and the most appropriate group structure determined. This class organization for testing depends to a great extent on the kind of test and the characteristics of the group to be tested. No one plan can be adapted to all situations.

There are the following 3 main ways to organize the class:

a. Squad Method—This method involves all the students at the same time, but the class is divided into squads and each squad works independently. This method works best when each station operates on a comparable time basis so that all the squads may rotate together. If squads are already organized for instruction, it is a simple matter to have each squad tested on a particular test item by the squad leader or by a trained assistant. Either squad cards or individual cards may be used to record scores. After each squad member has been tested the squad can rotate to the next test station and begin testing there.

This method works best when all stations require about the same amount of time for administration, or when multiple stations are used for the slower-moving items. If squads are not already organized, some simple method of dividing the group may be used. For instance, if there are 30 pupils and 5 test items and if individual score cards are used, the cards may be divided into 5 groups and each group can be marked with a different colour. As the class assembles, all students holding red cards are designated as 1 squad. This red squad can report to 1 station, the green to another, the blue to another, and so on.

b. Mass Testing—The most effective use of time allotment is made when a large number of students are tested at one time. Many tests can be administered on a mass basis. For example, one examiner can explain, demonstrate, and administer all tests to all students. There are 2 variations of this method:

(1) The students may be paired into partners, and while one partner is tested, the other partner serves as scorer and recorder after which the partner's exchange roles. This method saves time and may be used whenever the test items are adaptable to its use.

(2) All members of the class may take the test at the same time, which makes it even a greater time-saver. However, this system can be used only when it is feasible for the students to score themselves.

c. Station-to-Station Method—Sometimes when groups are large in number and the order of events is not important, or when some stations require more time than others, the best method of organization and rotation is on a station-to-station basis. Here the students rotate from 1 station to another as individuals and do not remain with any particular group or squad. They are scored by a trained assistant and carry with them an individual score card. In this system it may be that some test items are slower to administer than others. In this event once again, 2 or more testing stations can be set up for the slower-moving items. This prevents a massing of students waiting to be tested at any 1 station. The age of the student has some influence on the use of the station-to-station plan. This approach is sometimes not feasible when younger children are tested.

Combinations—On some occasions it may be effective to combine 2 or more of these methods of organization. For example, the squads can rotate from 1 test to another on a station-to-station basis. On other occasions, the mass technique of testing may be used for 1 or 2 items and then a shift can be made to the squad or station-to-station method for the other items. No single plan of organization will fit all situations. In any event, each test item should be explained and demonstrated to all members of the class before testing is actually started. Frequently, it is possible to set up 1 or more testing stations adjacent to the playing floor, court, or field. The instructor may then test 1 group, squad, or team while the others participate in the regularly scheduled-activity.

For example, if a class is divided into 5 squads or teams, 1 group may be tested while the other 4 compete or engaged in drills. If the testing environment and procedures are kept constant for each group, this may be an effective approach for class organization.

viii. Scoring—Two of the most important considerations are the observation of performance and the recording of scores. Testing results may be carefully observed by the scorer and recorded quickly and accurately. Many tests require the scorer to possess specialized skills and training. For example, if the test assistants are to operate a stopwatch or a dynamometer, they should have some instruction in its use. Sometimes test administration is expedited in events like throwing and jumping when 2 persons, a spotter and a recorder, assist with the scoring. Time is saved if only the best effort out of 3 trials is actually measured or marked. This method usually works more effectively when the contestants like their 3 trials in succession. When markers are used, such as tongue depressors with the thrower's name on them, a number of students, perhaps an entire squad, can take their throws and only the best effort of each student is eventually marked. When all members of the group have completed their trials, all can be measured at the same time.

In judging scores and recording results, there are 4 main methods. Naturally, there is some relationship between the organization of a class and the method of scoring. The methods are as follows:

a. By Instructors. This method is perhaps the most time-consuming and should be used only when the situation dictates. The instructor may do the scoring when 1 squad is being tested while the other squads are participating in regular class activity, or when the nature of the test is such that only a highly specialized person can administer it. Posture and nutrition tests fall into this category.

b. By Partners. This method is generally used when the tests are administered on a mass basis. The class is divided into partners and, while an examiner administers the tests and supervises them, scores are judged and recorded by the partner who is not taking the test at the time. Partners may also do the scoring within the squad. When this partner method of scoring is employed, the director of testing, in his explanation, must emphasize the scoring techniques to be followed.

c. By Squad Leaders. When tests are administered

on a squad basis, generally they are administered and scored by a squad leader. The training of this squad leader may be done at a training session prior to the testing period. This system is especially effective when a student leadership program is in operation and when student leads are already trained in the leadership techniques.

d. By Trained Testers. When tests are administered on a station-to-station basis, scoring is generally done by trained examiners who have been instructed in methods of judging and scoring at a training session prior to the testing day. These trained individuals may be students, faculty members, professional students from a teacher-training institution, paraprofessionals, or interested, nonschool personnel, e.g., parents.

ix. Orientation of Students—Some orientation of the students is necessary to obtain satisfactory results. The students should be instructed in the purpose of the tests and the manner in which the test results will be used by the teacher. In general, students should be told what they are striving for and the outcomes to be achieved. If practice is desirable or necessary, the test item may be explained and demonstrated days in advance of the actual testing period. Special direction should be given to students regarding equipment, dress, shoes, pencils, score cards, and the like. Students are frequently motivated when they are told that test scores will be posted, but in some cases this might be poor psychology. Negative attitudes are not conducive to best performance.

Student's past experience with taking tests may influence their attitude toward taking them again. For example, they may have suffered nausea, or they may have become extremely stiff and sore following strenuous tests. Also, they may have learned that their scores were not being used for some viable use and no purpose was behind the testing. If the students receive proper orientation, however, they will know that the test results will be employed for useful purposes. Furthermore, they will have some understanding of the testing procedure: how the scoring is done, the general design of the testing area and what goals are expected of them. All of these factors should contribute to a more positive attitude on the part of the student.

x. Training of Student Leaders and Scorers—If highly qualified people are available, they should be used to assist in the testing program. Experienced assistants are especially important when the testing procedures and techniques are complicated and difficult. Some experience is mandatory in the use of some equipment such as stopwatches and dynamometers or in the use of techniques such as counting pulse rates in a cardiovascular test. However, many times it is necessary for the students to assist in administering tests and keeping records of results.

The use of student leaders is not only a necessity from the standpoint of administration, but also it is an educationally sound procedure. It provides one of several ways the students can share in the measurement program. A great deal more training is required to administer tests than to judge results and record scores. When students are used to assist in the test administration process, some training is necessary. One or more training sessions are necessary if the students are to have a complete understanding of the tests and the testing procedures.

Students who are to assist must be trained in the administration procedures, the techniques for each individual test item, the demonstration techniques, and the method of scoring. They should be impressed with the need to be accurate, consistent, explicit and alert.

The standardized directions mentioned previously should be followed explicitly. Instructions should be so simple and definite that any examiner might carry on testing procedures at any other station. If possible, the student assistants should experience taking the entire test as subjects. This enables them to learn the correct techniques more effectively and at the same time increases their familiarity with the tests. It also provides an opportunity for them to share in the testing process in the same manner as their classmates. Special emphasis should be placed on scoring procedures. This is especially true when employing specialized equipment such as stopwatches, dynamometers, and calipers. Some practice in the use of these instruments is essential.

Duties During Testing

Once the advanced preparations have been made in a thorough manner, the teacher can move into the testing period with a great deal of confidence that the producers will move efficiently. However, some important considerations must still be emphasized during the testing period itself. Several of these are mentioned in the following sections:

Last-Minute Check. Time is of essence and becomes one of the most valuable factors in a physical education class. A good instructor is always alert for ways to gain valuable minutes for teaching and participation. When the testing period is at hand, the instructor should arrive early and make a last-minute check of equipment, supplies, and facilities that are to be used. When the class has assembled, everything should be ready and in place so that the actual testing may start immediately. If the group to be tested is unorganized, such as a group from study hall or a large group during orientation at the beginning of the year, some effort should be made to see that students report to the testing area in an orderly and punctual manner. If the group is quite large, the students should be ordered alphabetically or in some other comparable way.

Explanation. The standardized directions that have been prepared previously as written directions should be made available to the examiners and followed exactly as written. The directions to the instructor serve as a guide in the demonstration, and the directions to the students should be read or given to the students in an interesting and enthusiastic manner. Generally, it is more effective if the instructor memorizes the explanation so the directions to different groups are consistent. Combining the explanation with the demonstration is an efficient and timesaving method of presenting the test battery.

Demonstration. A demonstration of each test item is usually desirable. Technique to be demonstrated should be planned and learned by the demonstrator in advance. The demonstration may accompany the explanation or follow it. The examiner who is doing the demonstration should first present the test battery as a whole in order of item occurrence, if there is an order, and then he/she should stress the more important details. The attention of the class should be captured and all members arranged so they can observe the demonstration and hear the explanation. The usual procedure is to demonstrate all of the items before any testing is started. Students should be given an opportunity to ask questions.

Warm-up and Practice. As soon as the explanation and demonstration are completed and before testing is begun, a short warm-up exercise period should be administered to everyone. This is not only a safety precaution but it also enhances performance on the tests. There are really 2 types of warm-ups: one of a general nature and one specific to the tests. Many motor tests require a special kind of warm-up such as throws and kicks for distance, running, and jumps. It is the responsibility of the test administrator to see that all students are properly warmed up both before testing starts and later for specialized events. There must be consistency in this pretest practice. In certain tests it is desirable to provide space for warm-up and pretest practice.

Administration. During this period all the planning and preparation are brought to fruition. The testing period should always be conducted in a positive and efficient manner. The matter of student discipline is an important consideration. Administration should be planned so that all students may be kept active most of the time. Crowding around a particular station is an invitation to behaviour problems. In situations where leadership is limited or facilities are lacking so that only a few students can be tested at one time, the rest of the group can be organized into some activity that keeps them occupied within the framework of the curriculum while they are waiting their turn to be tested. Multiple stations may be set up if leadership is available and practice areas may be provided for those who are waiting. If the preplanning has been thorough, preparation of the testing area adequate, and the orientation of the students appropriate, test administration should proceed in a smooth and orderly manner. However, certain situations inevitable arise which need immediate attention, such as a broken piece of equipment to be repaired or replaced, a chalk line to be replenished, fresh making tape to be put in position, a missing score card to be replaced, or overcrowding at stations to be relieved.

Motivation. It has been pointed out previously that students have not been tested until they have given maximum effort. They are several suggestion on how to motivate students to give their best effort: The tests should be presented in an interesting manner so the student will be stimulated and want to excel. On some age levels, however, it is sometimes necessary to encourage the student to exert greater effort.

In general, students perform better when they are told the purpose of the test and the method of scoring. They also want to know the various levels of achievement for which they are striving, and they try harder when they perceive the importance of the tests as a part of the overall program. Therefore, all students should be instructed in the purpose for testing and the way test results will be used. Proper attitude and genuine enthusiasm on the part of the teacher are usually reflected in a good attitude by the students. Assistants should be given some definite suggestions on how to motivate students to greater effort during test administration. Some suggestions are: showing an interest in a student's performance, encouraging greater effort, praising good performance, and reminding students of the correct technique and rules. For example, the student may be reminded in the medicine ball put to 'put' the ball rather than throw it or to keep behind the restraining line. The poorly skilled should never be embarrassed by having attention called to their poor performance or be ridiculed for their lack of form or effort. If some degree of motivation appears to be needed, it should be uniformly and consistently applied to all.

Safety. Testing is accompanied by excitement and enthusiasm on the part of most students. They like self-testing activities and the challenge presented by most physical tests. They are stimulated and eager to excel as they test themselves. Safeguards must be observed to prevent accidents. This can be done in a number of ways. Safety precautions may be emphasized during the orientation period. Class discipline must be maintained, although student enthusiasm should not be stifled. A proper warm-up and prepractice are essential to prevent pulled muscles. If students have weak joints at the knees or ankles, certain tests may be indicated.

Leaders should be warned to look for certain hazards and should be trained to prevent accidents. Spotters may be indicated for some events. The entire class must be instructed in any special precaution that may be necessary owing to the nature of a particular test or facility. Precautions are necessary, not only in the placement of particular stations, but also in the routing of the traffic flow between stations. Care must be taken to use soft markers and protective mats when common sense indicates possible hazards. As a rule, medical examinations should preceded the administration of all strenuous tests. In the event medical exams have not been given, any student who is permitted to schedule an activity class in the regular instructional program probably should be permitted to take the test. When there is doubt, and once again common sense should prevail, a student should be excused. Proper conditioning should precede the administration of those tests that require great efforts of strength or endurance.

Duties after Testing

At the end of the testing period a number of considerations should be of concern to test administrators. Some of these are immediate and some may be performed more at leisure. However, feedback of test results to the students has more meaning and values when it is immediate. Therefore, the sooner all of these suggested steps can be implemented, the more effective the test results will become.

Collecting Score Cards. If class or squad cards are used, the collection of score cards presents little problem. When individual score cards are employed, they may be collected by the squad leaders from their respective squad members, by the trained student assistants at the last station where the student is tested, or at the gate or door by an assistant as the students leave the testing area.

Converting Raw Scores. When tests are administered and the results recorded, a raw score is obtained. These raw scores are generally meaningless and usually impossible to interpret until they have been converted to some kind of norm-referenced or criterion-referenced standard. The most common methods of conversion to a norm-referenced standard are to percentiles, some type of standard score, or a weighed score based on standard scores. The actual conversion is usually accomplished through use of norms in the form of scoring tables. These tables should be made available in advance and in such manner that scores can be identified and quickly converted. Score cards should have space for the raw scores and the converted scores. When criterion-referenced standards are employed, raw scores may be compared with a single predetermined standard. Criterion-referenced standards are usually established on a pass-or-fall basis and are set at some level that can be met by a given percentage of the group, usually from 80 to 90%.

Comparing Test Results with Norms and Constructing a Profile. Sometimes converted scores are more useful when they are compared with additional standards. Many tests are accompanied by these. For example, in Morrison's Test of Basic skills, the raw scores for both batteries are first related to norms through the scoring table of T-Scores. These T-Scores for each battery can then be summed for each student taking the tests and a composite-score obtained. These composite scores, in turn, are referred to a composite norm table for placement of students into levels or categories. This provides norms for the composite scores. If it is feasible, the score cards should contain the norms so the student's rating can be checked directly on the card. When there are several items in the test battery and especially when the items have diagnostic value, scale scores can be placed directly on the card and a profile constructed on the student's achievement. Process evaluation scores are frequently placed in profile also.

Constructing Norms and Standards. In some cases the test administrators must analyse test results and prepare their own norms or standards. They need to understand statistics so they may effectively analyse their test results. This analysis generally includes finding the average and spread of the scores. For the norm-referenced standards some type of table is devised, generally a percentile table or a standard scoring table. For the criterion-referenced standard, a cutoff point is generally determined to indicate successful performance.

3

ENVIRONMENTAL FACTORS AND SPORTS PERFORMANCE

Environment plays an important role in the quality of athlete's performance. There are many things the athlete can do or adaptations he can make to prepare him better for variations in the environment, either expected or unexpected. The athlete who trains at sea level is forced to make rather extensive physiological adjustments to compete successfully at higher altitudes. Training in cool climates does little to prepare the athlete to compete under conditions of extreme heat and humidity. Similarly, sudden exposure to cold can have a drastic influence on athlete's performances if they have not had an opportunity to acclimatize to the colder environment. Environment factors include exposure to extremes of heat, cold, humidity and contests at high altitudes.

VARIATION IN TEMPERATURE

The temperature by itself is not an accurate index of the physiological stress imposed on the athlete. As the temperature of the surrounding environment increases, the gradient between the athlete and environment decreases i.e., the temperature of the environment approaches the skin the deep body. The body produces considerable amount of heat as it generates energy to perform various physical tasks. In cold environment, this metabolic heat production in necessary to assist in maintaining the body temperature. In hot environments, however, it is a liability since it adds to the body's heat load.

Body temperature is controlled in the brain by the hypothalamus. The major process to regulate the body's temperature is convection, radiation, conduction and evaporation. At rest even under considerably varying environmental conditions., body temperature is maintained at a relatively constant valve of approximately 98.40F. Temperature receptors in the skin assist the hypothalamus in maintaining this temperature constant with exercise, body temperature increase in proportion to the intensity and duration of activity. Moderate exercise can raise the core body temperature. The body appears to select a new thermostatic "set-point" as the athlete goes from rest to strenuous exercise. This allow him to function more efficiently, since chemical reaction rate and oxygen availability are increased. When these regulatory mechanism fail the body still performs under various environmental temperature and cope with environmental extremes.

Exercise in the Heat : The ability of the athlete to successfully perform in the heat depends on the degree of heat, the humidity, the air movement, intensity and duration of effort, and the extent of his previous exposure to similar environmental conditions. An athlete should acclimatize to heat. The major importance is the athlete's fluid and mineral intake schedule both prior to, as well as during competition.

Four physical processes remove excess heat from the body are radiation, conduction, evaporation, and convection. Since the body temperature is usually higher than air temperature, the human body radiates heat rays to the environment. But during the warmer days of summer, heat is absorbed by the body through radiation.

There are two kinds of heat loss through conduction to the air and to objects. When swimmers lose body heat to the water, very little heat is lost through conduction during exercise.

Convention is the term applied to air movement – wind. It plays a major role in heat loss by both conduction and evaporation. During exercise sweat conducts an enormous amount of heat from within the body to the skin surface. The heat dissipates when the convention currents evaporate the sweat.

In the presence of high environmental temperature, evaporation and convection provide the only relief from heat stress. On hot days when humidity is high and there is little or no wind, evaporation is dangerously reduced.

Clothing is an important consideration for the problem of heat stress. It is recommended by the exercise scientists and sports physicians that the athlete, wear loose, light – coloured cotton or nylon mesh clothing to allow the skin beneath to breathe. Light colours reflect heat; dark colours absorb it. This physical principle also applies to skin, dark skin absorbs more heat.

Physically fit people tolerate heat better than the unfit, because their cardiovascular system are more stable and they dissipate heat more efficiently. They also become acclimatized more quickly. Simply loosing weight will increase heat tolerance. Overweight individuals suffer more in heat and humidity because their fat insulates them and interferes with heat loss.

Dehydration : Dehydration is one of the greatest problems associated with exercise in the heat, particularly under conditions of high humidity. Since sweating is the major avenue of heat loss when exercising in the heat, the total amount of fluid loss becomes very important as the duration of activity is extended over time. Man sweat at the rate of 2 litres per hour for short periods of time and at the rate of the one litre per hour or more for long periods. Dehydration is a serious threat to the human beings. The deep body temperature rises from 0.30 F to 0.50F for every one percent loss in body weight. This rise is the result of the ioss in blood volume i.e. a large percent of the water lost in sweating comes from the blood volume. It also causes kidney failure.

Acclimatization : Repeated exposures to hot environments help the athlete to adopt better to thermal stress, thus improving his athletic performance. Repeated exposure to heat causes a gradual adjustment that enables the athlete to tolerate the associated stress better. It is clear that total acclimatization can occur within 5 to 15 days period. The acclimatization require more than just exposure to hot environment, i.e. exercise in the heat. Teams or individuals that are training in environments cooler than those in which they will be competing, it is important to achieve thermal acclimatization prior to the competition. This would improve the individual's performance, in addition to reducing the associated physiological stress. Normally 5 to 7 days. Provide total acclimatization.

Heat Disorders : When the body is unable to successfully adopt to thermal stress.

(1) Heat Cramps : It is the result of dehydration and the salt loss accompanying high rates of sweating. It is characterized by sever cramping of the skeletal muscles, primarily those muscles used in the exercise.

(2) Heat exhaustion : It is characterized by a body temperature of 101-1040F, extreme tiredness, breathlessness, dizziness and rapid pulse rate. These symptoms appear to be the result of a reduced sweat

production thus limiting the body's major avenue of heat loss.

(3) Heat Stroke : It is the most serious heat disorders and is characterized by a body temperature of 105-1060F, or higher, cessation of sweating and total unconsciousness. If left untreated the victim of heat stroke is likely to die. While few people under normal, non-exercising conditions in the heat experience either heat stroke or exhaustioh, many athletes push themselves to the point where they are extremely vulnerable to a serious heat disorder.

PREVENTION OF HEAT DISORDERS

1. Competition and practice should not be held when the temperature is over 98°F. It reflects the humidity as well as the absolute temperature and is more sensitive indication of the physiological stress. Schedule the practice and contest either in the early morning or at night to overcome the severe heat stress of mid-day.

2. Fluids should be made readily available and the athlete drinks as much as he can, stopping every 10 to 20 min in the higher temperature for a "fluid break".

3. Clothing should be loose-weaved, and of light colours, since dark colours absorb heat while light colours reflect.

Exercise in the Cold

Exercise in the cold or winter sports and outdoor activities like skiing, hiking, hunting, mountaineering, jogging etc. has increased the risk of cold related problems like abnormally low body temperature. Additional clothing can always be worn during the athletic contest to maintain the athlete in a warm and comfortable environment. The extremities particularly the hands and feet, are most subject to discomfort and injury from exposure to cold.

As with the heat, the temperature alone is not a valid index of the degree of stress felt by the individual. The wind creates a chill factor, and the more moist the surrounding air, the greater the physiological stress. A dry, still day at 100F in the direct sun can be quite comfortable yet on a moist, windy day with complete cloud cover at 400F, the cloud can be quite penetrating.

Acclimatization to cold does occur as a result of repeated exposures. It is of relatively little valve with regard to athletic performance. The greater significance are the protective measures taken by physicians, trainers, and coaches to assure the most favourable circumstances for the athlete. Proper protective clothing is important, tightly woven garments will help to maintain a small heat pocket between the skin and clothing. Gloves, hats, or caps, and double pair stockings are also helpful. Thermal underwear is recommended for the arms, legs, and torso in extreme cold, but as the temperature rises and metabolic heat builds, a serious heat problem could develop. Once the athlete starts to warm up and starts to sweat, he should remove his excess clothing. Sweat-soaked wet clothing can create problems in an dry environment where evaporation occurs naturally with its resultant clothing effect.

Humidity

An additional factor that is of a considerable importance with regard to exercise in the heat is the relative humidity, or the degree of moisture in the surrounding air. Sweating contributes in the loss of body heat only if the sweat evaporates from the skin. Man is capable of sweating upto two liters or more per hour. If the surrounding air is totally saturated with water vapor, i.e, 100 percent humidity, it is impossible for seat to evaporate, since there is no dry or unsaturated air available to pick up the resulting water vapor. When the temperature is 1000F, and 10 percent relative humidity the body sweats profusely, but evaporation occurs so rapidly that the individual is not conscious of the fact that he is sweating. When the temperature is 800F and 95 percent relative humidity, only a limited amount of sweat can evaporate, since 95 percent of the surrounding air is filled with water vapor. The result is a continuous bath of sweat, which never seems to stop.

Evaporation is the major method of regulating body temperature in the heat. If the air is saturated with water vapor, no evaporation can occur even at the lower environmental temperatures and at the higher temperatures, the body has no way of losing heat, so the body temperature will rise until death results.

Temperature by itself is not an accurate index of the total physiological stress imposed on the athlete. Humidity, air velocity, and the degree of cloud cover, as well as temperature, all directly influence the degree of stress felt by the athlete. This stress varies with changing environmental conditions. As the humidity increases, the problem becomes considerably more serious. Work performance in hot, humid weather is somewhat limited because of cardiovascular system due to the ineffectiveness of the evaporative mechanisms for heat dissipation.

The heat rate and sweat rate are both higher in hot, humid conditions as compared to the hot, dry weather. In hot and humid weather the heart has to work much harder than normal because the amount of blood flowing through the skin is generally increased and highly saturated with oxygen. Less oxygen is available to the working much lower intensity of work. Because of the added strain on the circulatory system to provide sufficient blood to the working muscles and to the skin for heat dissipation, it is quite obvious that exercise in high temperature and high relative humidity can place severe strains upon the cardiovascular system. In certain activities where repeated, short, quick work-outs over an extended period of time are carried out in heat and humid conditions also adversely effect and may not be performed at optimal levels. Some of the adverse heat effect on performance is psychological and not physiological. That is why some people are less motivated to work and perform in heat than others, and therefore, they fail to perform up to their maximum capacity.

Altitude

An increase of altitude has several practical consequences for the athletes. It reduces the density of the air, thus lowering wind-resistance, it reduces the oxygen presence in the air that is breathed, thus restricting maximum oxygen transport, and it lowers atmospheric temperature. There is also small decrease in the force of gravity. If the athlete remains at high altitude, adjustment of body physiology such as reductions in tissue bicarbonate levels, increase in haemoglobin and progressive improvement in endurance performance.

At altitudes of over 5000 feet the ability to perform physical work is effected – the higher the altitude, more serve the effect.

Wind resistance accounts for a substantial fraction of energy expenditure in all events that produce fast movement of man or objects in air e.g. running, cycling, speed-skating and throwing. In the 1968 Olympics the altitude of MEXICO City successful competitors exceeded the best world marks, in running events records were broken and deterioration in the events which last longer than one minute. Altitude mainly affect endurance or aerobic activities rather than sprints on anaerobic events. Fit person will be able to perform better, just as they can at sea level, than the unfit.

Altitude Acclimatization

It refers to certain physiological adjustments which are brought about through continued exposure to altitude and which significantly improve performance. For un-acclimatized person, additional oxygen is essential at 18,000 feet above the sea level.

Longer you remain at altitude, better becomes your performance, but that is not equal to or reaches to that which is obtained at the sea level. This improved performance during stay at altitude is brought about through acclimatization. The number of week or days to acclimatization depends on the altitude e.g.

For 10,000 feet about 7 to 10 days.

12,000 feet about 15 to 21 days.

15,000 feet about 21 to 25 days.

It depends on individuals, some people will never acclimatize and they suffer mountain or altitude sickness. The symptoms of altitude sickness are pulmonary edema, nausea, vomiting, headache, rapid pulse and loss of appetite, fever and congestion of lungs. Treatment of mountain sickness is administering oxygen or removal to lower altitude or both.

As we ascend above sea level, the barometric pressure decreased as the weight of the atmosphere becomes less. The main reason for lessened performance at altitude is a consequence of the lowered oxygen partial pressure. The lowered PO2 results in hypoxia i.e.. lack of adequate oxygen. Hypoxia stimulates the acclimation mechanisms, depending upon the altitude and duration of stay.

Physiological changes that take place during acclimatization to altitude :

(i) Increase Pulmonary ventilation. This is immediate upon the arrival at altitude, being more pronounced during the first four days, then stabilizing after about a week.

(ii) Increased number of red blood cells and haemoglobin concentration. This is also rapid during the first few weeks at altitude. The function of this increase is to increase the oxygen content of the arterial blood.

(iii) Elimination of bicarbonate. This adjustment requires several days. Its main function is to maintain blood pH at near normal valves. With hyperventilation and loss of CO_2, the blood pH will increase; eliminate of bicarbonate is offsetting, causing a decrease in pH.

(iv) Tissue level changes. These changes are :-

a. Increased muscle and tissue capillarisation;

b. Increased myoglobin concentration

c. Increased mitochondria density;

d. Enzyme changes, that enhance the oxidative capacity. These cellar changes take more time.

They are seen most developed in the long time resident of high altitude regions.

PHYSICAL PERFORMANCE AT ALTITUDE

Spring-type or anaerobic activities are generally not influenced to a great extent by altitude. These are activities that require only a matter of seconds for completion. Consequently, the demands on the oxygen transport system are minimal, that is why performance is generally unaffected. At the higher altitudes, 8,000 feet and above, sprint type or throwing performance may even be enhanced due to the decreased air density which reduces the frictional resistance of air to running or to the objects beings thrown.

Following are the main effect of high altitude on Physical Performance

(a) Decrease in Total Barometric Pressure – As we ascend to higher and higher altitudes, the total pressure decrease because of the decreased weight of the atmosphere. The force of gravity is smaller at high altitude than at sea level, the energy required to lift the body as in the pole vault an high jump would decrease. However the effect on physical performance is quite small.

(b) Decrease in Partial Pressure of Oxygen :- The decreased barometric pressure causes the partial pressure of oxygen to be decreased. The decreased oxygen pressure at high altitude decreases the arterial oxygen saturation of blood which, in turn decreases the amount of oxygen available to the working tissues. Physiologically, the decreased PO2 is the most critical factor of high altitude because the individual's work capacity depends largely upon his ability to take in and utilize oxygen rapidly. Because of this, pilots and mountain climbers are required to take oxygen at altitudes over 20,000 feet.

(c) Decrease in Density of Air – The decreased density of the air reduces the resistance of the airways to the flow of air into and out of the lungs. This permits greater volumes of air to be taken in during work with no significant increase in ventilation cost. In which air resistance is a factor, the reduced density of the air acts in favour of those performances e.g. sprint types activities, jumping, pole vaulting, throwing etc.

(d) Cool and Dry Air – The air is generally cooler and

dry at high altitude. Although the cooler temperature makes work more pleasant, and in fact, can help performances involving prolonged exertion, the dry air can also increase the water loss from the respiratory tract which may contribute to the dehydration. Also, dryness of the throat is often experienced by athletes as a result of the dry air.

(e) Sunburn and Snow Blindness – It is common for skiers and mountaineers to experience sunburns and snow blindness at high altitude. Because solar radiation is much moiré intense at high altitude than a sea level and because the skin tends to be dryer at high altitudes, as the winds generally blow harder at higher elevations. Skin burn at high altitude are also related to the decreased density of the air.

PHYSIOLOGICAL FUNCTION AT ALTITUDE

The human body adjusts to the decrease in pressure gradients of oxygen by altering its respiratory and cardiovascular responses to exercises and work in several ways. They are –

(a) Pulmonary Ventilation – Pulmonary ventilation is increased at higher altitudes, both at rest and during exercise. Since the air at higher altitudes is less dense, the increase in ventilation is a compensatory mechanism to bring the same number of molecules of oxygen into the lung as the individual would taken in at sea level. Since the number of molecules of oxygen for a given volume of air is less at higher altitude, an additional volume of air is necessary to supply the same total number of molecules of oxygen. The increased ventilation acts much the same as hyperventilation at sea level, in that the CO_2 in the alveoli is reduced, causing more CO_2 to diffuse from the blood, which results in an increase in pH of the blood.

(b) An Enlarged Haemoglobin Concentration in the Blood – In this acclimatization an increase in the number of red blood cells causes rapid production of these cells by the bone marrow. The haemoglobin concentration also increases and this increase is due to the overall decreases in plasma volume. The formation of many new cells is a slow process requiring at least several weeks to help to acclimatize a person to high attitudes.

(c) Greater Diffusing Capacity of the Lungs – The normal diffusing capacity for oxygen through the pulmonary membrane increase during exercise at sea level or at high altitude. This increase is due to an augmented pulmonary capillary blood volume, which expands the capillaries increases the surface through which oxygen can diffuse into the blood and augment lung volume, which presumably expands the surface area of the alveolary membrance.

(d) An Increased vascularity of the Tissues – In this the increase in the number of capillaries along-with a better distribution of blood to the areas such as the muscles, heart, brain and other organs that normally require large amounts of oxygen increases where gas changes is needed for optimal performance. The hemoglobin molecule comes into much closer contact with the active tissue cells and provides a supply of oxygen to each cell even with a somewhat lower oxygen tension. A slight increase in arterial blood pressure has been found along-with a drop in total peripheral resistance as a result of vasodilatation. This is a better overall distribution of blood to the tissues and is brought about by the opening of new capillaries in the small blood vessels in order to suit the character of the blood flowing through them.

4

THE ROLE OF MEASUREMENT AND EVALUATION IN EDUCATION AND PHYSICAL EDUCATION

Measurement and evaluation in at least some elementary form are common everyday practices. In one sense they reflect man's incessant curiosity about the world he lives in and his concern and speculation about himself. Since time immemorial control over environmental conditions improved as better ways of measuring were found.

Even today there is a strong relationship in a field between the sophistication of its measurement techniques and progress in that field in general. This fact is probably revealed more dramatically by advancement in medicine. Thus, progress in an emerging culture was keynoted by more advanced measurement. There are number of reasons why evaluation and measurement are such significant elements of the education spectrum.

AN ERA OF ACCOUNTABILITY

Today is an era of accountability and education is not immune to his societal mandate. Most facets of the educational process will be supported by the public only when educators can show, generally through evaluation techniques, why those facets can be justified in terms of funding and time allotment.

Society places value on certain qualities and behaviour, and these are placed in the educational matrix as goals, but it is the responsibility of administrators and teachers to establish an environment where these can be transmitted to students. This places a compelling responsibility on educators to select suitable environments and procedures and then through measurement to show the extent to which this responsibility has been met.

Therefore, the public demands accountability not only in the output of their teachers in terms of how well they are bringing about that desired student output. In education, accountability becomes a 3-part system that begins with the statement of objectives or proposed changes in the learners, then establishes a plan or a set of experiences to achieve these objectives, and ends with a provision for continual assessment and reporting of results.

It should be pointed out here that accountability is not a simplistic cause-effect type of system to student learning and achieving. Accountability is concerned with a continuing measurement process to determine the extent to which student/teacher objectives are being met, the adequacy of the instructional process, and the adaptability of the process for achieving those objectives.

In many cases, some facet of the educational processes is influenced negatively by factors over which the teacher and administrators have little or no control. Therefore, accountability can become a double-edged sword for the teachers if it is taken too literally.

MEASUREMENT RELATES THE PRODUCT AND THE

PROCESS

A useful purpose of evaluation is to relate the product and the process through some tangible means. Educational processes should always be related to the ends desired or they lose their educational significance. Those values inherent in the process depend on the benefits derived by the product.

It is assumed that a good product results when a good program is developed in relation to formulated objectives, and when appropriate adaptation of methods and materials in instruction occurs, along with efficient administration. This phase of the process should be followed by effective evaluation.

The primary purpose of evaluation is to serve the needs of the students just as other processes and procedures do. It can be justified in the educational spectrum only when it serves useful purposes. When the follow-up after measurement is proper, it is generally reflected in an improved process. Therefore, the needs of the product and the quality of the process are inextricably interwoven.

When the process is evaluated, it is possible the outcomes in the product may be predicted to some degree. When the product is measured, it is equally possible that the process is also revealed. The product and the process should reflect each other. It is only through measurement, however, that relationship can be revealed.

In the final analysis, society is ultimately interested in the product. Any change brought about in the process must be accompanied by desirable and positive changes in the product. The growth, change, and development in the product in those areas valued by society are the criteria of all educational practices. This concept once again emphasized the continuity of the education cycle.

MEASUREMENT REVELS INDIVIDUAL DIFFERENCES

Another important facet of evaluation deals with the diversity of the student. Since each student is viewed as unique, the principle of individual differences must become a reality in education. If this principle is to become functional, the abilities and the needs of each individual must be established.

One of the chief functions of education is to understand the student, and an important purpose of measurement is to identify and recognize needs that will help in that understanding. Students differ in many ways. However, these differences can be translated into needs only when they have been revealed through measurement.

It is important to identify the gifted student as it is the retarded and the average student. When needs have been identified, a program can be planned to meet them. Thus, measurement is indispensable in planning a program to meet individual needs; it is also indispensable in recognizing when such needs have been met.

MEASUREMENT IS A UNIVERSAL PRACTICE

Measurement is a universal practice since it is employed in all fields of endeavour and used in its varied forms by all individuals. Much of the time those individuals who use some form of measurement may not even be aware of their actions.

For example, the final outcome of all games and contests is based on measurement to determine winners and losers. In a broader sense, many evaluations are made daily in carrying out one's normal activities. For instance, in all sport, evaluations are made whenever a player must make a choice: when a golfer selects 5-iron rather than a 6-iron in an approach to the green, when a basketball player passes to a team-mate rather than shoots, or when a batter takes a low pitch for a ball instead of swinging. Such evaluations occur many times daily in our professional, business, political, or social life.

In general, most intentional human behaviour concerns the establishment of some value or criterion, the exercising of judgement, and a follow-up involving a choice. All individuals face a lifetime of choices involving the values and criteria they have established for themselves and the judgements leading to choices based on these.

MEASUREMENT IS THE BASIS OF RESEARCH

If accurate measurement is a corollary to educational process, then research is an important aspect of the process, too, because valid tests are constructed by means of research techniques. Basically, research is a systematic search for finding the solutions to questions and problems in an orderly and logical way. More specifically, research is the scientific method of finding answers to questions and its methodology includes defining problems, formulating hypotheses, collecting, organizing, and evaluating data, making deductions, reaching conclusions, and testing conclusions.

The fundamental purpose of research, then, is to attack the cutting edge of knowledge and extend the boundaries of those horizons through scientific investigation and creative scholarship.

Research is not only closely related to the discipline of physical education, but to the profession of physical education as well. In the discipline it is concerned with understanding those segments of reality that make up a particular field of study.

In the profession it is concerned with modifying or changing those segments. Therefore, research becomes a primary tool to the discipline as it achieves its goals of understanding reality and adding to the body of knowledge in the discipline. On the other hand, research becomes only a secondary tool of the profession since a profession's primary tool is the technology produced by research.

Tests and measurements are part of the technology produced by the research in the discipline. It is through measurement tools and other technology produced by research in the discipline of physical education that the professions effects and evaluates change, growth, and modification.

If research in a discipline produces technology that alters or modifies those segments of reality in that discipline, then research becomes a double-edged sword. Not only does it increase the body of knowledge in that discipline, but it also serves to improve and enhance practices in the profession.

Scientifically constructed tests have been developed through research in fitness, motor, ability, sport skills, knowledge, and values, and these have become invaluable as components of the teaching/learning process. Frequently the data collected for evaluating the product or the process as a part of the education cycle can be used for research. Scientific data can therefore serve 2 primary purposes.

Research and measurement are related in another important way. Much research is possible only because of the technology produced by research. In finding answers to hypothetical questions, objective evidence is needed on which to base conclusions. This evidence comes through the use of valid tools of measurement. Therefore, research and measurement have a symbiotic relationship. One is necessary for the other. Valid tests are constructed through scientific research and scientific research always must depend on valid tests for securing objective data.

Succinctly stated, measurement under-girls man's comprehension, interpretation, and control of his environment. Since it is the basis of technology, it is also the key to research. The acceptance of a profession by other professions and its prestige with the public is dependent in part on the quantity and quality of the research produced by its professionals.

The worth of the research is proportionally related to the validity of those data on which its conclusions are based. In turn, the validity of the data is dependent on the accuracy and preciseness of its measurement instruments.

MEASUREMENT PROVIDES FOR SELF-EVALUATION

An important function of education is to help the students assume more responsibility for their education. To achieve this principle, the students must be furnished with self-knowledge as a part of the learning process. For example, in learning motor skills, the students can be furnished, through either extrinsic or intrinsic feedback, some knowledge of how they are progress to higher levels, they should be taught to engaged in self-analysis while they perform.

This self-analysis ultimately leads to self-evaluation, and self-evaluation leads to self-knowledge. Such evaluation can be either subjective, where the students have a clear goal in mind of the correct performance and they can subjectively estimate their progress in the frame of reference of their goals, or the self-knowledge can be provided in a more objective manner through the use of objective tests to measure the level of achievement toward the specific goal.

Helping students make evaluations about themselves is an important teaching and coaching strategy. Testing can foster self-evaluation by providing self-knowledge, which further enhances the learning of skills, knowledge, or values. Basically, students should be taught to establish their own criteria. In the motor skill area, this could be mental image of the correct performance they want to execute

The good teacher/coach projects this mental image in many ways. Then, the students, through self-evaluation and self-analysis, check on their progress. The self-analysis in physical education is not limited to the movement area. It can also be applied to attitudes and social behaviour relating toss sports and participating.

A most important aspect of teaching is to help students make evaluations in this area which will result in choices that are socially acceptable and which will afford them an opportunity for achievement, success, and satisfaction both immediately and in the future. To this extent, evaluation is education and education is evaluation.

RELATIONSHIP OF PHYSICAL EDUCATION AND EDUCATION

There should be no conflict between education and physicals education in the matter of either the product or the process. The product, objectives, and program of physical education are in harmony with those of general education and are recognized as a part of the educational cycle.

Physical programs are related to educational objectives. In fact, the aim of physical education itself is generally listed as one of the objectives of education. Modern programs of physical education have the same goals as education, although the physical educator must understand that this specialized area is just one of many disciplines that contribute to these goals.

It can be shown that physical education serves most of education's objectives. For example, in the Seven Cardinal Principal of Education. Physical education can contribute directly to the objectives of health, worthy use of leisure, and ethical character and indirectly to the objectives of citizenship, command of the fundamental processes, worthy home membership, and vocation.

In the 4 groups of objectives of the Educational Policies Commission—self-realization, human relationships, economic efficiency, and civic responsibility--physical education can contribute its share towards the realization of these broad goals. For example, physical education may contribute to the objectives of self-realization in several ways.

It contributes through the teaching of knowledge concerning health habits, through the teaching and development of skills and knowledge of sport and exercise, through the development of interest in and appreciation for sports and exercise from both the participants and spectators' standpoint, through an increased appreciation of one's own body and through a philosophy of life that includes play as an important aspect of the good life.

Physical education may contribute to the objectives of human relations by providing a richer social experience for all students through games, sports, and dance, by teaching cooperation in the frame work of competition, by providing training for leadership responsibilities, and by encouraging an increased emphasis on sportsmanship.

Physicals education may contribute to the objectives of economic efficiency by teaching that one's success in any vocation or profession is dependent on health and fitness, as well as industry, that work should have meaning and significance, and that one should buy and use many of the material things of life with a view toward good health and fitness.

Physical education may contribute to the objectives of civic responsibility through the teaching of democracy and citizenship. Sports and games offer fertile fields for the development of qualities of both leadership and "followship" that are necessary for living in a democratic society.

Thus, the needs of the physical are inextricably related to the activities of the mental. At the same time movement does not take place without something happening to personality and social behaviour. The product is an entity and the physical must take its place in the educational spectrum along with the aspects of the mental, social, and spiritual.

Each of these must make its contribution toward a unified, integrated, and effective individual. Succinctly stated, the ultimate end of physical education is the good of the whole individual and no conflict can exist between the aspect of the whole in either the direction or the process.

WHAT IS PHYSICAL EDUCATION?

Physical education may be defined as an education through the physical where many of educational objectives are achieved by means of big muscle-play activities. It is a vital phase of education and an integral part of the total educational process. First, values are conceptualized leading to a mythical individual with the qualities and characteristics of a physically educated person.

Just as in education, the next logical and mental aspects as well as the physical. Then, the physical education process must be determined to translate the established needs and values into learning experiences and to relate them to the objectives. These objectives, when achieved through the process, should lead toward the previously established value: a physically educated person. Such persons have the necessary qualities to become intelligent and interested participants and thereby more affective members of society.

WHAT ARE MEASUREMENT AND EVALUATIONS?

When values have been determined in physical education to lead to an envisioned product, when goals have been designed to elicit desirable changes in that product, and when experiences have been established, then it becomes essential to find out how well those goals have been met, how efficient the product is, and how effective the process has.

This phase of the educational process is concerned with tests, measurements, and evaluation. These involve techniques to student status and progress in growth, adjustment, development, and achievement. The results of such application indicate not only changes in the product in these aspects, but also the magnitude of such changes as well as the direction they have taken. By the same token, appropriate techniques are employed for process appraisal. Results of product appraisal may be used to reveal not only status and progress of the product, but also the process.

The 3 terms—tests, measurement, and evaluation—do have some common elements, but since each also has unique differences, they do not always have the same connotations. For clarity of use in physical education, the following definitions are suggested:

A test is a specific tool, procedure, or technique used to elicit a response from the student in order to gain information to be used as a basis for appraisal of the quantity or quality of elements such as fitness, skill, knowledge, and values.

Measurement is a technique of evaluation that uses tests and other procedures and instruments, is generally precise and objective, generally results in quantitative data, and characteristically can express its results in numerical form when indicating ability or capacity in some trait or characteristically can express its result in numerical form when indicating ability or capacity in some trait or characteristic involving fitness, motor skill, knowledge, value, or process..

Evaluation is a process of education that uses data gathered from the product and the process by means of measurement techniques. It is expressed in either a subjective or objective manner and can be used for comparisons with preconceived criteria to make judgements.

From these definitions its is clearly evident that these terms are not synonymous, but are closely related. Evaluation is a part of the dynamic process of education, measurement is a technique of evaluation, and tests are specific tools of measurement. Evaluation is broader in meaning than the other 2 terms, and its results may be expressed in more qualitative terms.

The definitions imply that measurement merely indicates status and its results may have little significance in themselves. However, when status data are used for comparison with predetermined criteria. Measurement answers specific questions related to quantity and quality, but evaluation appraises these answers in relation to some of the above criteria.

Measurement is terminal since there is no requirement that results be used. Evaluation, however, is a continuous process, for it determines the value or lack of value of process, an action, a characteristic, or a device, and a follow-up is implied. This follow-up is a process of feeding measurement data back into the educational cycle for re-study, re-evaluation, and revision of other segments of the cycle.

In the final analysis, evaluation becomes a process for judging how effective the educational experience has been for the student. It is related to philosophy because it indicates the extent to which objectives are met. It is also related to science since it employs scientific techniques and procedures.

Measurement is fact-finding because it merely provides raw data. Evaluation implies the use of those data for assimilation and interpretation of results, prescription for future use, and a follow-up. It reaffirm the idea that evaluation is a continuous process and is a feedback mechanism that keeps the educational cycle moving in the sequential pattern.

Evaluation should provide a knowledge of how

effective the teaching/learning process has been in achieving the goals that have been established for the product. Judgements must be made constantly about both the product and the process and important decisions are based on these judgements. Since it is highly desirable that these judgements be based on as much objective evidence as possible, scientific measurement should become the most important data-gathering procedure.

MEASUREMENT AND EVALUATION IN PHYSICAL EDUCATION

In sport and physical education, as in life, teachers, and coaches are constantly measuring and evaluating. They measure their students, players, associates, opponents, programs, teaching strategies, coaching techniques, and many other facets of the educational continuum.

The least valid forms of evaluation they might employe are hunches or calculated guesses. The most valid form is the use of well-established criteria as basis for comparison. Usually this is done by means of tests and measures that have been developed through research and validated against suitable criteria.

Physical educators, likes educators in general, should be prepared to submit to those who need or request it objective evidence obtained through valid measurements that physical really educates—educates in the sense that the degree of attainment can be shown in the goals, both general and specific, that have been established. Measurement techniques can be applied in both the product and the process.

HOW MEASUREMENT ARE APPLIED?

Measurement can be applied in several ways. In

evaluating the product, the teacher and coach can do the evaluation or the students may evaluate each other. In some cases the students may evaluate themselves. This student participation in the evaluation procedure is one of the great challenges in the field of teaching. When the process is evaluated, evaluation techniques may be applied by the administrator, by teachers, or by an evaluation team. In some cases, students and parents participate.

Measurement in physical education can be applied for two basic purposes. First, in may be used to measurement status. However, when this same measurement is repeated on the same group 1 or more times, then progress or achievement may be noted. Generally, both status and progress are compared with other values such as norms, standards, or criteria.

Thus, a status measurement repeated at any given time not only reveals how students have progressed, but also how they related to goals and to other students. In both the product and the process, measurement can show status, changes, and significances.

In measurement of the product, evaluation becomes a temporal matter. For example, tests may be given during the ongoing instructional program where they become a part of the procedures of instruction. On the other hand, they may be administered at the end of the instructional unit or term where their resulting data can only be used to evaluate the process or to inform the students of their final status or achievement.

When tests are used during the learning period, they become in integral part of the learning process. Their results are diagnostic and therefore can be used in formative evaluation, whereas tests administered at the end of a term are useful only for summative evaluation.

Formative measures can better serve the immediate needs of the students because their results are diagnostic and can become feedback and input into the learning cycle as they provide the means for self-analysis and self-knowledge. Formative evaluation furnishes students a realistic assessment of their present status, and if given often enough can reveal successive stage of progress. This feedback showing progress provides the students with the self-knowledge and motivation needed for self-satisfaction, and therefore provides more effective reinforcement and identification of errors leading to correction.

Summative measurement at the end of the unit or period is important for evaluating the final status of the students and the worth of the process, but it loses much of its value as a feedback mechanism for positive learning on the part of the students. Since evaluation of the product is perhaps the most viable way to judge the worth of the process, cumulative results are valuable in process evaluation. If the product is shown to be satisfactory through cumulative measurement, the need for process measurement directly may not be necessary

MEASUREMENT APPLIED TO THE PRODUCT

Effective utilization of evaluation occurs in physical education in 2 ways. First, it occurs when measurement procedures are applied directly to the product in order to measure accomplishment in a hierarchy of objectives that have been agreed upon historically by practically all authorities in the field.

These objectives are:

(i) organic development including fitness,

(ii) psychomotor development with emphasis on sport skills,

(iii) cognitive learnings, including knowledge and understanding concerning sport and exercise, and

(iv) psychoment, including social learning involving sports and participation with emphasis on sportsmanship.

Basically, a good program of physical education includes skills, fitness, knowledge, and values to be evaluated.

MEASUREMENT APPLIED TO THE PROCESS

Second, evaluation occurs when special techniques are used to measure the process of physical education directly. The teacher/administrator must know the degree to which the program and other aspects of the process meet acceptable educational standards.

In evaluation of the process, techniques are used to measure the procedures of education and these procedures should be investigated at all educational levels according to the required program, the individual program, the intramural program, and the interschool program.

Process measurement has several approaches, all of which provide the means for an improved service to the product. However,, it should be pointed out here that the evaluation of the product is one of the best means of assessing the quality of the process.

5

FLEXIBILITY, FITNESS, AGILITY, BALANCE AND SPECIFIC MOTOR ABILITIES TESTS IN PHYSICAL EDUCATION AND SPORTS

Flexibility, often referred to as suppleness, is usually defined as the measure of the range of the motion of body parts about their joints, attainable without undue strain to those joints and their muscular attachments. Most tests of flexibility have been of two types: (1) range of motion about a single joint and (2) degree of twist or bend of the body or its parts involving the flexibility or extensibility of two or more joints. Examples of sports movements that require or are enhanced by flexibility of body parts are back handsprings and "splits" in gymnastics, dolphin stroke in swimming, high hurdling in track, and competitive diving. Early flexibility testing consisted of single-joint evaluation in which some form of goniometry was used.

More reported that goniometry had been practised since the turn of the century. Numerous types of goniometers have been devised since that time. The goniometer consists of a 180° protactor with two extended arms, usually 15 inches in length. The stationary arm is fixed to the zero point of the protractor whereas the other arm is movable. A winged nut at the centre point at which the two arms meet may be tightened when a measurement is desired. The centre point of the goniometer is placed over the geometric centre of the joint to be measured, and the two body segments about the joint to be measured from the two legs of the angle recorded on the protractor.

A comprehensive review of the literature on flexibility was published by Wiechec and Krusen, who discussed the problems of measurement, nomenclature, and the need for standardization of norms used in the clinical setting. More recently, a device called the flexometer was devised by Leighton to measure range of motion of the trunk, neck and extremities. Even more recently, an electrogoniometer has been recording angles in joints during various body movements. As the development and maintenance of general body flexibility has been accepted as a physical education function, practical tests of gross flexibility, rather than tests for individual joints, have been emphasized. These tests, in general, do not require special or expensive equipment. A few will be described briefly.

The Cureton Flexibility Tests

This battery of four tests of gross flexibility was first described by Cureton in 1941. The subjects are allowed to warm up thoroughly before taking any of the tests.

Trunk Flexion Forward

Equipment. Sliding wood calliper or measuring stick.

Description and administration. The subject sits on a flat surface, legs 18 inches apart, hands interlaced behind the neck. The forehead is bent slowly forward and downward as far as possible. The knees are kept straight by an assistant.

Scoring. The distance is measured in inches (or centimetres) from the forehead to the surface. The best of three trials is recorded. For this and the following three tests, the subject must remain in position at least two seconds.

Trunk Extension Backward

Equipment. Sliding wood calliper or measuring stick.

Description and administration. The subject lies in a prone (face down) position on a flat surface, hands interlaced behind the neck. The hips are held firmly to the surface by an assistant straddling the legs and pressing forward and downward on the buttocks. The subject lifts the head and chest slowly and backward as far as possible.

Scoring. The distance is measured in inches (or centimetres) from the chin to the surface.

Shoulder Flexibility

Equipment. A sliding wood calliper or measuring stick; a small round wooden rod 24 inches (60.96 cm) in length.

Description and administration. The subject lies in a prone position on a flat surface, the chin touching the floor, and the arms extended forward shoulder-width apart. The rod is grasped and the elbows and wrists kept straight. The rod is raised the maximum distance possible from the floor.

Scoring. The distance is measured in inches (or centimetres) from the underside of the rod to the surface.

Average Ankle Flexibility

Equipment. Paper; long pencil; ruler; solid 3/8-inch (9.5 mm) thick plywood board is 18 inches × 18 inches (45.72 cm × 45.72 cm); protractor; compass.

Description and administration. The subject sits on a flat surface, keeping the legs flat on the surface. A board is placed vertically against the outside edge of a foot, with a piece of paper between the board and the foot. A pencil held horizontally traces the top of the foot at maximum flexion and maximum extension. The lines are drawn long enough to intersect and points are marked with a compass on each line 2 inches from the point of intersection. The legs of the angle are formed by drawing a line from the point of intersection to the 2-inch points.

Scoring. The angle is measured with a protractor and the right and left ankles are averaged.

Reliability and validity. Cureton reported test-retest reliability coefficients of .95, .71, .85 and .72 for college men for trunk flexion, trunk extension, shoulder flexibility and ankle flexibility, respectively. For the same tests in young boys ages 7-13 he reported coefficients of .87, .76, .70 and .55 respectively. Face validity is usually claimed for most flexibility tests, since it is generally agreed that little relationship exists among them.

An internally validity study by Cureton using an average T-score for the four flexibility tests as the test criterion, indicated that no single test had superiority in predicting performance in all four. In the same study, validity coefficients of .77-.88 for trunk extension, .29-.64 for trunk flexion, .23-.64 for shoulder flexibility, and .16-.38 for ankle flexibility indicated that the tests may have some validity in differentiating between expert and ordinary swimmers.

Normative information. Norms for all four tests for college men and for young boys were published by Cureton. Norms for college men and women for trunk extension and shoulder and ankle flexibility were also published by Johnson and Nelson, using slight variations in test administration and scoring.

Comments. The Cureton tests are practical and reasonably reliable tests of gross flexibility. One criticism of the tests is the failure to take into consideration the length of the trunk in the tests of flexion and extension of the trunk and the length of the arms in the shoulder flexibility test. This would cast doubt on the value of the use of his norms for making individual comparisons. However, the tests would still have value for assessing improvements in flexibility due to participation in physical fitness and sports programs when the subject is his or her own control. The norms published by Johnson and Nelson may be of more general value since they did include trunk and arm length in their scoring system.

Wells and Dillon Sit and Reach Test

This test is a modification of the Standing Bend and Reach Test described by Scott and French. The modification was made to eliminate the fear of falling, a common criticism of the latter test.

Equipment. A platform scale; two small benches, a rubber mat 4 feet square. The platform scale consists of a piece of plywood 8 inches × 24 inches with lines drawn horizontally at half-inch intervals. A centre line is marked zero, with plus and minus scales drawn on each side of the zero line. The support for the platform scale consists of an elongated plus sign made of 11-inch boards placed on their edges, a cross board, and a stem board. The platform scale is attached to the upper edges of the support in such a way that when the subject is seated on the floor, with the feet against the cross board, the zero line coincides with the near surface of this board and the minus values are toward the subject. The two benches are placed side by side on their sides about 12 inches apart, with their legs against the wall. The platform scale is placed between the benches with the cross board braced against them. The rubber matting is spread on the floor in front of the partially under the scale.

Description and administration. The subject sits on the rubber matting, legs separated enough to straddle the stem board, with feet pressed firmly against the cross board. The subject bobs forward four times and holds the position of maximum reach on the fourth movement. The knees must remain straight.

Scoring. The score is taken to the nearest half-inch of maximum reach. If the hands reach unevenly, the hand reaching the shorter distance determines the score.

Reliability and validity. The odd-even method of reliability was used, in which the sum of the first and third trials was correlated with the sum of the second and fourth trials. A reliability coefficient of .98 was reported, using 100 college women as subjects. A validity coefficient of .90 was reported, using the Scott and French Standing Bend and Reach Test as the criterion.

Normative information. No norms were published by the authors, although means and standard deviations were reported. Norms for college men and women have been published by Johnson and Nelson, who used a slight modification of the test. The new AAHPERD Health-Related Physical Fitness Test also includes norms for a sit and reach test for ages 6-17.

Comments. The Wells and Dillon Test is a practical and reliable test of back and leg flexibility. The use of the raised platform scale is criticized, however, since extremely flexible individuals would be hindered by it from bending all the way to the floor. The Jonhson and Nelson Sit and Reach Test overcame that problem by placing the measuring scale on the floor.

The Fleishman Extent Flexibility (Twist and Touch) Test

This test was one of six flexibility tests in an extensive factor analysis study of physical fitness components. The purpose of the test was to measure trunk rotation.

Equipment. A measuring scale is drawn on a wall. The scale is 30 inches long and is marked off in half-inch intervals from 0-30 inches. The scale should be sufficiently wide to accommodate differences in heights of subjects. A line is drawn on the floor, perpendicular to the wall and in line with the 12-inch mark on the scale.

Description and administration. A right-handed subject stands with the left side toward the wall, toes touching the line on the floor, and feet together and perpendicular to the line. The subject stands for enough from the wall so that he or she can just touch the wall with the left fist when the arm is held horizontally from the shoulder. The feet are kept in place and the right arm is extended to the side to shoulder height. The palm faces downward, with fingers extended and together. The wrist is kept straight. The subject twists clockwise as far as possible, so that the scale on the wall is touched with the right hand while an assistant assures that the subject's right foot remains in place.

Scoring. One practice trial is given and the second trial is scored to the nearest inch at the farthest point reached. The position must be held at least two seconds.

Reliability and validity. A test-retest reliability of .90 was reported for this test. An internal validity coefficient of .49 was reported, using a factor called "extent flexibility" as the test criterion.

Normative information. Percentile norms, by age

group, were published for boys and girls aged 13-18.

Comments. Although the test as described was practical and reliable, it obviously does not measure only trunk rotation. The test includes shoulder flexibility as well.

The Leighton Flexometer Tests

Through the development of the flexometer, Leighton has contributed probably the most comprehensive method of measuring the range of motion of various joints of the body including the trunk, head and neck, and extremities. Nineteen separate joint-range-of-motion tests may be made with the flexometer, for a total of 30 when the joints of both right and left extremities are included.

Equipment. A flexometer. This measurement consists of a weighted 360° dial and a weighted indicator arm, each of which operates independently of the other. The influence of gravity and the positioning of the extremity move both the dial and the indicator arm to the proper position for recording the joint angle.

Description and administration. The following general procedure applies for all joint movements. The flexometer is secured to the extremity with a one-inch webbed strap. When testing, the dial is locked at the starting position and the indicator arm remains free. The joint being measured is then moved through its full range. The indicator arm is locked at the completion of the joint movement.

Scoring. The difference in degrees between the locked dial at the starting position and the indicator arm at the completion of the movement is the actual range of motion through which the movement was performed.

Reliability and validity. Test-retest reliability

coefficients for 120 boys ranged from .91 to .99 for all tests. Face validity was claimed for the tests based upon the now recognized specificity of individual joint movements.

Normative information. No norms were published in the original study, but means and standard deviations for a group of 40 sixteen-year-old-boys, for all tests, were reported. Rating scales based on 100 sixteen-year-old boys were included in a dissertation by Forbes.

Comments. The Leighton flexometer tests are simple, practical and reliable tests of joint movements. Only the expense of the flexometer precludes its more widespread use in the typical school situation.

Tests of Agility

Agility refers to the controlled ability to change position and direction rapidly and accurately. Two conditions exist under which the ability of the performer may be influenced diversely: (1) a reaction, of a known type and in a known direction, to a stimulus that is anticipated; and (2) a reaction, of an undermined type and in an unknown direction, to a set of stimuli that may vary widely and, hence, be somewhat unpredictable; for example, a defensive halfback reacting to the changes in speed or direction of a pass receiver. Reactions of the performer under the second condition are inevitably slower and initially less precise, since the body is usually in a position that restricts rapid maximum reactions in almost all directions.

There are three types of agility items: (i) change of direction in running; (ii) change of hody position; and (iii) changes of direction of body parts. Examples of these types are, respectively, maze or dodge runs, squat thrusts, and various items demanding change of position of the hands or feet. Terminology is particularly confusing in this area, since various authors use the terms coordination and dynamic balance synonymously with agility.

In a factor analysis study of 20 agility items, Jennett identified at least six factors. These included reaction time, speed, strength, balance, change of direction, and change of position. All but two, strength and balance, can be subsumed under the definition we have used for agility, and these two have been treated as separate or specific motor abilities in this text. The few tests selected for brief review are predominantly tests of change of direction and position. These particular kinds of tests are in more common use in the field and are quite practical to administer.

Illinois Agility Run

The test is representative of the many dodge-run tests that have appeared in the literature over the years. It is recommended that the test be taken barefooted and practised at least once slowly and once rapidly.

Equipment. Four chairs; stopwatch.

Description and administration. The test is started from a prone position, hands at the sides of the chest and on the starting line. At the command, "go" the subject jumps to the feet and sprints, stops and reverses and sprints back toward the starting line. A left turn is made around the first chair, followed by a zig-zag around each other. A right turn is made around the fourth chair, followed by a zig-zag around each chair toward the starting line. A left turn is made around the first chair, followed by a 30-foot.

Scoring. The subject's chest is timed even with the finish line to the nearest half second. If time permits, the best of three trials should be used for best reliability.

Reliability and validity. The test was devised

originally for use with young men ages 17-26. Cureton did not publish reliability coefficients for this age group. However, Sterling reported a coefficient of .92 for this age group, and O'Connor obtained the same coefficient for high school girls. In later work Cureton reported a coefficient of .77 for young boys ages 7-13. For boys in grades 7-9, Gates and Sheffield reported a coefficient of .97 for a similar dodge-run test. Validity work is lacking on this test. In a factor analysis study, it ranked third in measuring a 5-item agility factor and correlated .33 with a 30-item battery composed of strength, balance, agility, flexibility, power and endurance items. O'Connor obtained a .46 validity coefficient with a similar battery composed of 19 items.

Normative information. Cureton published standard score tables for young men ages 17-25 and for young boys ages 7-13. O'Connor presented tables for high school girls.

Comments. This is a practical and reliable test of agility, involving change of direction and running. It is easy to administer, adaptable for both sexes and most age groups, and fun to take. However, more work needs to be done to determine the relativity validity of this particular test as a measure of agility, even though Mc-Cloy reported a validity coefficient of .82 for a similar type test against a 16-item agility to battery.

Burpee Test

This test has attributed to Burpee, although it had been used as a calisthenic exercise for many years before he advocated its use, and was known as the four-count squat thrust.

Equipment. Stopwatch.

Description and administration. From a straight-standing position, the subject moves to a squat-rest position, to a front-leaning-rest position, back to a squat-rest, and finally returns to the straight-standing position.

Scoring. One completed four-part performance is scored as one point. The final score is the total number of performances and fractions thereof completed in ten seconds. Scores for a partial performance are as follows: one-quarter for touching the hands to the floor; one-half for thrusting the legs backward; and three-quarters for returning to a squat-rest position with the hands still on the floor.

Reliability and validity. Test-retest reliability coefficients of .85 and .92 have been reported for high school girls and junior high school boys, respectively. The study on high school girls revealed an internal validity coefficient of .46 between the Burpee test and a 19-item criterion consisting of a number of motor ability components. The study on junior high boys revealed internal validity coefficients of .48 to .63 between the Burpee test and a criterion composed of 16 agility items.

Normative information. Norms are available for elementary school boys and girls, although the norms for high school girls are high compared to those reported by O'Connor. Norms for college men and women were published by Johnson and Nelson, who used a slightly different scoring technique.

Comments. This is a practical and reliable test of agility involving change of position but no running. It is easy to administer, applicable to both sexes, and fun to take. Its validity does not appear to be as high as common agility tests that include running.

Boomerang Run (Right)

This was one of 16 agility items investigated in the original study.

Equipment. One chair or similar object for the centre point; 4 Indian clubs or similar objects for the outside points; stopwatch; marking tape.

Description and administration. The centre point is placed 17 feet from the starting line. One Indian club is placed 15 feet on each side of the centre point. At the command "Go", the subject runs to the centre point, makes a quarter turn light, and completes the course.

Scoring. The score is the time taken to complete the course to the nearest tenth of a second.

Reliability and validity. Gates and Sheffield reported a test-retest reliability coefficient of .92 for junior high boys, and Sierakowski gave the same coefficient for high school girls. Sierakowski also reported an internal validity coefficient of .72 for girls, using the sum of T-scores for a 15-item agility battery as the test criterion. Gates and Sheffield reported validity coefficients ranging from .78 to .87 for junior high boys, using a similar 16-item battery.

Normative information. The original authors did not publish norms for this test. However, Johnson and Nelson presented norms for this test. However, Johnson and Nelson presented norms for junior high boys.

Comments. This is a practical, reliable and reasonably valid test of agility that includes running. Like most tests of agility, it is easy to administer, inexpensive, applicable to both sexes, and fun to take.

Gates-Sheffield Agility Batteries

Few batteries of agility tests have been developed, and these have been validated predominantly for small and select samples of population. In this study the subjects were boys from grade 7-9. A 16-item agility battery was subjected to regression analysis in order to arrive at a representative small battery.

Equipment. Nine chairs or similar objects; 6 Indian clubs or similar objects; stopwatch; marking tape.

Description and administration. Of the 16 items studied originally, six were included in a series of three, 3-item batteries. The description in the original paper of each of the six items will not be repeated here. These include the 40-yard maze, zig-zag side step, zig-zag run, loop-the-loop, boomerang right, and 30-foot shuttle run.

Scoring. Each of the six tests is scored by determining, to the nearest tenth of a second, the time it takes to complete each test. Tables are provided for converting raw scores to T-scores. The final three test batteries and regression coefficients were as shown here.

Seventh grade boys:

agility = .771 × 40-yd maze run + .409 × zig-zag side step + .205 × 30-ft shuttle run

Eighth grade boys:

agility = .389 × loop-the-loop + .449 × 30-ft shuttle run + .528 × zig-zag side step

Ninth grade boys:

agility = .397 × zig-zag run + .460 × boomerang, right + .453 × 30-ft shuttle run

Reliability and validity. Test-retest reliability coefficients for the six items ranged from .91 to .97. The internal validity coefficients for each of the six items against the 16-item agility criterion ranged from .73 to .92. Three additional validity schemes were employed. The first was correlation of the sum of T-scores against agility, i.e., scores obtained from the regression equations. The coefficient obtained was .86. The second was correlation of total T-scores against an external criterion consisting of a subjective judgment of games ability versus agility. The coefficient obtained was .80.

The third was multiple correlation of each of the three batteries against the 16-item criterion. The coefficients obtained were .96, .95 and .92 for the seventh, and ninth grade batteries, respectively.

Normative information. No norms were published in the original paper. However, since the sum of the weighted scores in each battery constitutes a total score, a T-score of 50 would be average, and deviations higher or lower would be indications of above or below average performance, respectively.

Comments. These batteries of agility tests are practical, reliable, and valid. They are easy to administer, applicable to both sexes, and fun to take. If time permits, the batteries are recommended over individual test items, even though there is probably some overlap, since intercorrelations among all 6 items used in the batteries ranged from .56 to .82.

Tests of Balance

"Static balance" involves the ability to maintain the body's centre of gravity over the centre of its supporting base. Two main factors determine the degree of stability of a body: (1) the larger the area of the base, the greater the range of stability; and (2) the closer the centre of gravity of the body is positioned over the centre of the base, the greater is the degree of stability. Ability to maintain static balance is critical in such activities as gymnastics balancing and in defensive positions in wrestling. Similarly critical is the ability to disturb momentarily the body's balance in a controlled movement that is immediately followed by the recovery of a similar or dissimilar position of balance.

Thus, all human motion is generated by the disturbance of the body's balance, and motion largely ceases when the body's stability is regained and maintained. For practical purposes, balance is considered here as a "specific" component of motor ability. However, it probably results from complex combinations of kinethetic responses, visual responses, and semicircular canal function. Muscular strcngth is a factor in some tests of balance. A few representative tests are selected for brief review because of their practicality. Other tests requiring more expensive and/ or complex equipment are also available.

Bass Stick Test of Static Balance

This test is also performed with the supporting foot crosswise on the balance stick. Except for the obvious difference, the crosswise test is administered identically to the lengthwise test.

Equipment. Several wooden sticks 1 inch × 1 inch × 12 inches; a watch with a second hand; adhesive tape to secure the sticks to the floor.

Description and administration. At the word "Ready", the subject places the supporting foot lengthwise on the balance stick, i.e., with the long axis of the foot parallel to the long axis of the stick. At the word "Go", the subject raises the free foot and holds this position as long as possible to a maximum of 60 counts. The time counts aloud one count per second. A trial is terminated if: (1) either the heel or toe of the supporting foot touches the floor; (2) the free foot touches the floor; or (3) balance is maintained for 60 counts. No more than three practice trials are recommended.

Scoring. The score of the test is the sum of the times for six official trials of the test.

Reliability and validity. A reliability coefficient of .86 was obtained on a sample of 270 college women. Years later, Fleishman obtained a coefficient of .82 on a slight modification of the test. Three validity schemes were presented in the original paper: (i) correlation of the test with a subjective rating of rhythmic ability; (ii) correlation with a subjective rating of general motor ability; and (iii) factor analysis in which the test correlated .45 with a battery of balance tests involving use of visual cues. Years later, Fleishman obtained a coefficient of .64 between a slight modification of this test and a very similar balance battery.

Normative information. No norms were published in the original paper. Since that time, however, Johnson and Nelson, using a slight modification of the test, presented norms for boys and girls ages 13-18.

Comments. This is a practical, reasonably reliable, and valid test of static balance. It is easy to administer and adaptable to both sexes and various age groups. With sufficient sticks, a large number of subjects can be tested simultaneously. The number of trials can probably be decreased from six without seriously compromising the test's reliability.

The Stork Stand

Equipment. One stopwatch or watch with a second hand.

Description and administration. The performer stands on the dominant foot, places the other foot flat on the medial aspect of the supporting knee, and places the hands on the hips. At the signal "Now", the performer raises the heel of the supporting foot and maintains balance as long as possible without moving the ball of the supporting foot or letting its heel touch the floor.

Scoring. Three trials are given. Time is counted in

seconds from the time the heel is raised to the time the balance is lost or the hands are removed from the hips. The highest of the three scores is recorded to the nearest second.

Reliability and validity. A test-retest reliability coefficient of .87 was reported for the best of three trials given on different days. No validity study was attempted. Face validity was claimed by the authors.

Normative information. T-score norm tables were included for college men and women.

Comments. This is a most practical and reasonably reliable test of static balance. It is easy to administer and adaptable to both sexes and various age groups. If time is a factor, subjects may be tested in pairs by having one person perform and the other note the seconds as they are called aloud by the timer. This test needs to be studied as to its relative ability to measure static balance, i.e., it should be correlated against a battery of other tests purported to measure static balance. Finally, norms are needed for school-age groups other than college students.

The Springfield Beam-Walking Test

This is an example of a "dynamic" balance test, according to our definitions.

Equipment. The test utilizes 9 hardwood beams 4½ inches high and 10 feet long, but with varying widths for walking surfaces of 4, 3½, 3, 2½, 2, 1½ and ¼ inches. Short cross pieces are needed to keep the beams steady. A simple foot-measuring board is used to classify all subjects into six categories of foot length, ranging from those having foot lengths between 7 and 8 inches to those between 12 and 13 inches. Six starting points are painted in different colours on the sides of the beam, such that if ten heel-to-toe steps are taken, the subject will finish the tenth step at the end of the beam.

Description and administration. A standardized practice is recommended. The subject is placed at the starting point on the beam according to shoe length, so that he or she could walk a maximum of ten steps from the starting point to the end of the beam. The subject attempts to walk ten steps in heel-to-toe fashion and with hands on hips. Subjects who fall off or drop their hands from the hips before completing the ten steps are allowed to continue from that point until they fall off or drop the hands a second time. The second "fall-off" terminates the trial on that particular beam.

Scoring. The walking surfaces of the beams are marked in quarter lengths. Since different people start at six different places, depending on shoe length, there are six different colour markings of quarter lengths. Thus, the score of a person on a particular beam is the score value of the segment of the beam in which the second fall-off occurs. Since the maximum score on each beam is four quarters and there are nine beams, the maximum score on the entire test is 36 points. In the original study, for reliability purposes, the average of six trials was used as the final score.

Reliability and validity. Reliability coefficients were obtained by correlating the three odd trial scores against the three even trial scores. This was done on samples of 30 boys each for each year of age from years 5-18. Coefficients ranged from .75 to .89. No validity work was reported in the original paper, although the author cited the works of others who correlated modifications of this test with other balance tests. The "validity" coefficients were generally very low.

Normative information. No norms appeared in the original paper. However, the author published for each age group means, standard deviations, medians, and first and third quartiles from which standard score and percentile tables could be constructed easily.

Comments. This appears to be a practical and reliable test of dynamic balance. Attempts should be made to determine if the number of trials could be shortened without compromising the reliability of the test. The validity of the test needs to be explored more fully. Norms should be developed for various age groups and for both sexes.

6

TEST AND MEASUREMENT OF MUSCULAR STRENGTH

Physical capabilities depend upon muscle strength as well as skill and stamina. Muscle strength depends primarily on the true cross-sectional area of the muscle(s) and its state of running. The externally measured force produced by any given muscle group depends upon a number of factors:

—There is an optimal muscle length for maximal force production. It is therefore necessary a standardised joint positions during the measurement.

—There is a force-velocity relation such that the muscles produce more force when shortening slowly than when shortening rapidly, more still when they are prevented from shortening. It is therefore necessary to standardise the speed of the moment.

—The produced force is also influenced by the mechanical advantage of the muscles both internally, depending on their attachment to the bony levers of the skeleton, and externally depending on the arrangement of the recording apparatus. The force in the tendon is usually any times greater than the externally recorded force.

—There is little justification for assuming that the measurement of one muscle group provides a measure of strength for that individual. There are correlations between the strength of the muscle group and another but they are not always high. One reason for this is that the effects of training are specific to the muscles used. If a full description is required then of many muscle groups as possible should be measured and the results displayed as a rifle.

—The choice of muscle group should be guided by the functional relevance of the movement at the reliability of the measurement. In some studies the social acceptability of the measurements and the portability and cost of the equipment may also be critical.

—The flexors and extensors of joints with a hinge movement such as the knee, ankle and foots can be measured as functionally separable muscle groups. Provided care is taken to mercendise the body position so that other against muscles cannot contribute to the measured for the reliability of such measurements is fairly good.

—The reception is the power grip of the hand. This does require the combined action of a centre of muscles in the hand and forearm, however, it is a familiar action and of functional importance. It depends upon a closed system of forces operating between the fingers and the thinner eminence, so it is measurable with light-weight equipment. Most other measures of strength require a fixed, and therefore heavy, frame against which to exert force and so are not easily portable.

Although the relevant to lifting ability, the extensor strength of the back muscles should not be subjected to maximal strength tests in those who report serious low back pain during the last 6 months or damage at any time to the vertebral discs. This is common in older adult Caucasians. The three measurements recommended below, hand-grip, knee extension and knee flexion have been found in isometric tests of young adult Causasian males to relate well to aggregate measures of muscle strength derived from many muscle groups. Knee extension relates better than knee flexion.

Isometric Measurements

Externally applied isometric force can be measured mechanically by the slight extension or compression of a strong spring. However, these dynamometers often suffer from hysteresis and temperature sensitivity. Better methods depend on strain-gauges which detect the slight bending or deformation of a steel bar produced by an applied force. These dynamometers are inherently more sensitive and more reliable. A negligible amount of muscle shortening occurs, and temperature sensitivity is negligible after the electronic circuits have warmed up. The strain-gauge must be tightly bonded to the bar at the position of maximal deformation when force is applied.

Electrical power is required from a stepped down mains supply or a battery. The strain-gauge form part of a Wheatstone bridge circuit and the applied force is proportional to the imbalance in the bridge. This can be detected electronically in a number of ways. The simplest system consists of a potentiometer, an amplifier and a dial. The observer reads the transient maximal position of the needle swinging over the dial. A light-weight tell-tale pointer can be pushed round by the active needle to serve as a peak hold device.

The friction in the tell-tale pivot must be slight so that the movement of the active needle is not damped. Rapid force generation may then lead to over-reading of the tell-tale due to its importance. More sophisticated systems can provide a digital display with a peak hold facility for the maximal detected force, storage of data in a microcomputer and a hard copy from a printer. Mechanical or electrical dynanometers can be arranged in numerous ways depending on the muscle group of interest using inextensible cables and pulleys. A variety of satisfactory force transducers and load cells using strain-gauges or hydraulic principles are available commercially.

It is advisable to check their calibration characteristics for sensitivity, linearity and repeatability. There are also a number of custom-built chairs, tables and couches which provide the fixed external frame. Sphygmomanometers have been adapted for measuring hand-grip strength as the maximal pressure which can be registered by squeezing the partially inflated cuff. However, this is not easily standardised and it is not clear how to calibrate them appropriately.

Isokinetic Measurements

If the muscles of interest are acting round a joint with a well-defined axis of rotation then the externally applied force can be measured isokinetically as torque. This is done using a lever arm connected through a gear/clutch/worm system driven at the worm end by a constant speed motor. When the subject is moving the lever arm fast enough to match the motor speed, force is transmitted through the clutch and recorded. It is important that the motor speed does not vary when the system is subjected to high forces during strength measurements. The original system was developed by Cybex. A range of isokinetic speeds can be used so that the force-velocity characteristics of the muscle are described. The force can be detected in a number of ways, for instance, using strain guages at the lever arm or a load cell bellow the worm wheel.

Microcomputer systems are available for controlling the motor, collecting and analysis the data and providing hard copy. This approach is versatile, a large number of different muscle groups can be assessed, and a wide range of forces can be accurately measured. The disadvantages are the cost and the size and weight of the equipment. Electrical stimulation either via the motor nerve or directly to the muscle has also been used in studies of muscle strength. It should not be undertaken without recourse to detailed advice not provided below, is similar to the electrically stimulated strength. This confirms that well-motivated subjects are able to activate their muscles fully.

Observation to be Made

Hand-grip

This is an isometric test. Both hands should be tested. The test is best carried out using a strain-gauge dynamometer which is not sensitive to the position of application of the force.

Knee-extension

This test measures the strength of the quadriceps muscle group. It can be carried out isometrically using a cable and strain-guage system, or both isometrically and isokinetically at a range of speeds using a motorised system.

Knee-flexion

This test measures the strength of the hamstrings muscle group. It can be measured similarly to knee-extension as described above. A large number of other tests can be carried out using isometric strain-gauge systems and isokinetic systems.

Sampling and Methods of Testing

Strength tests are of interest in population studies in relation to the growth of children, bodily physique, working capacity, nutritional status and health. They are also of interest for characterising an individual or monitoring interventions in selected groups in clinical, sports or rehabilitation studies. The sample size will be determined in the usual way paying attention to the variation in the measurement which is attributable to factors other than those under examination.

The instrument should contribute only a small amount of variation provided it has been properly calibrated, the mechanical dynamometers being the least reliable. There is a considerable intra-subject variation in maximal voluntary strength measurements even with one tester who endeavours to give maximal encouragement during each effort. Inter-individual variation in well nourished adults is mainly due to body size, sex and state of training.

In children, age and state of sexual development which both affect muscle cross-sectional area are important. Samples may be grouped according to these factors. For children, grouping for stature as a measure of body size in 10 cm intervals that been recommended by Asmussen and Heeboll-Neilsen. A double logarithmic plot of stature against mean strength in each 10 cm class interval gives a straight line relation. Sample sizes of 100 individuals in each sex for each 10 year age group are required to describe the population. Dynamometer tests yield interval data which is continuous and usually fairly normally distributed.

Therefore, statistical tests such as Students t for differences between groups and Pearson's product-moment for relations between variables can be used. If the investigation requires the detection of differences of no less than 5% either between independent groups or longitudinally within a group and the measurement has a coefficient of variation on retest of ± 10% or better than sample sizes of 20 will suffice provided they are randomly drawn. In the tests described below, standardisation of the body position in which the movements are made is of the utmost importance.

It has been shown that the difference between muscle groups on the right and left sides of the body is about 5-10% of the strength of the stronger side, with a standard deviation of about 4-11%. This difference is most pronounced in the lower extremities. Subjects must be allowed to rehearse the manoeuvre required submaximally to their own and the tester's satisfaction before any maximal efforts are made. All trials should be recorded and the best of three entered as the maximal voluntary strength provided the two highest are within 5 of one another.

If this requirement is not met then a further two trials are permissible. A rest of 2 min between each trial is essential to prevent the effect of fatigue on the measurement. Subjects must in all cases be exhorted to do their best. It has been shown that results obtained using the shout technique of exhortation may exceed the results obtained without such encouragement by as much as 20%. Effective motivation of the subject is tiring work and the tester should not attempt to make measurements for more than an hour at a time nor for more than 3 hours per day. Testers need to be trained and their measurements compared with those of the experienced tester. Agreement of the order of the intra-individual re-test variation should be achieved. All dynamometers must be calibrated regularly.

The calibration should extend over the full expected range of measurement, and repeated calibrations should vary by not more than 5%, after controlling for temperature, warm-up time and potential hysteresis. If the calibration curve is linear with good repeatability, then 6 points will describe it satisfactorily and weekly checks using 3 points across the range will be adequate. Cross comparisons of results recorded with different types of dynamometer should not be cross-vandation. Mean differences of 50% have been recorded between a mechanical and a strain-gauge hand-grip dynamometer. All results should be recorded as Newtons for isometric measurements, or Newton-metres for isokinetic measurements, according to the System International.

Hand-grip strength

The size of the dynamometer should be adjusted to the size of the hand to bring the second joint of fore-finger approximately into a right angle. This is usually consistent with subjective impressions of the optimal size of the dynamometer. The subject should sit comfortably with the elbow at a right angle, the arm abducted against the side of the trunk, the forearm in neutral rotation and the wrist in about 15 degrees of extension.

Knee-extension and flexion

The subject should sit with a firm back support and restraining straps across the chest and the thigh. The knee is at 90 degrees. The arms should be folded across the chest during the measurement. If there are no straps then the subject should lean forward during the measurement. For some isometric measurements the strain-gauge cable is attached perpendicularly to the lower leg, using a padded strap, at a fixed distance from the axis of rotation of the knee. For isokinetic measurements the axis of rotation of the knee joint must first be lined up with the axis of rotation of the lever arm of the dynamometer.

The lower leg is then attached as above to the lever arm. Torque should always be recorded at a specific angle. The torque profile recorded during a maximal effort will contain an impact artefact. This occurs at the point when the leg catches up with the motor and force is transmitted through the clutch. This is an inevitable mechanical property of such systems. At slow speeds it is unimportant as it occurs before maximal torues are reached and is relatively small.

However, at fast speeds it can obscure the true torque. The problem is not solved by damping which may be provided by the manufacturer. This distorts the signal as well as smoothing the impact spike. The only solution is to measure the torque late in the movement when the impact spike is over. This also ensures adequate activation time for the muscle. For either type of measurement the force produced by the mass of the relaxed leg should be added or substracted as appropriate to forces recorded when the knee is at any angle other than 90 degrees.

Equipment

(a) Hang-grip dynamometers

Mechanical

C.H. Stoelting Co., 424 N. Homan Ave., Chicago, IL 60624, U.S.A. Details in "Standardized Test of Fitness" Operations Manual, Canada Fit, 2nd Edition (1981).

Electrical

Bio-Med Engineering Ltd., 1 Headlands Rd., Liversedge, W. Yorks, WF15 7NT, U.K.

Tel: 0924-405386

MIE Medical Research Ltd., 6 Wortley Moor Rd., Leeds LS 124JF, U.K.

Tel: 0532-7937100.

This is insensitive to the position of force application and is available with a software for IBM or BBC microcomputers (MIE only).

(b) Isometric knee extensor dynamometers

Details in: Tornvall, G. (1963); Edwards, R. et al (1997); and Maughan, R.J., Watson, J.S. and Weir, J. (1983).

Supplies and information on strain-gauges available from

R.S. Components Ltd., P.O: Box 99m Corby, Northants NN179RS, U.K.

Tel: 01-3608600 or 0536-201201.

(c) Multi-purpose dynamometers

Isometric

Tornvall, G. (1963) as above, or Asmussen, E. and Heeboll-Neilsen, K. (1959 and 1961).

Isokinetic

Lumex Inc., Cybex Division, 2100 Smithtown Ave., Ronkonkama, NY 11779, U.S.A.

Tel: 516-585-9000 or Numeq, 23-24 Thornhill Rd., North Moons Moat, Redditch, Wore. B9H9ND, U.K.

Tel: 0572-64222

Data Collecting Sheet

Name:

Serial Number:

Ethnic and Tribal Origin (Or nationality):

Age:

Sex:

Place of Examination:

Date of Examination:

Occupation:

Observer:

Weight (kg):

Height (mm):

Record to nearest N-the best of 3 trials:

Grip strength (left hand):

Grip strength (right hand):

Dominant hand:

Instrument used for grip strength:

Knee extension (left):

Knee extension (right):

Knee flexion (left):

Knee flexion (right);

Instrument used for knee strength:

7

TEST AND MEASUREMENT OF MOTOR PERFORMANCE

The Measurement of Power

Power may be identified as the ability to release maximum force in the faster possible time, as is exemplified in the vertical jump, the broad jump, the shot put, and other movements against a resistance in a minimum of time.

The measurement of power in physical education has recently become controversial enough to warrant recognition of two types of such measurement. The two types are identified as follows:

Athletic power measurement—This type of measurement is expressed in terms of the distances through which the body or an object is propelled through space. Such tests as the Sargent jump broad jump, and vertical arm common tests of athletic power.

While such tests involve both force and velocity, other factors, also influence testing results. However, the factors of force and velocity are not measured as such; thus, only the resultant distance is recorded in athletic power measurement.

Work-power measurement—In measuring power for research purposes, special efforts are usually made to eliminate extraneous movements, thus placing maximum effort on the specific muscle group to be studied.

Then the result is usually based on computations of work or power. Example of this type of measurement are the modified vertical power jump, and the vertical arm pull.

Athletic power tests are quite practical for the majority of schools and have been widely used in physical fitness and motor ability testing programs. New tests, the modified vertical power jump and the vertical arm pull, have also been developed for practical use in physical education programs and for research.

Because power includes the important factors of strength and speed of movement, it may become confused with the those types of tests. However, strength tests are concerned only with the force exerted or the number of pounds successfully lifted, and speed tests are concerned in a specified distance or the distance covered in a specified amount of time.

In power tests the distance, force, and time factors should be specified, while the resistance is usually either body weight or a specified number of pounds. The 60-yard dash and the 30-yard shuttle run have been used as tests of power and this has caused confusion in an understanding of power measurement. However, since these tests are more characteristic of speed and agility, they should not be considered as power tests.

Practical Test of Athletic Power

Several practical tests of athletic power in terms of time, equipment.

Vertical Jumps

Chalk Jump

Sex—Satisfactory for both boys and girls.

Age Level—Satisfactory for ages nine through adulthood,

Objective—To measure the power of the legs in jumping vertically upward.

Reliability—Has been reported as high as .93.

Objectivity—An objectivity coefficient of .93 was obtained by Jack Clayton, 1969.

Validity—A validity of .78 has been reported with the criterion of a sum of four track and field event scores.

Directions—The performer should stand with one side toward a wall, heels together, and hold a 1 inch piece of chalk in the hand nearest to the wall, keeping the heels on the floor, he should reach upward as high as possible and make a mark on the wall. The performer then jumps as high as possible and makes another marks at the height of his jump.

Equipment and Materials—A yardstick, several pieces of chalk, and a smooth wall surface of at least 12 feet from the floor are required.

Additional Pointer—(i) A double jump or a "crow hop" should not be permitted upon takeoff. (ii) The chalk should not be extended any further than necessary beyond the fingertips to make the standing and jumping marks. (iii) The reliability and validity of the test can be slightly improved if the performer practices the jump unit it is correctly executed before being tested. (iv) Body weight may be included to score in terms of foot-pounds.

Scoring—The number of inches between the reach and the jump marks measured to the nearest half inch is the score. Three to five trials are allowed and the best trial is recorded as the score.

Two-Hand Medicine Ball Put

Sex—Satisfactory for boys and girls.

Age Level—Ages twelve through college.

Objective—To measure the power of the arms and shoulder girdle.

Reliability—An r of .81 was found for college girls, while an r of .84 was found for college men.

Objectivity—Reported as high as .99 as found by Gene Ford, 1969.

Validity—An r of .77 was obtained by correlating distance scores with scores computed by the power formula.

Directions—From a sitting position in a straight back chair, the performer holds the ball in both hands with the ball drawn back against the chest and just under the chin. He then pushes the ball upward and outward for maximum distance.

The rope is placed around the performer's chest and held taut to the rear by a partner in order to eliminate rocking action during the push. The performer's effort should be primarily with the arms.

Equipment and Materials—A 6-pound medicine ball, marking material, small rope, chair, and a tape measure are needed for this test.

Additional Pointers—(i) Each of three trails should be taken in succession. (ii) Distance is measured from the forward edge of the chair to the point of contact of the ball with the floor.

Scoring—The distance of the best of three trials measured to the nearest foot is recorded as the score. One practice trials may be taken before scoring.

Standing Broad or Long Jump

Sex—Satisfactory for both boys and girls.

Age Level—Ages six through college.

Objective—To measure the athletic power of the legs in jumping forward.

Reliability—Has been reported as high as .963.

Objectivity—An objectivity coefficient of .96 was obtained by Jack Clayton, 1969.

Validity—A validity of .607 has been reported for this test when a pure power test was used as the criterion.

Directions—With the feet parallel to each other and behind the starting mark, the performer bends as far forward as possible.

Equipment and Materials—Either a mat or the floor may be used for this test. Marking material is needed for the stating line, along with a tape measure to mark off increments of distance along the landing area.

Additional Pointers—(i) If the performer falls backward upon landing, the measurement is made between the starting line and the nearest part of the body touching the landing surface. (ii) The jump should be practised until the movement can be executed correctly, since validity and reliability can be improved thereby.

Scoring—The number of inches between the starting line and the nearest heel upon landing is the score. Three trials are permitted, and then the best trial is recorded as the score.

Vertical Arm Pull Test

Sex- -Satisfactory for boys only.

Age Level—Ages fourteen through college.

Objective—To measure the power of the arms and shoulder girdle in a vertical rope pull. This test may be used to indicates potential in pole vaulting and gymnastics.

Reliability—An r of .97 was found for this test.

Validity—An r of .80 was found when the distance score test was correlated with the vertical power pull test.

Objectivity—An r of .99 indicated a high degree of objectivity.

Directions—Record the performer's name and then have him assume a sitting position on a chair or bench and grasp as high up the rope as possible without raising the buttocks from the chair or bench seat. Concerning the grasp, the hand of the preferred arm should be just above the opposite hand.

The tester should place a piece of marking tape around the rope just above the uppermost hand. The performer should then pull and reach as high up the rope as possible and grasp and hold the rope until the tester can again place piece of marking tape above the uppermost hand.

The tester should allow each performer three trials and disregard any trial where the feet touch the floor during the pull. On the third trial, say "This is your last pull. Try to beat your last two pulls."

Equipment and Materials—A climbing rope, marking tape, a tape measure, and a chair are required for this test. Students are required to dress in shorts, light shirt, and no shoes.

Additional Pointers—(i) The tester must have marking tape ready to immediately place above the uppermost hand as it grasps the ropc. (ii) The performer should be instructed to vigorously pike the hips as he makes the pull. (iii) The performer may close his legs in around the rope following his pull and grasp. (iii) The rope should hang directly downward so that it touches the front edge of the chair between the legs of the performer, (v) As the performer's seat leaves the chair, the tester may step upon the chair to mark the heights of the performer's search. (vi) From the starting position, the uppermost hand will become the reaching hand during the pull, keep in mind that this is a one pull and grasp test, nota climbing sequence test.

Scoring—Record the score of the best pull as measured to the nearest quarter inch.

Work-Power Test

Vertical Power Jump

Sex—Satisfactory for both boys and girls.

Age Level—Ages ten through college.

Objective—To measure power of the legs in jumping vertically upward.

Reliability—Has been reported as high as .977 for college men.

Objectivity—Was reported as high as .99 by Steve Long, 1972.

Validity—Has been reported as high as .989 with the vertical power-jump as the criterion with college men.

Directions—Record the performer's weight and then have him assume a standing position facing sideways to the jump board, the preferred arm behind the back, and the other arm raised vertically with the hand turned outward and fingers extended. Holding the described position, the performer should stand as tall as possible on the toes so that the height of the extended middle finger of the raised arm can be recorded. Chalk dust is then placed on the middle finger, and the performer adopts a full body in balance.

The performer is then told to jump as high as possible

and to touch the board at the top of the jump. The tester must watch and disregard any jump in which balance or position is lost.

The tester should record the height of the chalk mark on the jump board. Each performer is allowed three trials. On the last trial the tester should say, "This is your last jump. Try to beat your last two jumps."

Equipment and Materials—A jump board marked off in half inches, chalk dust, and weight scales are required for the test. The subject must be dressed in shorts, light shirt,, and no shoes.

Scoring—Using the measure of the best jump.

Uses of Power Tests

Several ways in which power tests can be utilised in physical education classes are listed as follows:

(i) As a means to motivates students to improve their status within the class.

(ii) As a measure for determining achievement and grades when improvement in athletic powers is a specific objective in a physical activity class.

(iii) As a means to indicate an individuals potential for varsity athletics.

(iv) As a factor in motor ability tests.

Findings and Conclusions from Power Measurement and Research

Power has been measured and studied in various ways. For example, it has been studied by the following methods: (i) athletic power method where extraneous movements are not eliminated and (iii) motion photography where recordings of force, distance, and time were collected to calculate power based on its mechanical principle.

Studies have shown that systematic weight training can improve athletic power performance. However, Muller concluded that strong muscles do not necessarily indicate better performance. Since dynamic training was found to be effective in improving athletic power performance, it was theorized that static training might equally be as effective.

However, several studies failed to obtain gains in jumping performance to accompany static strength increases at the end of training programs, although other studies have found that isometric training improved both strength and speed performance.

Obviously, studies are in conflict concerning the effectiveness of isometric because of variations in testing or training procedures. In isometrics training it is important that a measuring devisable used each day so that subjects will known how hard they are straining, and it is important to train subjects at the angles where the greatest force is needed in power performance. Otherwise, mediocre results are more than likely to occur.

Several studies have shown that previous activity such as basketball and swimming have a negative effect on jumping tests. Therefore, rest prior to athletic power jump tests should be considered if optimum results are to be achieved.

In studying age, height, and power, the following findings have been reported:

(i) Power was found to increase during the early years until the approach of middle age, after which there was a decline in power performance.

(ii) Power measures were not found to increase of decrease with the increased age and growth of junior high girls enrolled in ungraded classes.

(iii) The Sargents Jump was found to be better means of classifying girls for individuals athletic performance, since age, height, and weight alone were found to be of little value for such classification.

A number of studies were related with the relationship of strength and speed to power. The results of such studies are listed as follows:

(i) Several studies indicate that speed was significantly related to power and that it was more important than strength in athletic performance.

(ii) Two studies found static strengths and dynamic strength significantly related to leg power, thus indicating strength as an important variable in power measurement.

Concerning physical activities, Mccloy found the Sargent jump significantly related to the total point score of select track and field events, and Bushey found a significant relationship between vertical jump scores and modern dance performance.

In studying the effects of various positions on vertical jump performance, Martin and Sttull found that the most effective knee angle is approximately 115 degrees, while foot spacing should range between 5 to 10 inches laterally and slightly better than 5 inches anteriorly posteriorly.

Powers Associated with Power Testing

Several of the problems associated with power testing are listed as follows:

(i) Vigorous activity prior to jumping performance tests seems to have a significantly negative effect upon performance. Therefore, more consideration should be given to rest for participants prior to jumping performance.

(ii) The level of motivation must be controlled so that all students are tested under the same conditions. The conditions which are usually considered standard are a knowledge of results, tested in the presence of peers, and the avoidance of cheering and other unusual circumstances.

(iii) The common tests of athletic power are inadequate for use in experimental research since learning to perform could be misinterpreted as increased power. Therefore, such tests as the vertical power jump and the power lever should be used since extraneous movements have been eliminated.

(iv) There is a need for norms at all grade levels for both boys and girls on certain power tests.

(v) Practice and coaching tips seem to affect the reliability and validity of athletic power tests due to the improved use of extraneous movements rather than of an actual increases in power itself. Thus, it seems necessary to either eliminate the extraneous movements or practice them until all movements are executed correctly before recording scores.

THE MEASUREMENT OF SPEED AND REACTION

Speed of movements and quick reactions are prized qualities in athletics. Coaches are frequently heard to praise certain players or an entire team for their quickness.

In football a player who is extremely fast poses a constant threat to break away for the long run; in baseball the fast runner causes hurried throws and adjustments in pitching and defensive strategy; the full-court press is a potent weapon in basketball if a team has the speed to make it effective; and, of course, in track speed is the essence of the sport.

However, despite these commonplace observations, the study of speed of movement and speed of reaction is much more complex than it might appears. Speed of movement, for example, entails much more than mere running speed.

The speed with which a wrestler executes a reversal, the lighting flash of a boxer's jab, the explosive spring of the shot putter's move across the throwing circle, and the graceful swiftness of the swimmer and skater are but a few of the many different kinds of movement speeds that are involved in physical performance. Speed of movement shall thus be defined as the rate at which a person can propel his body, or parts of his body through space.

Reaction time is the interval of time between the presentation of the stimulus and the initiation of the response. While reaction time was initially thought to be a rather simple and easily measured phenomenon, it has been shown to be influenced by a number of variables. Strictly speaking, and individual cannot be described as having a single reaction time without specifying the conditions under which have been found to influence reaction time are the following: the sense organ involved, the intensity of the stimulus, the preparatory set, general muscular tension, motivation, practice, the response required, fatigue, and one's general state of fatigues, and one's general state of health.

Analysis of speed of movement and reaction time when combined together is even more complex. It has been fairly well established that some individuals react quickly but move slowly; and some react slowly but are able to run or move very rapidly once they get started.

However, even though speed of movement and speed of reaction may not show a significant relationship when these traits are measured separately and then correlated with each other, they cannot be separated in actual performance. A line-backer in football, for instance, might react quickly in diagnosing the play, but he still has to move fast enough to be able to make the tackle if he is to be a successful performer.

Therefore, while it may be highly desirable to measure each factor separately for diagnostic purposes and for research, it would seem more practical for the coach and physical educator to measure them together in test situations that duplicate response-movements that are required in the activity in question.

Speed and reaction time are considered to be largely innate abilities; however, both can be improved through practice and training. Consequently, it would seem only logical that the practice and training would be performed with reaction time and speed of movement combined in a game-like sequence of movements.

Generally, speed has been measured by short dashes. Distances of over 100 yards are usually not recommended because endurance then becomes a factor. Naturally , the age, sex, and characteristics of the subjects should be the major consideration in selecting tests of speed.

Reaction time has usually been more complicated and more expensive to measure because of the timing device that has been employed. The device usually has a stimulus presenting mechanism such as a light or buzzer, and a switch that the subject presses or releases in response to the stimulus.

A precise timer then measure the interval of time from the stimulus to the response. Recently, Nelson developed a measuring device that is both simple and inexpensive. The Nelson Reaction Timer is based on the law of constant acceleration of free failing bodies and consists of a stick that is scaled to read in time as computed from the following formula:

Practical Test of Speed and Reaction

The physical educator is ordinarily not able to justify the purchase of an expensive timing device. Therefore he is somewhat limited in his measurement of speed of movement and, particularly, in his measurement of reaction time.

Nevertheless, armed with only a stopwatch and imagination, the physical educator can obtain value measures of both of these traits which are both meaningful and sufficiently accurate.

The test that are presented here include a hand reaction test, a foot reaction test, several dashes, and a choice-response accuracy test. None of the tests require expensive timing devices or elaborate equipment.

The Nelson Speed of Movement Test

Objective—To measure combined reaction and speed of movement of the hands.

Validity—Face validity as long as no attempt is made to separate reaction time and speed of movement.

Reliability—A reliability coefficient for college men was found to be .75.

Directions—The subject sits at a table with his hands resting on the edge of the table. The palms are facing one another with the inside border of the little fingers along two lines which are marked on the edge of the cable 12 inches apart.

The tester holds the timer near its top so that it hangs midway between the subject's palms. The Base Line should be positioned so it is level with the upper borders of the subjects hands.

After the preparatory command "ready" is given, the time is released and the subject clapping the hands together. The subject must be careful not to allow his hands to move up or down when he is clapping the hands together. Twenty trials are given.

Safety Precautions—None

Test Equipment and Materials—Nelson Reaction Timer, table and chair, chalk or tape and ruler.

Additional Pointers

(i) The pointers listed for the hand reaction time test are applicable for this test.

(ii) After the subject has his hands in the ready position, a 12-inch ruler should be utilized to make sure the hands are the correct distance apart.

(iii) A small mark exactly between the two marks should be made to facilitate the positioning of the timer prior to release.

(iv) The subject should remove any rings to prevent the denting or marring of the timer's surface.

Norms are incomplete at this time. Average time has been found to be about. 24 for college men.

Scoring—The score for the combined response movement is read from the timer at the point just above the upper edge of the hand after the catch. The average of the middle ten trials, after the slowest five trials have been discarded, is recorded.

The Nelson Hand Reaction Test

Sex—Boys and girls.

Age Level—Any age from kindergarten upward. The only limiting factor would be the subject's ability to catch the falling stick with the fingers.

Objective—To measure the speed of reaction with the hand in response to a visual stimulus.

Validity—The validity of the timing device is inherent, since the earth's gravitational pull is consistent; therefore, the timer falls at the same rate of acceleration each time.

Reliability—A reliability coefficient of .89 was obtained using average scores taken on two separate test administrations.

Directions—The subject sits with his fore forearm and hand resting comfortably on the table. The tips of the thumb and index finger are held in a ready to pinch position about 3 or 4 inches beyond the edge of the table. The upper edges of the thumb and index finger should be in a horizontal position.

The tester holds the stick timer near the top, letting it hand between the subjects thumb and index finger. The Base Line should be even with the upper surface of the subject's thumb.

The subject is directed to look at the Concentration Zone and is told to react by catching the stick when it is released. The subject should not look at the tester's hand; nor is he allowed to move his hand up or down while attempting to catch the falling stick. Twenty trials are given. Each drop is preceded by a preparatory command of "ready."

Safety Precautions—None.

Test Equipment and Materials—Nelson Reaction Timer, table and chair, or desk chair.

Additional Pointers

(i) The testing environment should be such that the

subject is able to concentrate.

(ii) Allow the subject three or found practice trials to make sure he understands the procedures and becomes familiar with the task.

(iii) The interval of time between the preparatory command of "ready" and the release is extremely important. It should e varied in order to prevent the subject from becoming accustomed to a constant patter. ON the other hand, this interval should remain within a range of not loss than one-half second nor longer than approximately 2 seconds. If too short, it catches the subject before he is ready, and if the interval is too long the subject loses his optimal state of readiness. For standardization the tester could have a specific order of these intervals. For example, on the first trial he could say "ready," then count to himself .1,001, then, release; on the second trial, after "ready," he might mentally say, "one," then release, etc.

(iv) Obvious anticipation should be careful that the trials.

(v) The tester must be careful that the subject's thumb or index finger is not touching the timer.

(vi) If the subjects are young children, the test should be conducted like a challenging game.

(vii) The subject's dominant hand should be used if only one hand is to be tested.

(viii) The thumb and index finger should not be more than 1 inch apart at the start.

Scoring—When the subject catches the timer, the score is read just above the upper edge of and the five fastest trials are discarded, and an average of the middle ten is recorded as the score. Number on the timer represent thousandths of a second. Scores may be recorded to the nearest 5/1000 of a second.

The Nelson Foot Reaction Test

Age and Sex—Same as with the hand reaction test.

Objective—To measure the speed of reaction with the foot in response to a visual stimulus.

Validity—Face validity. Same as with the hand reaction test.

Reliability—A reliability coefficient of .85 was obtained with college men as subjects.

Directions—The subject sits on a table which is about 1 inch from the wall. With his shoe off, the subject positions his foot so that the ball of the foot is held about 1 inch from the wall with the heel resting on the table about 2 inches from the edge.

The tester holds the reaction timer next to the wall so that it hangs between the wall and the subjects foot with the Base Line opposite the end of the big toe. The subject looks at the Concentration Zone and is told to react, when the timer is dropped, by pressing the stick against the wall with the ball of this foot. Twenty trials are given.

Safety Precautions—None.

Test Equipment and Materials—Nelson Reaction Timer, table or bench, wall space.

Additional Pointers—Same as with hand reaction test.

Scoring—The reaction time for each trial is the line just above the end of the big toe when the foot is pressing the stick to the wall. The slowest five trials and the fastest five trials are discarded, and the average of the middle ten trials is recorded.

Six-Second Dash

Sex—Satisfactory for both boys and girls.

Age level—There are only norms for high school and college students, but the test could be used for junior high students.

Objective—Although this event has been used as a measure of running endurance, it would seem to be appropriate as a test of speed, at least for older students. Except for the extremely fast high school or college student, the distance covered would rarely be over 50 yards and endurance should not be a factor.

Validity—Face validity is accepted.

Directions—The subject starts from a standing position with both feet behind the end line. The starter uses the preparatory commands of "get set" and "go." On the command to go the subject runs in a straight line as fast as possible until the whistle is blown at the end of 6 seconds.

The subject does not have to come to a sudden stop at the sound of the whistle, he merely begins to down at his own rate. Two trials are given, 5 minutes apart.

Safety—Precautions should be taken to allow sufficient warm-up to avoid strained muscles. Adequate space should be provided along the sides of the running lanes and at the end of the lanes. Proper footwear should be insisted up-on.

Test Equipment and Materials—Stopwatch, whistle, running space of at least 70 yards to allow for a gradual stop, and approximately fourteen markers placed at 2-yard intervals from 34 to 60 yards.

Additional Pointers

(i) The main advantage of this type of run is that

several subjects can be tested with one stopwatch. Therefore, it is recommended that more than one runner be tested at a time. Otherwise, running a specific distances for time is a more precise measure.

(ii) Each spotter must be impressed with the necessity of watching only his runner and not look to see who is winning.

(iii) In judging the exact spot at which the runner was when the whistle sounded, the spotter should use the subject's sounded, the spotter should use the subjects chest as the point of reference.

(iv) The tester should keep his eyes on the watch and not on the runners. He should count loudly the seconds 3, 4, and 5 to alert the spotters as to the approximate point at which their runners will be.

(v) Chalk or painted lines across the running lanes at the 2-yard intervals will facilitate scoring.

(vi) Although a period of 5 minutes is suggested as the interval between trials, more time should be allowed if fatigue is adjudged to be possible influence on the seconds trial.

Scoring—A spotter is assigned to each runner and is positioned about of the whistle the spotter immediately runs to the place where the runner was at the time the whistle was blown. This point is then measured from the nearest marker. The score is recorded to the nearest yard, and the best of the two trials is used.

Fifty-Yards Dash

Sex—Satisfactory for both boys and girls .

Age Level—Ages six through seventeen.

Objective—To measure speed.

Reliability—None reported.

Objectivity—None reported.

Validity—Face validity is accepted.

Directions—It is advised that two subjects run at the same time. Both start from a standing position. The commands, "Are you ready?" and "Go!" are given. At the command to go the starter drops his arm so that the timer at the finish line can start the timing. The subjects run as fast as possible across the finish line.

Equipment—Two stopwatches, or a watch with a split-second timer is needed. A suitable running area to allow the fifty-yard run plus extension for stopping is also required.

Scoring—The elapsed time from the starting signal until the runner crosses the finish line is measured to the nearest tenth of a second.

Nelsons Choice-Response-Movement Test

Sex—Satisfactory for both boys and girls.

Age Level—Satisfactory for ages ten through college.

Objective—To measure ability to react and move quickly and accurately in accordance with a choice stimulus. It was believed that this type of test stimulated movement patterns found in a number of sports.

Validity—Face validity is accepted.

Reliability—A reliability coefficient of .87 was found for college men, using the test-re-test method.

Objectivity—An objectivity coefficient of .83 was obtained with two testers scoring the same individuals. However, much of the disagreement was believed to be due to the difficulty of synchronizing the start with two watches.

Directions—The subject faces the tester while

crouching in an on-guard position at a spot exactly between the two sidelines. The tester holds the stopwatch in his up-raised hand. The tester then abruptly waves his arm to either the left or right and simultaneously starts the watch.

The subject responds to the hand signal and attempts turn as quickly as possible, in the indicated direction, to the boundary line. The watch is stopped when the subject crosses the correct line. If the subject should start to move in the wrong direction, the watch continues to run until the subject reverses directions and given, five to each side, line. Ten trials are given, five to each side, but in a random sequence. A rest interval of 20 seconds is provided between each trial.

Safety—The teacher should insist upon adequate foot were and should provide warm-up exercises. The testing area must be kept free from obstructions.

Test Equipment and Materials—Stopwatch, measuring tape, and marking equipment.

Additional Pointers

(i) Several practice trials should be given to acquaint the subject with the test procedures.

(ii) The tester should practice the starting signals to attain proficiency in synchronizing his hand signal with the start of the watch.

(iii) In selecting the sequence of direction, the tester can simply put five slips with right on them and five slips within left on them in a hat for a random draw. This procedure prevents the subject for anticipating the direction from one trial to the next.

However, the subject should not be told that he will have five trials in each direction. In fact, the subject should probably be told that this is not the case—that the distribution of trials is entirely based on random than another. There should be several prepared sequences so that students waiting to be tested cannot memorize the order of directions.

(iv) This test could be adapted so as to be more applicable to the specific activity in question. For example, tacking dummies could be placed at each sideline that the subject must hit to stop the clock.

(v) As in all speed and reaction tests, the interval between the command, "ready," and the starting signal should be within a range of approximately ½ to 2 seconds.

Problems Associated with Speed of Movement and Reaction Time Testing

Some of the problems and limitation that are associated with speed and reaction time measurement were mentioned. It was pointed out that equipment would be major obstacle if the physical educator wished to secure very precise measures for a variety of response-movements. Quite obviously the need fors elaborate equipment would depend upon the purposes for which the measures were to be used.

When speed of movement and reaction time are to be studied separately, the specificity of each must be considered, as well as how each may operate in relation to the movements involved and the task. In other words, it would not make much sense to measure reaction time by having the subject release a telegraph key device upon hearing a buzzer and speed of movement by the 100-yard dash, and then attempt to make conclusions regarding the reaction and movement speed of a defensive line-man in football.

THE MEASUREMENT OF AGILITY

Agility may be defined as the physical ability which enables an individual to rapidly change body position and direction in a precise manners. Agility is an important ability in many sports activities, as exemplified in a fast game of badminton by two experienced players or by the trampolinist executing a triple twisting back somersault. By the proper use of test which rate high in validity and reliability, it is possible for the physical education teacher to determine which individuals in class are most agile and which ones need work in agility in order to better perform the particular activity.

Practical Test of Agility

Purpose Test

Sex—Satisfactory for both boys and girls.

Age Level—Ages ten through college.

Objective—To measure the rapidity by which body position can be changed.

Reliability—Has been reported as high as .921.

Objectivity—An r of .99 was obtained by Doyle Mammons, 1969.

Validity—With the criterion of general athletic ability, an r of .553 has been reported for boys and .341 for girls.

Directions—From a standing position (i) bend at the knees and waist and place hands on the floor in front of the feet, (ii) thrust, the legs backward to a fronts leaning rest position, (iii) return to the squat position, and (iv) rise to a standing position. From the signal "go" repeat this movement as rapidly as possible until the common "stop" is given.

Equipment and Materials—Stopwatch or wristwatch

with a second hand.

Penalty—There is one-point penalty for the following faults: (i) if the feet move to the rear before the hands touch the floor, (ii) if there is excessive sway or pike of the hips in the reward position, (iii) if the hands leave the floor before the feet are drawn up in position number three, and (iv) if the stand is not erect with the head up.

Scoring—The test is scored in terms of the number of parts executed in 10 seconds. For example, squatting and placing the hands on the floor is one part, thrusting legs to the rear is two, returning to squat-rest position is three, and returning to the standing position is four.

Right-Bootmerang Run

Sex—Satisfactory for both boys and girls.

Age Level—Ages ten through college.

Objective—To measure the agility of the performer in running and changing direction.

Reliability—Has been reported as high as .93 for boys and .92 for girls.

Validity—Has been reported as high as .82 for boys and .72 for girls using the sum of T-scores for sixteen and fifteen tests of agility, respectively, as the criterion.

Objectivity—An r of .98 was obtained by Steve Long, 1972.

Directions—Upon hearing the signal "go," the performer runs to the centre station making a quarter right turn and continues through the course.

Equipment and Materials—One jumping standard or chair for the centre station, four Indian clubs or small similar objects for the outside stations, one stopwatch, and marking tape.

Penalty—There is a 1/10 second penalty for each object touched at the various stations.

Additional Pointers

(i) Stress running as hard as possible across the finish line.

(ii) Stress importance of not touching the object at each station.

(iii) Re-test a performer when it is obvious that he could have done better.

(iv) Allow the students to jog through it once to become familiar with the pattern.

Shuttle Run

Sex—Satisfactory for both boys and girls.

Age Level—Ages 9 through college.

Objective—To measure the agility of the performer in running and changing direction.

Reliability—Not reported in test booklet.

Objectivity—Not reported in test booklet.

Validity—Not reported in test booklet.

Directions—The performer starts behind the starting line on the signal "go" and runs to the blocks, picks up one, returns to the starting line, and places block behind the line; he then repeats the process with the second block. Allow some rest between the two trials.

Additional Pointers

(i) Stress importance of running as hard as possible across the finish line with second block.

(ii) Marking tape should be used to designate the starting and finishing line.

(iii) A person may blocks since blocks may be tumbled, dropped, kicked, or thrown and thus require an additional testing or problems in standardization.

Scoring—The score for each performer is the length of time required to complete the course. Record only the best trial.

Findings and Conclusions from Agility Measurement and Research

In the past it was generally believed that agility was almost entirely dependent upon one's heritage; however, measurement and research revealed that it could be improved through practice, training, and instruction.

Sells, in testing primary-grade children, found a moderately high positive correlation between physical growth and agility performance in boys and girls. Espenschade noted that both boys and girls increase in agility performance up to 14 years of age, after which girls seem to decline while boys rapidly gain in agility performance.

Concerning body types, there is general agreement among investigators that endomorphs have the least potential of the somatotypes concerning performance in agility. However, some disagreement exists concerning whether mesomorphs. While Sillss found the mesomorphs superior, Bookwalter noted that thin boys of average size perform better than medium physique boys of average size.

Moreover, Solley found no significant evidence to support the claim that boys who are big for their age or small for their age may be expected to perform better or worse on agility items.

PERCEPTUAL MOTOR PERFORMANCE AND KINAESTHESIS

Although theories advocating the value of motor activity experience in the child's perceptuals development are by no means new, there has been a great upsurge of interest recently among physical educators in the relationship between basic motor patterns and intellectual growth. Much of this interest has been stimulated by the work of Kesphart and Dalacato who utilized motor therapy with children with language and reading readiness problems.

Much controversy has ensured as to the relative merits of the various therapeutic programs which emphasize developmental movement experiences and the practice of basic locomotor activities. The evidence has been contradictory, due in large part to a lack of objective evidence.

The instruments used in assessing movement behaviour and perceptual functions have been questioned with regard to their validity and reliability. Other facets of the controversy concern the appropriate age level, whether all children should be kinds of motor activities that should be incorporated in the programs.

In studies concerning the slow learner, many of the children were found to be of normal and above normal intelligence, yet they were found to perform poorly on motor ability test items. According to Kephart, poor motor coordination involving laterality and directionality must be overcome through practice of various movement patterns if the child is to be able to cope with the more complex activities of reading, writing, and arithmetic.

It has been said that the children of today are denied many of the opportunities to climb, run, jump, explore, and manipulate their environment that were afforded children of previous generations. Hence, come workers in this area maintain that a real need exists for a wide variety of movement experiences for all pre-school and primary grade children.

Space does not permit us to present an adequate discussion of the rationate behind the perceptual-motor "movement" and the research evidence supporting and discounting the claims that cognitive functioning can be improved through motor activities. It will surface to say that there is general agreement that a child's self-image and level of aspiration may be aided through improved motor skills and that, because of the interaction between perception and functions, certain parts of the overall educational program may be affected positively through movement activities

Therefore, although there may be disagreement as to the extent of direct and indirect enhancement of intellectual functioning as a result of movement, we can conclude that perceptual-motor activities should be provided for all young children.

The stated objectives in the various perceptual-motor programs may differ in terms of emphasis, but essentially they seek to provide the child experience in the following areas:

(i) To develop skills basic to movement and gross motor performance such as balance, agility, flexibility, strength, and endurance.

(ii) To provide opportunities for the child to utilize various sense modalities, auditory, visual, tactual, and proprioceptive, in gross motor activities.

(iii) To develop and utilize skills of locomotor movement such as walking, running, jumping, hopping, sliding, skipping, climbing, etc.

(iv) To develop and utilise eye-hand and foot-hand coordination skills of throwing, catching, striking, and kicking.

(v) To develop a functional concept of body size and space requirements in terms of height, depth, and breath for one's body to perform in a variety of situations.

As was mentioned before, one of the problems in establishing evidence of the effectiveness of perceptual-motor programs is the lack of precise measuring devices for evaluation.

This is certainly understandable, since the teacher is interested in the quality of the movements perhaps more so than the quantify. In other words, the evaluative criteria may stress as the "how" of performance as well as the "what."

The teacher is interested in observing the child as he performs in terms of his confidence, coordination, relaxation, etc., and not just how quickly he negotiates the task. Subsequently, the assessment of quality is by necessity largely subjectives. The child's performance has generally been scored either as "pass" or "fail" or on a "good," "average," "fair," or "failure" basis.

8

TEST AND MEASUREMENT OF CARDIOVASCULAR FUNCTION

The cardiovascular system is normally the limiting link in the chain of conductances transporting oxygen from the ambient air to the working tissues. Good cardiovascular function is thus vital to physical fitness and the performance of endurance work. The maximum conductance of the cardiovascular system is influenced by nutritional status, growth, physique and ageing; adverse environmental influences include cigarette smoking, exposure to high altitudes, hot or cold environments, and dehydration, while the impact of disease is seen in acute bacterial and viral infections, valvular dysfunction secondary to chronic disease, various manifestations of coronary vascular occlusion, and myopathies, secondary to ischaemia, disease, malnutrion or alcoholism. Where possible, assessments of cardiovascular function should thus be linked to a review of individual factors adversely influencing the performance of the cardiovascular system. Unfortunately, the preferred measures of cardiovascular function are invasive, and cannot normally be applied under field condition.

However, depending upon the available level of technical support, there are a number of indirect indices of performance which—while of limited precision—can be applied with minimal inconvenience to the subject. These measures include determinations of haemoglobin and iron stores, waking or resting heart rate, oxygen pulse, heart volume, cardiac output, myocardial contractility and blood pressure, together with an examination of the electrocardiogram.

Haemoglobin and Iron Stores

A rearrangement of the classical Fick equation shows that in the "steady state", the maximal oxygen intake (VO_2 *l.* min^{-1}) is determined by the product of the maximal cardiac output and the maximal arterio-venous oxygen difference (Ca, O_2-C_v, O_2, ml. l^{-1}). $VO_2 = Q$ (Ca, O_2-C_v, O_2).

The arterial oxygen content is strongly influenced by the haemoglobin concentration, each gram of haemoglobin permitting the uptake of up to 1.34 ml of oxygen. Thus, unless an increase of red cell count increases blood viscosity enough to decrease the maximal cardiac output or local tissue perfusion, any given individual in a given state of training will show a close proportionality between haemoglobin level and maximal oxygen transport. In populations where the iron intake is marginal, the haemoglobin level at certain seasons of the year may appear adequate, but a laten iron deficiency can nevertheless be brought to light by determinations of the iron saturation of serum transferring; a saturation of less than 20% raises suspicion, and a saturation of under 15% is diagnostic.

Waking or Resting Heart Rate

Under quiet resting conditions, the cardiac output is relatively constant from one person to another. Values have traditionally been expressed relative to body surface area, with norms of 3.0-3.5 *l.* min^{-1} per m^2, although if body composition data is available a fat-free mass standard is preferable. The resting stroke volume index of the heart can thus be estimated from the resting, or preferably the waking heart rate.

$$Qs/m^2 = 3300/fh \ (ml/m^2)$$

while the corresponding FFM value is given by

Qs/kg FFM = 103/fh (ml/kg FFM).

If measurements are made in the supine position, the healthy person shows little change of stroke volume from rest to maximal effort, and the maximal cardiac output can thus be approximated rather crudely from the product of the resting stroke volume and the observed maximal heart rate:

Qmax = Qs. fh (max).

Oxygen Pulse

The oxygen pulse is the quantity of oxygen transported per pulse beat:

Oxygen pulse = VO_2/fh.

The arterial oxygen content is determined largely by haemoglobin level, and the mixed venous oxygen content becomes relatively low during vigorous physical activity. The quantity of oxygen transported by a single heart beat thus bears a fairly simple relationship to the corresponding stroke volume. While there are theoretical objections to comparison of what is a simple ratio over a wide range of heart rates, the oxygen pulse can be used as a simple means of comparing cardiac performance from just sub-maximal to maximal effort. If stroke volume is well-sustained, a constant oxygen pulse may be anticipated, but if there is difficulty in sustaining pump function, the oxygen pulse, blood pressure and other indices may all decrease as the subject approaches exhaustion.

Heart Volume

Radiographic estimations of cardiac volume have for long recognized the large heart of the endurance athlete. Unfortunately, there is some potential to confuse the positive finding of cardiac hypertrophy with a substantial deposition of epicardial fat or the dilated, failing heart of disease.

Possible distinguishing features of hypertrophy are: (i) shape, (ii) the vigour of the cardiac pulsation on the x-ray screen, (iii) electrocardiographic evidence of ventricular strain and (iv) the relationship of heart volume to power output.

Cardiac Output and Myocardial Contractility

Determinations of cardiac output and myocardial contractility assume a substantial level of technical support. CO_2 rebreathing determinations of cardiac output have been undertaken in remote field stations, although the cost of flying in the necessary equipment is fairly high. In the future, the Doppler method or impedance electrocardiography may also provide a semi-quantitative index of cardiac performance, although in a hot environment sweating tends to alter the impedance characteristics of the system. An increasing number of hospitals are equipped with echocardiograms, and where access to such apparatus can be arranged, examinations of the cardiac ejection fraction and myocardial contractility may be undertaken on at least selected in samples of a population.

Blood Pressure

Careful calibration of equipment and training of observers, is vital to accurate field measurements of blood pressure. Nevertheless, the relationship of resting blood pressure to age provides a useful commentary on the overall cardiovascular health of a community. Changes of blood pressure which develop during exercise offer valuable additional information. If myocardial contractility is good, the systolic pressure continues to rise steadily with an increase of power output, until the subject reaches exhaustion. However, if myocardial function is impaired by ischaemia or disease, the pressure plateaus or even shows the ominous sign of a decrease as the work-rate is augmented.

Conversely, in a well-compensated hypertensive subject, the terminal pressure response to a progressive exercise test may be greater than in a normal person. The product of maximal systolic pressure and maximal heart rate or maximal systolic pressure times maximal heart rate times ejection time provides a simple index of myocardial power output. It is particularly useful to record his figure if a progressive exercise test is halted by anginal pain or electrocardiographic evidence of excessive myocardial ischaemia before a true maximum of oxygen consumption is reached.

Electrocardiogram

The resting electrocardiogram may provide evidence of problems such as a recent myocardial infraction or a viral myocarditis which are contraindications to exercise testing. During exercise, particular interest attaches to evidence of acute myocardial ischaemia, including the development of deep horizontal or downsloping depression of the ST segment and/or frequent ventricular premature contractions.

Observations to be Made

In addition to the primary observations noted above, the following ancillary observations are advised:

(a) general medical examination, with special reference to cardiac symptoms, cigarette and alcohol consumption, risk factors for coronary vascular disease, parasitic infections, sickle-cell disease and acute and chronic conditions leading to impaired cardiovascular function.

(b) assessment of nutritional status

(c) morphological data

(d) where possible, information on working capacity, hydration, blood volume and habitual activity.

Sampling

The number of subjects studied will be influenced by the precision and complexity of the measurements to be undertaken, the requirements of the survey, and constraints of time and finding. Among adults, a stratified, random sample of 10 men and 10 women in each decade might be appropriate for the study of cardiovascular data in a homogeneous population, but where sub-groups are evident, the size of samples should be expanded to include adequate representation of each category. In children, the required numbers per category are similar, but individual age-categories must be narrower. The best tactic seems a preliminary grouping of children in terms of biological rather than calendar age.

Techniques

Apparatus

To carry out the analyses proposed above, it may be necessary to transport a number of pieces of sophisticated equipment from the base laboratory, and before investing in such an expense, the equipment should be critically reviewed for its durability in a tropical environment. The electrical frequency and stability limits of the local power supply should be ascertained, and where necessary generators and voltage stabilisers should be imported. Humidity and/ or heat may cause electrical failures, and where necessary, a dehumidifier and/or refrigerating unit should be purchased. Key pieces of equipment should be carried in duplicate, together with full circuit diagrams and repair manuals. A modular design with potential for rapid replacement of a faulty circuit is to be preferred. The x-ray machine for the estimation of cardiac volume will likely be of a small portable design, but should be purchased with a view to minimizing irradiation and permitting chest films at the required standard distance.

The CO_2 monitoring equipment used for cardiac output determinations should be compatible with the needs of oxygen consumption measurement, the one additional requirement being a "breathe-through" cell or equivalent trickle-sampler to permit the continuous analysis of CO_2 concentrations during expiration. The electrocardiograph will also likely be a portable machine without such luxuries as ST-segment averaging; however, it should meet American Heart Association minimum standards for fidelity of recording, and problems of impedance variations at the contacts between skin and electrodes should be minimized by abrading the skin surface with "Sotch-brite" or a battery-operated dental burr. In some countries, there may be difficulties in obtaining customs permits for the import of complicated items of equipment.

Documentation that the observers involved in the study are donating their services to the host country for a health project may facilitate matters; where funding permits, an alternative tactic might be the ultimate donation of the equipment to a local hospital.

Training of Personnel

Use of indigenous personnel is increasingly becoming a condition for the approval of research projects. Adequate time must be allowed for the training of such personnel in the use of unfamiliar technology;

for example, in blood pressure determinations, observers must be taught to recognise a common end-point and to avoid such sources of error as digit bias and inappropriate rates of cuff deflation; residual inter-observer errors must be recognised, documented and entered into the analysis of data. In communities where a standard 5-day working week is not an established custom, some trained personnel should be held in reserve. All cardiovascular measurements are very susceptible to emotional bias.

It is thus very important, not only to provide subjects with preliminary "habituating" sessions in the test laboratory, but also to ensure that all data are collected in a calm and unhurried manner.

Environmental Conditions

It is important to note the temperature, absolute water content and wind-speed at the test site, particularly when working in a tropical environment. If near an airfield or a road, it may be possible to organize an air-conditioned laboratory or vehicle as the test site. If not, measurements should be made in the early morning, rather than during the heat of the day. Data are also susceptible to circadian variation; thus the time of observation should be held as consistent as possible, and this information should be reported with the data.

Details of Measurements

Haemoglobin and Iron Stores

The haemoglobin is determined by the internationally standardized ferricyanide method, using 20 l specimens of capillary blood. These can be collected in heparinized micro-pipettes from the sterilized finger tip or ear lobe. A vigorous scab with a disposable lance causes less pain than a slow and tentative puncture. Blood must low freely; attempts to obtain the required sample by squeezing cause expression of serum rather than blood. After wiping the tip, the contents of the micropipette are transferred to a test-tube containing 5.0 ml of the standard Drabkin's ferricyanide reagent; the resultant cyanmethaemoglobin reaction is relatively stable, and the intensity of the coloration developed at a wavelength of 540 nm is read on a colorimeter. The reference solution is provided by an international standards laboratory, and coincides with a haemoglobin concentration of 15.6 g dl^{-1}.

In one particularly convenient form of spectrometer, a direct reading is provided in concentration units; if this is calibrated initially against the standard preparation, subsequent results can be obtained easily by personnel with little technical knowledge. Venous blood samples can be analysed in a base laboratory to examine the iron content of the serum—globulin transferrin. Normally, this is 33% saturated with iron; figures below 20% saturation are suggestive of a latent iron deficiency, and a saturation of less than 15% is diagnostic.

Waking or Resting Heart Rate

The waking heart rate is the preferred measurement, as there has been a long period of supine rest; if the resting value is to be substituted, a minimum of 30 minutes supine repose is desirable. Potential intefering variables include:

(a) a hot room; (b) emotional disturbance; (c) recent strenuous exercise, meals, consumption of cigarettes, alcohol or coffee. Particularly in fit individuals, the waking or resting heart rate can show substantial variation due to sinus arrhythmia, and the count should thus extend over a full minute. If the pulse is palpated, rather than measured from an e.c.g. record, the first beat should be counted as zero.

Heart Volume

The heart volume is estimated from standard PA and lateral chest films, taken at a distance of two metres; while the precision of measurements can be improved by a barium swallow, this is not essential.

Cardiac and Myocardial Contractility

The PCO_2 rebreathing method of estimating cardiac output has been described fully by Jones and Jones and Campbell, but attention may be drawn to specific details, as follows:

(a) in field situations, the arterial CO_2 tension is most conveniently estimated from end-tidal CO_2 and tidal volume (VT):

$$Pa, CO_2 = 5.5 + 0.90\ P_{ET}, CO_2 - 0.0021\ VT.$$

(b) in vigorous exercise, a substantial downstream correction has often been applied to the estimate of mixed venous CO_2 concentration; while there is no general agreement on the need for this correction, it is very important to indicate clearly whether it has been made or not; and

(c) in tropical populations it is important to adjust the assumed slope of the CO_2 dissociation curve for differences in haemoglobin levels.

Impedance cardiography remains in the developmental stage, despite a long history, and cannot at present be recommended for field surveys. The topic has been reviewed by Denniston et al. Myocardinal contractility is examined by M-mode echocardiography. Measurements include end-systolic and end-diastolic volumes, the cardiac ejection fraction, and the velocity of circumferential fibre shortening. Details of procedures are discussed by Abbasi and Feigenbaum.

Blood Pressure

In the field situation, readings are best obtained by a clinical sphygmomanometer cuff, fitted with a recently calibrated aneroid gauge. The cuff should completely encircle the arm, and it should be of appropriate width. It is also important that the relaxed arm is supported at heart level during measurements. The cuff should be inflated to some 5 mm Hg above systolic pressure, and then deflated at a steady rate of some 2 mm Hg per sec. Care must be taken to avoid digit preference and bias errors in recording. If resources permit, a randomized readout device may be used to eliminate these problems. The fifth phase is now preferred to muffling as the index of diastolic pressure. During exercise, body involvement makes all types of measurement difficult. The diastolic reading is particularly hard to determine, and it may be necessary to record only systolic values; these also have an error of at least ±15%.

Electrocardiogram

A multiplicity of lead systems has been proposed for electrocardiography. Under resting conditions, the standard clinical 12 lead recording should be obtained. During exercise, the preferred location of leads differs for arm and for leg work. In leg exercise, a neutral electrode is applied to the nape of the neck, a second electrode is attached to the manubrium semi, and a belt containing three exploring electrodes is strapped around the chest at the level of the fourth interspace. It is important to ensure that the connecting cable is long enough to avid traction on the electrodes; however, at the same time the cable must not be so long as to become entangled with the feet or pedals during exercise. When stepping, the subject can conveniently support the cable with one hand. If the arms are to be exercised, two of the electrodes may be attached in the iliac region, and the exploring electrodes are best displaced to a level immediately below the pectoral muscles to avoid interference from muscle action potentials.

Evidence of ischaemia is commonly attached to a horizontal or downward sloping ST segmental depression of more than 0.1 mV during or following exercise to at least 85% of maximum oxygen intake. Problems can arise from a wandering baseline, particularly if the skin has been inadequately prepared, and some so-called averaging devices achieve stability at the price of a distortion of the ECG waveform. There are many other sources of false positive tracings.

Some causes of false positive and false negative readings are as follows:

a. False negative results: Insufficient exercise intensity, resting ST elevation, use of nitroglycerine and other vasodilators, abnormalities of ventricular conduction.

b. False positive results: Resting ST depression, hyperventilation, cigarette smoking, use of diueretics, potassium, glucose and carbohydrate loading, abnormal stress of left ventricle, abnormal conduction, anti-dysrythmic drug, digitalis therapy.

Premature venticular contractions are noteworthy if more than 3 occurs in a 10 second tracing. They are particularly likely to have an ischaemic origin if (a) they become more frequent with exercise; (b) they occur early in the repolarization cycle; and (c) they are multifocal in origin.

Date to be Recorded

The basic specification of subject and population group should be supplemented as follows:

Place of date of examination;
Time of day tests performed;
Environmental conditions
—relative humidity, water content
—air speed
—dry bulb, wet bulb, black bulb
—barometric pressure
—effective temperature or wet bulb globe temperature
Disturbing variables
—fluid balance
—emotional disturbances and extent of habituation
—posture for all tests
—last exercise, meal, cigarette, alcohol, caffeine intake
Nutritional status and dietary composition;
Physicuq
Growth, ageing, and biological age;
Cardiac risk factors;
Acute and chronic diseases relevant to heart;
Cardiac symptoms, including breathlessness, angina and premature ventricular contractions;
Cigarette and alcohol consumption;
Haemoglobin
Iron saturation;
Resting heart rate.

9

TEST AND MEASUREMENT OF AEROBIC POWER

Aerobic power is the maximal power output which can be supported by oxidative metabolism. It is measured by ergometry and expressed in watts or equivalent traditional units. However, difficulty arises because the work recorded as being done against the ergometer is not a constant proportion of the total work done. Instead it varies depending on the type of ergometry and the skill of the subject. The variation is reduced by expressing the aerobic power in terms of the associated uptake of oxygen. Accordingly, for the present account aerobic power is defined as the maximal quantity of oxygen which the subject can utilise per minute during heavy exercise.

The end point has been reached if a further increase in the rate of work does not materially increase the uptake of oxygen; verification requires that the subject can perform work beyond the aerobic maximum if only for a limited time. This is a feature of persons in whom exercise is limited by the capacity of the circulation to deliver oxygen to the active muscles. Circulatory limitation of exercise is usual in healthy persons at sea level, in patients with iron deficiency anaemia, and in parents with a low cardiac output unaccompanied by ischaemic pain, for example those with a defective function of the one or more of the valves of the heart.

Circumstances when Measurement is Impracticable.

The direct measurement of aerobic power is not practicable in subjects who far any reason are unable to continue exercise to the defined end-point. The inability is usually due to incapacitating symptoms and for these subjects the measurement is that of the symptom-limited maximal oxygen uptake. The symptom may be pain, which is usually either skeletal or circulatory arising from insufficient blood flow to the heart or limbs. Breathlessness limits exercise in healthy persons at high altitude and most patients with chronic lung disease. Dizziness may be a consequent of anxiety leading to voluntary over-breathing which in turn reduces the blood'flow to the brain. Fatigue may limit in persons not accustomed to exercise.

In addition most subjects who do not participate in competitive physical activity find the measurement disagreeable due to the effort that is required. Depending on the circumstances, some people are unwilling to complete the exercise procedure so the measurement is impractical.

Need for an Alternative to Direct Measurement

The measurement of aerobic power is well-tolerated by persons who are highly motivated and in good physical condition; for this reason the index is often obtained in athletes, participants in physical training programmes, military personnel, adolescent boys, and persons whose culture entails a high level of habitual activity. For others the aerobic power can be estimated indirectly from measurements made at test or during submaximal exercise. However, such extrapolations must be justified either by reference to previous studies on a similar population or by methods can also be applied where exercise is symptom limited; the result is hypothetical since the estimate will exceed that which is attainable but it may be informative, for example in the variation in persons with respiratory impairment. The indirect estimation of aerobic power makes use of the dependence of exercise capacity on structural and functional characteristics of the individual.

The accuracy of the estimate is greatest for factors measured during nearly maximal exercise and the acceptability is greatest for factors obtained at rest. In different circumstances either approach may be appropriate:

i. Functional Factors

The effectiveness of oxygen delivery and utilisation varies with use and on this account, after allowing for size, the aerobic power depends on the intensity and duration of the habitual daily activity. This directly affects the performance of the cardiopulmonary-muscular system. It also affects the structural dimensions, which tend to enlarge when the activity is increased and vice-versa. The principal exception is again the lung, where the ability to transfer gas, whilst responsive to an increase in customary activity during adolescence, is unresponsive during adult life.

The level of activity affects particularly the indices of performance of the heart and circulation, an active person having a relatively large cardiac stroke volume and low cardiac frequency compared with one who is inactive. The product of stroke volume and frequency is cardiac output which, relative to oxygen uptake, during maximal exercise, is almost independent of the physical condition. However, compared with the physically active person the inactive one attains his or her maximal cardiac frequency and hence maximal cardiac output at a much lower oxygen uptake.

The maximal frequency itself may be slightly greater

in the person with the small heart but this does not compensate for what can be large differences in stroke volume. The stroke volume is also related directly to body size and inversely to age. Together, these factors give rise to a more than threefold range in maximal output in healthy adults.

ii. Structural Factors

Aerobic power reflects the ability to deliver and utilise oxygen. The delivery system includes the lungs, heart, circulation and blood. The utilisation is by those skeletal muscles which can be brought into use. Under most circumstances the dimensions of all these structures are interrelated so a subject possessing a large muscle mass is likely to have a large muscular heart, a large blood volume, and a large lung surface area for gas exchange. The size of any of these organs can be used singly or in combination to estimate the aerobic power. The principal exception is when there is differential enlargement of one or more component, for example the lungs in some childhood asthmatics and the muscle mass in persons who have practised body building.

Other functional indices which reflect aerobic power include the extraction of oxygen from blood perfusing the active muscles and the total body haemoglobin. Muscle strength seldom contributes useful information. The relationships can form the basis for equations which describe the aerobic power; the parameters of the equation are determined experimentally. Many of the functional indices are obtained during a period of progressive exercise and reflect the physiological response to exercise.

Physiological Response to Submaximal Exercise

Aspects of the Measurement

Starting from rest the subject performs exercise of progressively increasing intensity on a treadmill, cycle ergomete or step. The increase in workload may be continuous or in increments which are usually each minute though longer increments can be used with or without intervening periods of rest. During the submaximal exercise test the subject wears a safety harness if on a treadmill, uses a mouthpiece and has electrodes attached over the cardial apes and top of the atrenium for recording the CM5 lead of the electrocardiogram. A reference electrode applied elsewhere on the sternum improves the stability of the record. A noseclip is worn. Each 30 seconds measurements are made of ventilation minute volume, respiratory frequency, the concentrations of oxygen and carbon dioxide in mixed expired gas and the cardiac frequency (FC). The ventilation and gas concentrations are used to calculate the uptake of oxygen and output of carbon dioxide, hence the respiratory exchange ratio, where RER = (CO_2/nO_2).

The World Health Organisation recommended units of exchange as $mmol.min^{-1}$, but traditional units are still widely used. Graphs are prepared relating the ventilation, cardiac frequency and respiratory exchange ratio to the uptake of oxygen and the ventilation to the tidal volume. The graphs provide a check on the quality of the measurement procedure are yield indices which can be used to estimate the aerobic power.

Graphical Representation of the Physiological Response to Exercise

The relationship of ventilation on oxygen uptake is initially rectilinear with a positive intercept on the y axis. On this account the relationship may be described by the ventilation at a specified oxygen uptake, but not by the ventilatory equivalent which would only be valid if the relationship were a proportionality passing through the origin. For description of submaximal ventilation and cardiac frequency, convenient oxygen uptakes are 45 $mmol.min^{-1}$ and 67 $mmol.min^{-1}$; the equivalents in traditional units are 1.0 $l.min^{-1}$ and 1.5 $l.min^{-1}$, the SI units may also be represented by $^{V}E_{1.0}$ (traditional units). The V_{E45} is accurated positively with age in adults and negatively with barometric pressure and the level of habitual exercise; it is increased by smoking and when there is disease of the lung parenchyma.

The point where the relationship becomes curvilinear is correlated with the maximal oxygen uptake. The upper limit of vegetation is the maximal exercise ventilation; this is usually approximately 20% below, but athletes may just exceed, the maximal ventilation which the subject can achieve the voluntary efforts at rest maximal voluntary ventilation. The MVV is highly correlated with forced extratory volume. The relationship of ventilation on tidal volume has a positive intercept on the x axis. The relationship is linear up to a tidal volume of approximately half of the vital capacity, after which any further increase in ventilation is achieved mainly by an increase in respiratory frequency.

The relationship may be described by the tidal volume at a given ventilation and the maximal tidal volume. Both of these variables are correlated with vital capacity. The relationship of cardiac frequency to oxygen uptake is nearly linear. The relationship intercepts the y axis and on this account the oxygen pulse is not a valid index. The cardiac frequency at specified oxygen uptakes may be used instead. The fC_{45} and fC_{67} are correlated positively with maximal oxygen uptake and negatively with fat free mass and level of habitual activity. The upper limit of cardiac frequency is the maximal cardiac frequency.

This is negatively correlated with age and, after allowing for age, with aerobic power. The respiratory exchange ratio changes throughout the progressive exercise test. At test RER is influenced by diet; it is usually approximately 0.83. At the start of progressive exercise there may be an initial increase reflecting hyperventilation. There is then a decrease when the carbon dioxide output lags behind the oxygen uptake. Subsequently, there is a linear rise up to maximal exercise; the rise is due to exercise hyperventilation. One factor is CO_2 liberated as a result of an increase in blood lactic acid concentration. The linear part of the relationship of RER on uptake of oxygen can be described by the oxygen uptake at a specific value for respiratory exchange ratio. $RER_{1.0}$ is highly correlated with maximal oxygen uptake and variables related to it.

Underlying Factors

The physiological response to exercise reflects the level and pattern of habitual activity and the functional dimensions of the oxygen transport and utilisation systems including skeletal and cardiac muscle, blood and lungs. Indices which describe these underlying factors are listed below. Habitual activity is rated with respect to work, leisure and sporting activity. A specific score can be based on the distance travelled or quantity of material handled per day; a non-specific score can be obtained using a visual analogue scale or as a four-point score in which 1 inactive and 4 is very active, for example, participation in competitive sport or engaging in very hard physical work. 2 and 3 are intermediate, and correspond respectively to moderate and heavy activity for at least part of most days. A 5-point scale should not be used as this leads to bias towards the middle point. The energy requirement of habitual activity is measured in terms of food intake or oxygen intake.

The food intake is monitored, the calorific equivalent calculated and the assumption made that body mass is constant over the period of observation which is usually one week. However, no direct information is obtained on exercise intensity. The measurement of habitual activity in terms of oxygen intake is based on a record of daily activities together with an estimate of the oxygen cost of each. The record may be by diary, score chart or continuously monitored cardiac frequency. The oxygen costs are obtained by measurement during the performance of selected tasks which need to cover the whole range of recorded activities.

The use of cardiac frequency can confer additional precision at whilst the relationship of frequency to oxygen cost is linear for each type of exercise separately, the frequency for a given cost is greater when this is achieved by small rather than by large muscle groups. On this account the energy cost of work with the arms will be estimated by approximately 10% if the relationship of cardiac frequency to oxygen intake during teadmill walking is used for the calculation. Due to differences in response times of different parts of the oxygen transport system the cardiac frequency may also be higher relative to oxygen intake during progressive compared with steady state exercise; however, error on this account is small, less than due to the type of work. The recording of cardiac frequency permits estimation of the duration of strenuous activity, for example, the total time per day when the oxygen uptake exceeds 50% of maximum. The quantity of body muscles may be expressed in general terms as total muscle, or for specific muscle groups.

The general estimate is based on stature and body mass and needs to take into account that these variables are usually highly correlated and so should not be included in a contradiction equation. Either may be used alone. Alternatively, stature may be used together with a function of body mass which is independent of stature. In adults, body mass/stature^2 meets the latter requirement but in children up to and including adolescence body mass/stature^3 is compartment. Total body muscle can be estimated as fat free mass obtained from body mass and skinfold thicknesses or by underwater weighing.

The derivation is based on the assumption that the non-fat tissue in the body has an identifiable density which is the same for all individuals. Neither assumption is correct but the fat free mass so obtained is non-the-less of practical use. The fat free mass can be expressed independently of stature in the same way as for body mass. Total body muscle can be estimated as active cell mass, of which muscle is the largest component. The measurement is made in a whole body radiation counter tuned to detect the naturally occurring isotope K^{40}; this serves as a marker for potassium which is present mainly in metabolically active cells.

Whole body counters are used in relatively few centres but the possibility should be borne in mind as the measurement can be made very accurately. Total body muscle can also be estimated from the excretion of creatinine released during muscle renewal which is a nearly continuous process. However, the estimate is imprecise as creatinine excretion is also influenced by other factors. The size of local muscle groups can be assessed anthropometrically. The result is usually expressed as muscle cross-sectional area or as muscle plus bone. The latter is estimated using skin calipers or an ultrasonic probe. In the lower limb the area is best measured at the maximal diameter of the calf, and in the thigh at a point one-third of the subischial height up from the lower femoral condyles.

In the upper limb the area is measured at the midpoint between the olecranon and acromion processes; there is no recommended site in the forearm. As an alternative to area the muscle plus bone volume can be measured instead. The quantity of muscle in the heart is reflected in the heart size; this can be measured radiographically. The functional capacity of the lungs is usually expressed as forced vital capacity which in most studies has been found to contribute more to the description of exercise capacity in health than any other lung function index. The additional inclusion of forced expiratory volume in one second, transfer factor or maximal voluntary ventilation seldom add much additional information. Smoking affects the exercise capacity directly through influencing the level of carbon monoxide in the blood; there is also an indirect influence from narrowing of blood vessels by atheroma and damaging the lungs.

The smoking history is usually scored as yes or no for current smoking; this method groups ex-smokers with lifetime non-smokers and is often adequate when the smoking history is considered in relation to the exercise capacity. However, the number of cigarettes per day and the time since the last cigarette influence saturation of haemoglobin with carbon monoxide; saturation in excess of 3% reduces the exercise capacity. The number and timing of cigarettes smoked and other information such as is needed for interpreting lung function tests, can be obtained using a questionnaire.

Alternatively the carboxyhaemoglobin concentration can be measured directly or estimated from the concentration of carbon monoxide in alveolar gas; the latter is obtained by analysis of a gas sample taken after the subject has held his breath for 20 seconds. The ability of the blood to transfer oxygen is usually expressed in terms of the concentration of haemoglobin; this is measured on blood drawn from a prick to the finger or earlobe or from a vein in the arm. The total body haemoglobin is a more useful guide to exercise capacity. It can be measured non invasively using carbon monoxide but the method is technically demanding; and should be considered for surveys of populations at risk of anaemia.

Maximal Oxygen Intake

Aspects of Measurement

The direct measurement of maximal oxygen intake can be a one stage or two stage procedure using a cycle ergometer or treadmill; the former is often more convenient but the latter yields a higher aerobic power. The exercise should be preceded by an enquiry into general and cardiovascular health. The enquiry is usually based on a questionnaire of symptoms and previous illnesses.

A full clinical interview and examination is seldom needed and a full electrocardiogram is only rarely required except for subjects aged 55 years or under. The ECG should be recorded if ischaemic heart disease is suspected on the basis of the initial clinical assessment. The blood pressure should be measured at rest and if appropriate during exercise in subjects aged 40 years and over; the measurement is optional in younger subjects. An ECG monitor, resuscitation trolley and cardiac defibrillator should be set out in the exercise laboratory and staff should have been trained in their use. The one stage estimation of maximal oxygen intake entails the continuation of the submaximal exercise test up to a pre-determined maximum. This procedure is sometimes convenient but is not recommended because the increments of work may not be optimal for obtaining both the nO_2 max and the physiological response to submaximal exercise.

It is better to take the two measurements separately. The submaximal information can then be of good quality and can be used to estimate the likely maximal end-point and hence the optimal strategy in attaining it in a suitable time interval. In the two stage procedure the second stage should rally last 5-7 minutes. The end-point will be when the oxygen intake reaches a plateau r the cardiac frequency reaches the estimated maximum or the subject experiences incapacitating symptoms. Occasionally the operator may need to terminate the exercise on account of circulatory abnormality, a faltering performance, or the subject being distressed. At the end of the exercise the observer should record why the subject stopped both from observation and in the subject's own words.

The subject should also be asked to rate the intensity of the exercise using a Borg scale. The preceding submaximal test is terminated after 10 minutes or when the respiratory exchange ratio reaches a value of unity or the cardiac frequency reaches 80% of the estimated maximum. Alternative protocols such as those developed by Bruce and by the European Coal and Steel Community are not recommended on account of their long duration.

Estimation from Resting Data

The maximal oxygen uptake is described with a standard deviation of approximately 17 $mmol.min^{-1}$ by a multiple regression equation containing independent terms for age, body size, sex, score for habitual activity and whether or not a current smoker. The body size may be in terms of stature and body mass, fat free mass, total body potassium, thigh muscle width or leg muscle plus bone. The additional use of stroke volume measured in a supine position might be expressed to improve the precision, though there does not appear to be evidence on this point.

Estimation from Results for Submaximal Exercise

Traditionally maximal oxygen uptake is obtained from the relationship of cardiac frequency to uptake of oxygen during submaximal exercise. The exercise is usually progressive and in these circumstances the oxygen intake should be recorded directly. Alternatively several periods of continuous exercise of increasing intensity can be performed each of 5 minute duration with rest pauses between; when this is done the oxygen intake can be replaced by the rate of external work. The highest rate of work should preferably be within 20% of the expected maximum.

The relationship so obtained is extrapolated to the age-related estimated maximal frequency for that individual and the corresponding oxygen intake or work rate obtained. The procedure depends on the assumptions that (i) the relationship of cardiac frequency to intake of oxygen or work rate is linear and (ii) the maximal cardiac frequency is described with acceptable accuracy in terms of age alone without recourse to other variables. Neither assumption is strictly correct; the relationship is seldom completely linear, especially at near to maximal exercise, and the maximal frequency varies with heart size, the extent to which the subject is motivated to continue exercise after the oxygen uptake has reached its maximum and probably other factors; these sources of variability can lead to systematic bias in the results.

For groups of subjects the error variance in maximal

oxygen uptake obtained by extrapolation is no less than that for estimation from variables obtained at test. Recently, alternative approaches to estimation of maximal oxygen uptake have been developed. These use either one or more indices of exercise performance or a combination of exercise indices and indices obtained at rest. The latter can lead to a useful improvement in precision which is then materially better than for the two methods described above. The choice of exercise indices is dictated by their acceptability, accuracy and practicability in the circumstances of the particular study.

The combination of the oxygen uptake at a respiratory exchange ratio of unity and the cardiac frequency at a specified uptake of oxygen is often optimal but there may be circumstances when the maximal exercise stroke volume or the blood lactic acid concentration at a specified rate of work or oxygen uptake can be used instead. The prediction equation should not include variables whose effect on the aerobic power it is proposed to investigate in the sub-population under study. For this reason age, habitual activity and smoking should not be included. For many applications the response to exercise is better used using a submaximal index which can be obtained in most of the population being investigation rather than the aerobic power itself which can usually only be obtained on a minority.

Measurement Strategy

Direct measurement of aerobic power is only practicable on all members of a defined population when the definition includes willingness to undertake a maximal exercise test and medical fitness to perform it. In all other circumstances there will be a material proportion of lapses especially amongst older subjects. The measurement is useful mainly for validating a procedure estimating the aerobic power from information obtained at rest or during submaximal exercise. For this purpose a sample size of some 30 persons is likely to yield a meaningful result. For assessing the physical condition of populations, the aerobic power can be estimated through results from a submaximal exercise test; alternatively one of the submaximal indices, for example fC_{45}, V_{E45}, oxygen intake at RER = 1.0 or anaerobic threshold can be used. These indices can be obtained on most apparently healthy subjects though the lapse rate will always be higher than for tests performed at rest. This has led epidemiologists to question the usefulness of including exercise amongst the battery of tests to be applied and it is up to the physiologists by careful technique and good public relations to ensure that the lapse rate is acceptable small.

Apparatus

Ventilation minute volume can be measured with a dry gas meter, or respiratory anemometer, or pneumotachograph and integrator. The equipment should have a resistant to flow of not more than 0.1kPa at a flow rate of 100 $l.min^{-1}$ and volumetric calibration should be carried out at several rates of gas flow using a gas syringe or pump. Respiratory frequency should be recorded. The concentrations of oxygen and carbon dioxide in the mixed expired gas are obtained by gas analysers sampling distal to a gas mixing chamber. The analysers should have ranges expressed as fractional concentrations respectively of 0-0.21 and 0-0.10 and be accurate to ± 0.0002.

Calibration should be carried out using prepared gas mixtures of known accuracy or a Wösthoff pump. Oxygen uptake, carbon dioxide output and respiratory exchange ratio are calculated from the ventilation and expired gas concentrations. Cardiac frequency, obtained electronically from the R waves of the electrocardiogram, is displayed each minute; the ECG is displayed on a visual monitor.

The interrelationships between the variables should be available for inspecting during or at the end of the test: the display is provided by a microprocessor or computer linked to transducers.

Sampling Strategy

Calculation of Results

(i) Ventilation

This is expressed as expired gas per min. in litres at body temperature accurated with water vapour. It is measured at ambient temperature either as expected gas when it is saturated with water vapour or inspired gas which is usually relatively dry. The partial pressure of dry gas is barometric pressure minus the pressure of water vapour.

Correction for temperature and pressure:

$$V_{BTPS} = V_{ATPS} \text{ x } \frac{273+37}{273+t} \times \frac{P_B - PH_2O\,(t)}{P_B - PH_2O\,(37)}$$

$$= V_{ATPD} \text{x } \frac{273+37}{273+t} \times \frac{P_B}{P_B - PH_2O\,(37)}$$

Conversion for V_I to V_E

V_E is equal to V_I when the volume of carbon dioxide excreted by the lungs is equal to the volume of oxygen which is absorbed. In other circumstances V_E and V_I differ by an amount which reflects gas exchange. Conversion is made on the assumption that there is no overall exchange of nitrogen, hence:

$$F_I N_2 = V_E . F_E N_2$$

where F_IN_2 and F_EN_2 are respectively the concentration of nitrogen plus rare gases in inspired and expired gas. The former is usually taken to be 0.7904. Tidal volume is usually calculated as V_E divided by respiratory frequency.

Gas Exchange

Oxygen and carbon dioxide are exchanged as gas molecules in solution for which the units are $mmol.min^{-1}$, hence nO_2 and nCO_2, hence VO_2 and VCO_2. From the gas laws:

mmol = 1000/22.4 *l* STPD for O_2

$VCO_2 = (F_ECO_2 - F_ICO_2) \times V_EBTPS \times 1000/22.2$ $mmol.min^{-1}$

where FCO_2 is the fractional concentration of carbon dioxide respectively in expired and inspired gas and 0.826 converts *l* BTPS to *l* STPD.

$VO_2 = (V_ISTPD.F_IO_2 - V_ESTPD.F_EO_2) \times 1000/22.4$ $mmol.min^{-1}$

where FO_2 is the frictional concentration of oxygen respectively in inspired and expired gas and the other terms are above.

Converting from V_I to V_E (*l* BTPS) yields the equation:

$V_2 = V_EBTPS \times (0.2648.\ F_EN_2 - F_EO_2) \times 0.826 \times 1000/22.4$ $mmol.min^{-1}$

laboratory exchange ratio (RER) = $nCO_2/nO = FECO_2/(0.2648.FEN_2 - FEO_2)$

Reporting the Results

The quality of the submaximal exercise test should be assessed in terms of the scatter about the graphical relationships. A wide scatter or a discontinuity in one or more of the relationships should lead to the test being reported. Subject to the test being technically satisfactory the result should be reported in terms of indices which have been described. Depending on circumstances the result is likely to include the ventilation, cardiac frequency and respiratory exchange ratio at an oxygen intake of 45 $mmol.min^{-1}$, the tidal volume at a minute ventilation of 30 $l.min^{-1}$ and the values for these indices in the left half minute of the test.

The oxygen intake at RER = 1.0 and the highest obtained oxygen intake should also be reported together with the reason why the test was discontinued. The method of obtaining aerobic power should be stated and the result reported both in absolute units and relative to body composition. Formerly, this was done by expressing the aerobic power per kg body mass or fat free mass which implied that power was proportional to mass.

10

MEASUREMENT TECHNIQUES IN PHYSICAL EDUCATION AND SPORTS

Since physical education has been defined as education through physical means, it implies change, but is something more than the physical aspects. Like education in general, its hierarchy of goals takes into account the holistic nature of the student and its goals include much more than the physical training.

Traditionally, they cover the 3 domains of learning commonly referred to as psychomotor, cognitive, and affective. When these goals have been achieved by any given individual through these 3 areas of learning, they result in a physical educated person. This person has been described as one who has attained reasonable skill in a wide variety of activities, a high level of fitness, adequate knowledge of sports and exercise, and sufficient emotional maturity to become a good participant in sport and exercise, and sufficient emotional maturity to become a good participant in sport and exercise.

A physical educated person is one aspect of the totally integrated and effective person. When this aim of physical education has been achieved along with the many other objectives of education, a fully or totally educated person is emerging.

It is a premise of measurement that whatever exists in amounts; and if it exists in amounts, it can be measured. When this principle is applied to the ends product of physical education, it suggest that all important traits or components of the students are measurable.. Broadly speaking, these components include such qualities as organic fitness, fundamental skills, sport skills, knowledge, and understanding associated with sport and exercise, and the various types of social learnings emphasized in physical education as a part of the affective domain.

This concept suggests, however, that in the process of evaluating the product, the student must be divided into parts, and for the sake of convenience, each part evaluated separately. This practice has become traditional in education.

Since educators now view the students as a whole, but understand that they must grow; develop, and learn specially, this part method of evaluation is an educationally sound principle. However, this is true only if the teacher fully comprehends the unity concept and understands that, contrary to a well-known mathematical thesis, the sum of the parts does not always add up to the whole when dealing with human entities.

It is relatively easy to analyse the students into parts or elements, but when the process of synthesis is used to combine these same elements, but when the process of synthesise is used to combine these same elements into a whole, there are not enough to go around. Something is inevitably missing. When dealing with the human entity, the whole is something more than the sum of its parts.

For instance, this total concept of the individual is exemplified by the term "total fitness." Total fitness can then be analysed into several aspects including physical, mental, social, and emotional. Physical fitness is further reduced to the still narrower concept of motor fitness. Proliferation is carried still further when motor fitness is analysed into the components of endurance, strength, power, agility, flexibility, and the like. Virtually all of these identified elements involve measurement of specifics. However, when all of these specific elements are measured and the results are placed in a profile, the parts, do not add up to the whole. Something of this "wholeness" is not measured. In the process of synthesis, some of the parts, of the fitness music are inevitably missing.

When dealing with this product, the physical educator does measure specific aspects in most instances. Before starting the process of analysis and before dividing the students into parts, philosophically it might be well first to view them as a whole.

It is equally important to look at the pars in relation to the whole after measurements. These separate and diverse items, but are inextricably related. Most are not readily isolated and identified as unique, distinct factors. They really have meaning only when viewed in this context, which is one of synthesis rather than analysis.

These equalities and factors that are associated with them can generally be measured by one means or another. In addition, the different types of test and measures used to evaluate them will be presented.

The major factor or traits of the product of physical education have been enumerated and defined. This seems necessary in order for the student to have a better understanding of these many variables to be measured and to have an insight into how they are related to the whole individual.

The relationship and interrelationships of these variables have been explained and it has been clearly pointed out that each of these factors does not exist as an entity in itself.

Procedures, and techniques that are commonly used in measuring the listed qualities and factors. Specific tests will not be identified, but the general areas will be discussed. Over the years a great many techniques and procedures have been developed for measuring the various aspects of the product.

Many of these were developed for purpose of research and are not practical for use in the physical education class. Since emphasis in this textbook concerns tools and techniques that are usable in practical situations, only those types will be presented that are that are usable in practical situations, only those types will be presented that are readily adaptable to class use. No claim is made that these are all the techniques in use for the collection of data. No claim is made that these are all the techniques in use for the collection of data.

Autobiography

Various means are used by teacher to understand students. If educators are to make fullest use of their opportunities for guidance, they should understand more about each individual's needs, problems, and ambitions. A device designed to obtain some of this information is the autobiography.

It is similar to the ancedote except it is written by the student instead of the teacher. An autobiography is a self-written story about some phase of the students experience from which the teacher may wish to draw information. Its emphasis is generally limited to a certain topic over a specific period. If student's stories are well-done, they give the teacher a good picture of the student's attitudes, feelings, and actions concerning the indicated phase or area. For instance, the teacher may want to learn something about Jerry's autobiography will reveal much insight into what he has done to become fit and the importance he attaches to fitness.

Physical Performance Tests

Skills and fitness are they heart and core of the physical education program because it is through physical activities that all the other learning and accomplishments attributed to physical education become possible. This is the unique approach that physical education has to character development, social growth, and mental learnings.

This area is best measured through what is empirically called physical performance tests. The physical performance test may be defined as those objective tests used to measure human movement including motor ability, motor fitness, sport skill, posture, and nutrition.

Naturally, these qualities are composites of many variables. In general, all motor performance tests are developed along similar lines. All test-makers have made use of scientific and statistical techniques to improve the validity of their tests. Several important considerations in planning these tests are listed in their logical order below. However, the order may vary slightly in some cases.

The logical steps are: (i) choosing the criterion; (ii) selecting the test items; (iii) establishing the reliability and objectivity of individual test items; (iv) establishing the validity of the final test battery; (v) developing the norms; and (vi) writing the test report. There is no cut-and-dried way of arriving at any of these steps. Rather, a number of ways are considered acceptable procedures for each. The type of test planned and the nature of the variables dictate the choice of procedures to a great extent.

Checklist

A tool frequently used to gather information about both the process and the product of physical education, which cannot be obtained from any of the usual objective sources, is the checklist. It is sometimes combined with one or more other techniques such as the interview, observation, and inventory. In its simplest form, it is a list of things to look for as observations are being made.

The general procedure in the construction of a checklist is to select a list of items for which appraisal is to be made in terms of certain traits or criteria. Generally, there are columns in which the observer or the student places check marks. Yes or no, absent or present, and for or against, are the usual categories for checking.

Sometimes the checklist takes the form of an incidence chart where the number of times an incident occurs is checked or the absence of a particular behaviour or action is noted. Checklists area of psychomotor learnings as well. The latter is especially true where an the area of psychomotor learnings as well.

The latter is especially true where an activity as a whole is beings measured. For instance, in evaluating tennis ability, the observe establishes a list of tennis skills and activities that combine to represent the skilled tennis player. These items can be placed in checklist form and the observer can check their presence or absence.

Questionnaire

One of the most frequently used methods of

obtaining information directly from individuals about their present status and practices is the questionnaire. However, this tool should be employed only as a last resort when the information desired can be obtained in no other way. This technique is especially adapted to large groups when factual information is sought.

It is a quickly applied technique and when the items are well-constructed, it can reveal valuable data. This method of obtaining data has probably been overworked, especially in the area of research, and its use has frequently been employed when other techniques would have served the intended purpose better. This has brought some justifiable criticism and has cast some reflection on its use. However, in measurement areas other than research, it has proven a valuable tool for obtaining information about the student. When it is intelligently constructed and properly employed, and its results accurately interpreted, it can lead to valuable conclusions. The conclusions revealed should lead to follow-up procedures in relation to the original purposes of the test.

The questionnaire is especially useful in gaining information about the attitude and interest of students—an are where objective measurement is not feasible anyway. The success of the questionnaire depend on how well each question is constructed. Approved criteria can be applied to questions regarding both their form and their function.

Interview

The interview is a tool quite similar in nature to the questionnaire and might be rightfully termed an oral questionnaire. Their purposes are the same, and much of the same of the interview is such that it is better adapted to obtaining the more personal data of a confidential nature, although its use is definitely not restricted to this purpose. Frequently, the 2 techniques are used to complement each other, and they have both been used to supplement the information supplied by observation techniques.

The success of this procedure depends on several factors. First, the interview has to be directed toward a specific purpose and this purpose should be made known to the student prior to the time of the interview. Second, the physical climate for the interview should be adequate , with some thought given to sufficient time allotment and a private setting in a friendly atmosphere. Such a climate can help create the rapport that has to be established between the teacher and students are to talk freely about their feelings, aspirations, and problems. Third, the interview should be structured to some extent in order for the discussion to be consistent with the purpose of these interview and to help objectify the results as much as possible. The structuring cans be done in the form of a checklist. The information obtained through the interview technique is only as valuable as the skill displayed by the interview.

Inventory

Another tool that can be used by the physical educator in assessing the product is the inventory. It is used essentially for the same purpose as the anecdote and the autobiography, but can be focused a bit more definitely and can be controlled to a greater extent with regard to the information it can reveal.

The inventory, as its name implies, usually consists of a list of qualities, traits, or characteristics. It is frequently used in measuring health attitudes and also evaluating affective behaviour. In design it may be general or specific. For instance, its design may be such that the students analyse their own behaviour, attitude, or feelings in terms of general qualities, or they may be called upon to respond in a specific way to actual situations that arise in class.

In any event, the information found is about what the student does, or feels, or is interested in. Inventories might be classed as practice, attitude, or interest inventories. All reveal the student's social adjustment to a degree. Most inventories do not have the validity for such purposes of testing as grading and diagnosis, but their results may frequently be used to real certain strength and diagnosis, but their results may frequently be used to reveal certain strengths and weaknesses and conceivably could be used as screening devices for the maladjusted. Certainly they might be used as a basis for discussion in such activities as a value clarification period.

Observations

One of the most extensive means of evaluating the product is through observation. Not only is extensive from the standpoint of the kinds of information it can reveal, but also from the point of view of the ways observations can be taken. Observation in physical education may be defined as the act of watching the behaviour, actions, or status of students for a specific purpose by a trained observer. This implies that the teacher must have training and practice not only in the act of observing, but also in recording the findings and interpreting them with accuracy.

On of the big problems in the use of this technique is to objectivity, the results do not have great value. It is probably because of this apparent subjectivity of observations that its validity is questioned. However, suitable objectivity may be obtained if the observer knows his subject, concentrate on the specified problems outlined in his purpose, and applies the suggestions of how to make ratings more valid. Teachers, just as the learner of motor skills, must have a mental picture of the traits, qualities or acts they are specifically observing. It is valuable to have a list of things to look for as observations are made.

The use of checklists, rating scales, and charts helps to objectify observation results. Scouts in basketball games frequently use chart to guide and record their observations. Mechanical means are often to observe and record certain activities. In fact, this is now a common procedure in scouting athletic games. Formerly, football scouts observed opponents and recorded their observations.

They still do this, but the most effective technique in present-day scouting is the study of the actual game films that record action for more accurately than the scout and do it more inclusively. In addition, the films serve as a permanent record for reviewing questionable situations.

Observations are generally made in a normal setting where the observer makes no attempt to control the situations or the students being observed. However, under certain circumstances, he may wish to control one or both of these variables.

Rating Scale

One of the most valuable technique techniques in measuring the product is the rating scale. Like the checklist, the rating scale brings order to the processes of observation and self-appraisal, but goes a step further by providing for degrees of the quality, trait, or factor being examined.

It frequently serves as a recording device for observation, but on many occasions it is used for discrimination and interpretation. This is especially true in research when criteria are being developed for performance tests through the jury technique. A survey of the physical education objectives shows that many desirable outcomes are intangible and do not lend themselves to objective techniques of measurement.

Also, a survey of the tools and techniques used to measure certain factors shows that many of them are too time-consuming and impractical for use in a measurement program. The rating scale is the best means of measuring these subjective areas and factors where no adequate objective techniques are available or where existing techniques are administratively not feasible. It is possible also to use the rating scale to supplement objective measurement. In some cases, such scales may be used as the primary means of measurement while the objective measurement may be used as a supplement.

In function, the rating scale is a subjective estimate, but if it is properly constructed and used, it will help to narrow the gap between the subjective and the objective in physical education. They make observation far more accurate and serve as means of focusing the attention of the teacher and the student on the important outcomes of the program. There are numerous type of rating scales.

The type to be employed is dictated by the nature of the information desired and the characteristics of the individuals being rated, the rating scale enable the ratter to ascertain more accurately and precisely the degree to which the trait, factor, or quality under examination is present.

Such ratings are in common use in the measurement of attitudes and appreciations, sportsmanship, form in sports and dance, and the activity as a whole. The pattern is generally the same. A criterion is established, type of rating scale is selected, factors to be rated are identified, categories are defined, and observation and rating take place.

Sociometry

A technique that may occupy an important place in the are of affective behaviour is sociometrics. All physical activity has been described as a social experience. Through activities of sports and dance, socialization and personality development in students may be an outcome. In any group of students, social forces are at work that tend to promote certain relationships and interrelationship among students within the group.

The roles children play in the group and their relationship with other members of that group are significant factors in how nearly they realize their potential. It is human nature to work for significance and to desire prestige in one's group. Sociometrics is a technique or method of measuring the amount of organization of a social group in order to show the pattern of relationships and interrelationship. It is a practical means of quantifying to some degree these relationships and interrelationships within the group.

The sociometric test start by asking the group members to indicate their feelings about each other. It simply and graphically show who would like to be with whom for a particular activity. It can be carried one step further and can permit the students not only to choose those with whom they want to be, but also to reject others they do not want.

In the final analysis, it indicates which individuals

are accepted and which are not. On the basis of these findings a follow-up can be made. The analysis indicates several things. Leaders are located; the rejected, isolated and unwanted are identified; and a basis for classification into cooperative and productive unites is found.

It further can identify gangs and cliques which tend to promote social disintegration in the group rather than integration. When all of these facts are prevailed, the teacher can select techniques and experiences to help students adjust more readily in their social relationships.

One of the most important of these is to arrange the students into harmonious groups since they tend to reach their potential much more readily when they work with those they like. Also, the rejected and isolated students can be given special help in making social adjustments.

The sociogram is a tool used to show graphically these relationships and interrelationships within the group mentioned above. It diagrams the group organization and in graphic patterns show who accepts whom, who is rejected by whom, and the other forces that tend to prevent social integration in the group.

Written Tests

If the individual is to be evaluated as a whole, measurement techniques should be applied to all 3 domains of learning; psychomotor, cognitive, and affective. In the area of cognitive learnings, oral test and observation of the student in actual performance have been used, but in general both methods are too time-consuming for practical use. Written tests are the best means of measuring knowledge and understandings in evaluating the mental objective in physical education.

The Domains of Learning

It is possible to classify learning and performance in physical education in a number of ways. Such classification may be listed under the recognized learning areas or under the objectives inherent in those areas. In a traditional scheme of classification, learning has been divided into technical, associated, and concomitant, indicating respectively motor performance, mental learnings, and psychosocial patterns of behaviour.

This tripartition is really not all-inclusive since associated learnings refer to incidental learning, and concomitant refers to learning without intent. It is hoped that education can become more than incidental or without intent, although educators now recognize the role played by the school's so-called "hidden curriculum."

A more modern approach to learning categories is through classification according to the taxonomy of educational objectives. Taxonomy means a set of classifications and has been used successfully in the sciences for clarity, understanding, and communication. More recently it has been applied to educational objectives.

When taxonomy principles are applied to the goals of education, 3 broad areas or domains emerge, They are: cognitive, affective, and psychomotor. All educational objectives presumably can be fitted into this tripartite framework, although admittedly such classification is chiefly for convenience since no clear-cut lines of demarcation can really be drawn between them. In the learning process, once these objectives have been successfully achieved by the learner, the end product becomes a more completely educated person. By the same token, if the physical education objectives are successfully attained by any given learner, the result is a better physical educated person.

Perhaps the most important one of the these areas to physical education is the psychomotor domain because it is the medium through which the cognitive and affective domains are achieved through their work. However, it must be pointed out once again that before the student is empirically divided into segments or domains, recognition must be given to the unity, or whole-person concept. All willed propulsive movement is an integration of all 3 of these domains.

The domains do not exist as separate entities, but they are inexorably related and interrelated. Sometimes it is difficult to tell where one leaves off and the others begin. Each of these tripartite areas is unique to the extent that one cannot be predicted from the others. However, each is inexorably related to the others to such an extent that learning in one area is affected by learning in another.

They are characterized not by separation and isolation, but by continuity and interdependence. This inextricable intertwinement becomes a moving force in the education of the young and is irrefutably indicative of the holistic nature of man. Learning in physical education comes about through movement in the form of sports, games, dance, gymnastics, and other physical activities, but being physically educated is never singular. It involves the whole person.

The students learn specificities, but their whole being is affected and modification occurs. When they acquire a skill specifically, they acquire other learning as well, although the teacher and coach may be totally unaware of these sometimes unplanned acquisitions. Motor skill development is dependent on some knowledge and understanding as well as attitudes and motivation. One of the great challenges in teaching and coaching is how to project learning in the psychomotor domain in order to assist the students in transcending mere skill in movement.

The 3 domains of behaviour have been useful as frame of reference in establishing objectives. Since objectives are the keystones for planning the process, and the process is the environment where the chosen level of fitness, skill, understandings, and values are transmitted, their importance cannot be stressed too much.

The 3 domain schemes, when understood in terms of their hierarchical cumulative categories, can present the physical educator with a viable means of identifying the behaviour under which each might be considered as behaviour that is desired, the usual approach here is to write behaviour objectives for the myriad of learnings in each of the domains.

The laborious practice of writing behavioural objectives in great detail has become a debatable concern in the field of physical education and the students will be left to judge for themselves the merits of this time-consuming practice. However, it must be pointed out at this juncture that immediate outcomes of some kind seem to be essential if teaching is to be directive, if learning is to be a life adjustment, and if evaluation is to become effective.

Objectives are the real keystones for the rest of the educational cycle. It would seem that since remote and immediate objectives are only generally directives and are difficult or impossible to evaluate with any degree of accuracy, general objectives should be broken down into more specific goals and these outcomes should be stated in behavioural terms. This provides more meaningful goals for the student and more direction for the teacher. When goals are stated in behavioural terms, they are generally characterized by specifying precisely what the student's expected behaviour manifests itself, and how it can be observed and measured.

These 3 domains do not accommodate to the process of taxonomy with the same facility. Because of its quantitative nature and the great amount of previous work in the area, the cognitive domain lends itself well to a structural classification.

The affective domain, because of its intangible nature and the dearth of previous measurement, adapts itself somewhat less readily to structuring. The psychomotor domain is still in the formative stages of taxonomy although recent attempts by educators and physical educators seem to offer much promise.

Physical Performance Factors

Strength

All of the factors of motor performance described in this unit depend in varying degrees on muscular movement and thus, strength. Strength is a prerequisite to all activity since it takes a certain amount to be agile, to have, power, and to run fast. Strength is related to a type of endurance since the more efficient the muscle is in its work load, the longer it can function.

Although strength as a factor is inextricably related to other motor performance factors, it remains an entity in itself and is a salient element of the whole. Strength of and in itself is not an indicant of capacity, fitness, or educability, but is merely the ability to apply force. This force is revealed by the individual's ability to pull, push, lift, or squeeze an object, or to hold the body in a hanging position. Maximum strength is applied in these ways with a singular muscular contraction, and the strength of the muscle is in proportion to its effective cross section.

Strength of muscle is necessary if one is to perform normal daily activities in an efficient manner. Strength in excess of this amount enables the student to perform them more easily and effectively. This excess over daily demands is needed for 2 reasons. First, it is needed for emergency situations where survival is a factor.

Second, after daily normal activities are completed, the student should have sufficient strength to live life more fully and completely in leisure-time-pursuits. Strength can be measured by such test items as the chins, dips, push-ups, and hanging, and by pulling, pushing, and lifting various devices such as scales, dynamometers, and weights.

Speed

An essential for successful performance in many motor activities is speed. Generally, when speed is discussed, one thinks of leg speed in running activities. But speed, like reaction time, concerns many body parts and may vary from one part to another. In general, speed may be defined as the capacity of the individual to perform successive movements of the same pattern at a fast rate.

Speed of muscle contractions would appear to be an innate quality, but certainly speed of movement used in running the sprints or running in any game such as football can be improved through training in the proper techniques and through continued practice in the coordination of movement.

Strength is highly related to speed. This fact might

indicate that improving the strength of the moving part might result in a corresponding increase in speed. In any event, speed is an important element in most athletic performances. Generally, speed can be measured by a short dash of 40 to 60 yards. The distance depends on the age and condition of the person being tested. Sometimes a shuttle run is used where space is limited for sprints. As in all motor performance, there are limiting factors to speed.

The rapidity of movement is affected by body weight, body density, muscle viscosity, and such mechanical and structural features as length of limits and flexibility of joints.

Power

Power is recognized as one of the most basic components of movement. It is the capacity of the individual to bring into play maximum muscle contraction at the faster rate of speed. Power is an explosive action and it is equal to the product of force times velocity, where force has to do with muscle strength and velocity with the speed with which strength is used in motor performance.

Power is a forceful, explosive manner in the shortest period of time. It is the ability to release maximum muscular force at maximum speed. This power factors is a characteristic of the superior athlete. Speed and force are combined in athletic performance for high standards of excellence. Power is frequently measured by some type of jump, charge, or throw.

The vertical jump and the standing broad jump are most commonly used to measure leg power. A shot put or medicine ball put may be used to indicate power in the arms and shoulder. A charge at a blocking led measure body power.

Endurance

Endurance is the result of a physiologic capacity of the individual to sustain movement over a period of time. Endurance is of 2 kinds. One is associated with strength, whereas the other is associated with the circulatory respiratory system. The 2 types are related, however.

In the first type, associated with strength, the individual with endurance has the ability to continue successive movements in situations where the muscles or muscle groups being used are loaded heavily. Naturally, the stronger person is able to work over a longer period of time than the weaker person. However, strength in itself does not provide the entire answer to muscular endurance. A strong muscle can be improved in endurance by the developing more efficiency so that its recovery rate will be faster.

This phenomenon of recovery is related to the number of functioning capillaries that are present within the muscle, as well as the strength of the muscle itself. Such endurance is characterized by the ability to continue repetition actions with a heavy load at a maximum speed for a short period of time.

Such endurance can be improved by increasing strength through the application of some form of the overload principle. As muscles are taxed beyond the point of comfort, or are overloaded, endurance is developed. This endurance can be measured in several ways. An example is the chin-ups.

The kind of endurance associated with circulatory-respiratory systems is characterized by a physiologic fitness and is related to the phenomenon of "wind." In this instance, exercise is carried on with sufficient duration and intensity to place stress on the heart, circulatory, and respiratory-respiratory systems.

In this type of endurance there is an adjustment in the circulatory-respiratory systems to prolong action. Such endurance enables the individual to sustain moderate contraction of the skeletal muscles over a comparatively long period of time. The adjustment in the heart, lungs, and circulatory systems just mentioned can be made more efficient through training. The best tests to measure this facet of motor performance are distance running and the treadmill run.

Agility

One of the most important factors influencing movement is agility. This factor is revealed by the ability of the body or parts of the body to change directions rapidly and accurately. Measures of this quality test the ability of the student move quickly and accurately the big muscles of the body in a particular activity.

These rapid changes in movement patterns by the whole body or by some of its parts have been measured by such test items as dodge run, obstacle run, zigzag run, side step, and squat thrust. One's level of agility is probably a result of both innate capacity and training and experience. It is revealed to a great extent in sports involving efficient footwork and quick changes in body position.

Balance

Balance is an important aspect of efficient motor response and is one of the basis motor factors. It is ability of the individual to maintain his neuromuscular system in a static condition for an efficient response or to control it in a specific efficient posture while it is moving.

The first type of balance is movement under varying conditions. Each is perhaps made up of the same constituents, but in varying amounts. Both indicate a certain amount of steadiness and stability and are characterized by a certain amount of ease and poise in maintaining position.

The factors of balance is founded in several elements. First, it is related to the functioning of the organs of the inner ear where the semicircular canals are located. These are commonly recognized as the organs of balance. Second, it is definitely related to kinaesthetic sense located in the muscle and joints.

One must have the "feel" of an activity for stability. Third, it is partly dependent on visual perception. One is able to maintain a pose or control clearly in the item known as the "stork stand." In this stunt, one foot is placed against the opposite knee and the hands are placed on the hips. When the eyes are open, balance may be maintained rather easily, but it becomes much more difficult to maintain when the eyes are closed.

Dynamic balance is revealed by one's ability to move from one point or space to another and maintain equilibrium. For such efficient movement a certain amount of steadiness and stability is required. This is the same quality displayed by the lumberjack as he jumps from one log to another. Such activities as tumbling, stunts, apparatus, dancing, skiing, skating, and swimming depend to high degree on good balance.

Static balance is actually the same measure, but different degree. In this instance the range of movement is revealed through such activities as standing on a rail or beam, doing a handstand, or maintaining equilibrium after a fast ride. In both static and dynamic balance, stance is of vital importance in maintaining stability after the body has been placed in an unfavourable position by movement. The key point here is keeping the centre of gravity over the base of support.

Flexibility—Another factor that is recognized as basic to proficiency in motor movement is flexibility. It is significant in the performance of many skills and as a motor fitness factor. Flexibility may be defined as the range of movement in a joint. It concerns degree of movement and it limits the degree to which the body or body parts can bend or twist by means of flexion and extension of muscle. This degree of movement depends on the flexibility and extensibility of the muscles and the ligaments surrounding the particular joint.

The degree of flexibility needed by any student has not been determined. One generally thinks in terms of a full range of movement, but this full range of movements is desirable only when it can contribute to betters performance.

Flexibility is more a specific quality than a general one. For example, flexibility must be considered in terms of specific joints and for specific uses. There may even be variability from one joint to another. Within the same joint, flexibility may vary from time to time depending on such factors as warm-up, temperature, effort, relaxation, and pain tolerance.

A good range of movement in general has several advantages for the student. A high level of flexibility fosters a saving in energy during vigorous movement because of the better mechanical adjustment. Because of this better physiologic and mechanical adjustment of the joint and muscles, the individual may be less vulnerable to injury. Flexibility, like balance, play its part in maintaining good posture. It is related to such components as endurance, speed, and agility. Flexibility negates tension and thus is a positive force in motor ability.

Flexibility may be measured by testing the range of movement at specific joints. A great many devices have been used to do this, such as flexometers and tests that require touching the finger tips to the floor. These tests measure the ability of the body or parts of the body to extend or flex.

Coordination

Coordination is another of the factors that is basic to performance and especially to highly complex movements. It may be defined as the ability of the performer to integrate types of movements into specific patterns.

The requirements for different activities may be quite different. Coordination, like several other components, is interrelated with other factors and cannot be isolated for measurement.

Performing integrated patterns of movement with good coordination involves agility, balance, speed, and kinaesthetic sense. Interestingly enough, strength and endurance are not especially significant in coordination except to the extent that coordination is impaired after fatigue sets in. This integration into skill patterns not only plays an important in sports, but also in daily, normal activities.

The essential quality of this factor concerns the capacity of the student to perform specific movements in a series quickly and accurately. In this case a perform understands and can perform each part of the total movement and can change rapidly from one pattern to another for efficient execution. Such movements are revealed in activities like a gold swing, pole vault, the complicated pivot in the discus, and gymnastics.

The move complicated the movement, the greater is

the requirement in terms of coordination. Good coordination is associated with insight into the nature of the movement, with kinaesthetic sense, and with a learner's perception of relationship. It can be improved through training and practice. The bar snap for distance has been used to measure this factor.

Kinaesthetic Sense

A factor that is very much involved in movement and especially in learning specific skills is kinaesthetic sense. Kinaesthesis may be defined as the sense that gives the individual an awareness of position of the body or parts of the body as it moves through space. As a result of this information received from the senses, the individual is able to control his movements more accurately.

This position sense is found in receptors act as feedback mechanisms for making the individual aware of the intensity of stretch or contraction of the muscle, or the stress placed on the tendon, muscle fascia, or joint, With this information, the performer can tell with varying degrees of accuracy the position of the body and/or body part as it moves into space.

This awareness of movement position is an important factors in learning a movement. It operates to degree each time the body or part of it is called upon to challenge the forces of gravity in sports, exercise, and daily tasks. It is significantly related to balance, and plays a dynamic part in establishing and maintaining patterns of good posture.

In the highly complex skills encountered in diving, gymnastics, trampoline, and some forms of the dance, this sense enables the performer to distinguish his position in space with a degree of accuracy and consistency. As a result of this awareness, the performer can acquire the ability to execute the designated movement more accurately and effectively. A number of devices have been used to measure kinaesthetic perception.

Hand-Eye-Foot-Coordination

One of the most important factors in the performance of many sports skills is concerned with the coordination of the eyes with either the feet, hands, or head. Skilfulness in this area of movement is characterized by control, accuracy, and steadiness.

Many of these movements involve a ball or a similar object. All such movements involved a primary objective, and the performer must keep the eyes trained on this primary objective, and the performer must keep the eyes trained on this primary objective while the initial part of the movement is performed. This is frequently referred to as "keeping your eye on the ball." It is good advice to the performer and is necessary for judging such variable factors as speed, distance, direction, and size.

This factor is closely related to several other qualities, such as depth perception, kinaesthetic sense, rhythm, insight into learning, agility, and relaxation. The quality is evidently a combination of the innate and the acquired. Skills involving this factor can be developed through practice. Countless skills involve coordination of the eyes with hands. All activities involving hitting, batting, catching, fielding, and throwing belong in this category.

There are fewer activities for the eyes and foot, but they are still coordinated in many activities involving kicking skills. Even the head and eyes are coordinated in the soccer skill of heading.

In all cases, the quality involves the ability of a

performer to judge accurately the speed and direction of some object and, in most sports, it further involves the ability to adjust the body or parts of the body in relation to the object. These adjustments take several forms:

(i) hitting or kicking an object from a stationary position, such as hitting a gold ball from a tee, or kicking a football from a tee;

(ii) fielding, catching hitting, or kicking a moving object, such as catching a pass in football, or making a pass from a moving ball in soccer;

(iii) throwing, shooting, or kicking at a goal or distant target. In this case, the primary objective is the goal or target and not the ball.

The Psychomotor Domain

The psychomotor domain is concerned with movement and other closely related factors that influence it. Through sports, exercise, or dance, as well as all work and locomotor skills, students overcome both their own forces and the forces universally found in nature, such as the physical laws and principles governing force, gravity, friction, and motion.

Movement is the key to life processes. While it is associated directly with muscular contractions and involves muscular action in its myriad forms, it is also associated with neural involves muscular action in myriad forms, it is also associated with neural mechanisms—hence, psychomotor domain, or sometimes neuromotor or neuromuscular domain.

There are levels of utilization of the body's forces and there are many restrictions on movement. Some factors aid and help make more effective such man-made forms of movement as sports, exercise, and work skills. The purpose of this unit is to provide a greater appreciation and understanding of the many facets that make up movement and influence it. For purposes of measurement in physical education, human movement may be classified into a number of categories.

Movement is complex quality and is influenced by many factors:

(i) Physical performance factors underlie the action for all movement. These factors include speed, agility, strength, power, and the like as they are manifested through the fundamental skills of running, jumping, throwing, or hanging.

(ii) Structural factors either help or hinder movement. These factors include age, weight, height, body type, and structure.

(iii) Psychologic and sociologic forces influence behaviour and ultimately affect movement to a marked degree. These factors will be discussed under the affective and cognitive domains.

Physical educators generally measure the first of these when they interested in evaluating movements, although indirectly they may concern themselves with the second. For example, norms established for these movements are based on age, weight, and height, or combination.

The coach and teacher must also be cognized of the third group consisting of certain mental, emotional, and social factors, these also have great influence on movement, but they generally cannot be isolated, parcelled out, and measured separately and directly in tests of physical performance.

The physical performance factors are the ones most influential in this area. They are of 3 kinds:

(i) factors that are basic to all performance, such as agility, power, speed, arm and shoulder coordination, balance, and flexibility;

(ii) basic fundamental movements such as running, walking, jumping, throwing, lifting, carrying, climbing, and hanging, which are racial activities, are inherent in man, and are common to the performance of all people since they make up the basic patterns of motor movement;

(iii) highly specialized movements that are the result of training and experience and are not common to mankind everywhere. These include athletic or sport activities and skills, gymnastics, dance, and most works skills. These highly specialized movements are adaptations of fundamental skills and are influenced by the factor that are basic to all performance.

The fundamental skills are both cause and effect since they are result or the effect of the basic factors and are themselves basic or causal to the specific sport skills. The factors that are basic to all motor performance are causal and represent the first level of performance. In subsequent paragraphs these basic factors are elaborated upon in order to increase an understanding of total movement and to provide some insight into such traditional qualities as motor ability, motors fitness, and sport skill.

In addition to these, the processes of perceptions appear to be inexorably related to movement. Therefore, perceptual-motor, learning is another facet of the psychomotor domain. In addition, since one of the characteristics of the taxonomy scheme of classification is that all objectives and areas of learning fall within the parameters of these 3 domains, the structural factors of posture, nutritional status, and body type will be discussed as a part of the psychomotor domain. Indirectly these factors do come within the province of this domain since they are physical factors that may significantly influence movement.

In a sense, all of the above factors lie within man and are in some way or another involved with the functioning of the neuro-musculo-skeletal system. Man's movement, however, is subject to other that bear upon it, including one aspect that lies outside the human body. This involves the physical laws of the universe that govern all mechanical aspects of human movement as well as all object.

None of these is measured directly, but most of them have an influence on all types of movement patterns. Mechanical laws and principles area part of complex movement and are reflected in the psychomotor hierarchy.

Psychomotor Domain Hierarchies

Understanding human movement may become clear when the taxonomy concept is applied to the psychomotor domain. Most taxonomies presented so far are similar in nature and are highly related to the principles and theories of the psychology learning and the performance of motor skills.

Two such classification schemes have been presented respectively by Simpson and Jewett. Both of these approaches start with perceiving through the senses. Although they vary with respect to placement of subsequent elements into hierarchies, they vary with respect to placement of subsequent elements into hierarchies, they include such motor learning principles as cue selection, trial and error practice, imitation, goal setting, readiness, refining, and habituating.

Each taxonomy culminates with a level where skill becomes habitual and automatic, although Jewett carries it one step higher into a process of creating and inventing unique movement patterns.

These 2 schemes, like some of the others, fail to take into consideration, except in an indirect way, all of the many forces that bear upon human movement and that may indirect way, all of the many forces that bear upon human movement and that may come within the province of the physical educator to emphasize and evaluate.

For example, skilled performance is frequently highly related to such factors as posture, body type, nutritional status, and visual discrimination, yet it may be difficult for the student to fit these elements into the various hierarchical levels except to the extent that they may be related to total performance and cannot be parcelled out.

Perhaps the best arrangement of the movement mosaic in the psychomotor domain has been presented by Harrow. In this instance unique human movement has been classified into a hierarchical scheme with 6s 6-1. The arrangement was designed primarily for the teacher to establish behavioural objectives, but secondarily for curriculum construction and designing of teacher objectives, but secondarily for curriculum construction and designing of teaching strategies.

The first 2 levels designated as reflex movements and basic-fundamental skills age genetically based. Although they are necessary and important to voluntary willed human movement, they are more a result of the unfolding processes of maturation than they are learning. Therefore, they do not lend themselves to the development of behavioural objectives, but do provide a better understanding and appreciation of the remaining 4 levels of the hierarchy.

The third and fourth levels are entitled perceptual abilities and physical abilities. Between them, these-2 levels provide for countless movement and behaviours to be learned and performed and therefore are a fertile field for developing performance goals and teaching strategies.

The fifth and sixth levels of skilled movements and non-discursive communication represent higher and more specialized levels of learning and performance.

Little is new in the way of isolated information concerning these specialities. However, their arrangement into a hierarchical structure is unique and does provide a more lucid view of observable humans movement. A new perception might place learning and performance on a continuum beginning with the reflex action and culminating aesthetic and creative movements of the highest order.

Perhaps the students might like to construct their own psychomotor hierarchy from the following factors. These are the traditional factors and elements that have been observed and measured in physical education. Observation of those listed in the section to follow will show that most of them are included within Harrow's psychomotor dominate some level.

Fundamental Skills

Man's basic pattern of movement are embodied in the fundamental skills. These are frequently refereed to as the immemorial racial activities of man since they are racial in nature and are common to all mankind. These fundamental patterns of movement are expressed as walking, running, jumping, throwing, striking, hanging, and carrying.

Such activities with minor variations have no boundaries either geographically or racially. They are gross motor activities and are made up of most postural and locomotor movements as well as some manipulative movements. Their quality and efficiency are dependent on the underlying physical performance factors such as power or speed which were discussed in the preceding section.

These fundamental skills have formed the basis of man's work and play since time immemorial. They were prime instigators of the evolutionary processes and were the catalyst that lifted man to higher and more humane levels. They were the basis for survivals activities originally and they later developed into more propulsive work.

Man's play, games, gymnastics, and dance are adaptations, modifications, and elaborations of these basic patterns. In the process of evaluation an inextricable relationship was set up between these big muscle movements and man's organic and nervous systems.

The development and maintenance of these systems are even now dependent on known movements through these patterns. These patterns may be engaged in directly running, for example, or indirectly through participation in work, play, dance, and other activities that are organized and integrated out of the basic patterns and adapted to specialized purposes. These fundamental skills are universal in nature and common to all races, whereas their adaptation into games and dance makes a new product that is unique and specific and as different as the mores and customs of people.

General Abilities

It has been traditional for human motor behaviour to be divided into categories. In the light of more recent research some doubt now exists concerning the generally of movement. Some scientists believe that all movement is highly specific to the task and there can be no such thing as a general ability or capacity.

The issue has not been settled clearly, however, so for purposes of this text the traditional general qualities of motor capacity, motor educability, motor ability, and motor fitness will be presented.

Motor Capacity

Motor capacity is defined as the general overall quality which is indicative of an individual's potential or innate ability. As an isolated quality, the factors that undergrid it have been difficult to identify. Such factors must not be subject to modification through education since they are indicants of maximum potential.

McCloy did pioneer work in this area and presented a test of general motor capacity within a motor quotient that presumably was the motor analogue of the I.Q. McCloy isolated 4 elements that he considered indicative of capacity: size and maturity, power, motor educability, and agility and coordination. While tests of capacity would be desirable, the ones that have been developed have been used very little.

Motor Educability

It is obvious that some individuals learn skills more readily than others and that there are varying degrees of ability to learn. There appears to be an inherent aptitude for motor learning in the same way that there is for mental learning. This quality is associated with educability. Motor educability may be defined as the ease and thoroughness with which one learns new motor skills.

Since it is undoubtedly related to insight, it is perhaps as much psychologic as physiological. This might suggest that it is not a factor of motor learning in the same sense as the factors. However,, the presence or lack of it has a great deal to do with how quickly and effectively motor skills can be learned.

In the past this quality has been evaluated by presenting motor problems that are new to the student. Traditionally, this has been done through stunt activities where stunts involving performance of unfamiliar motor patterns are presented. A student who possesses a high level of this quickly. He usually has levels of achievement in the championship class.

Motor educability, like both motor ability and motor fitness, is affected by body size, body build, and most of the factors described previously. Maturation undoubtedly plays a role in the improvement shown by different individuals. Strangely, however, this quality is influenced very little by strength and endurance. Most of the items used to test motor educability are capable of being improved through practice.

Therefore, if the test is to be valid, the individual must not have previously practised the event. Naturally, it would improve these test if items could be found that were not subject to improvement through practice. This is hardly possible since all motor performance seems to improve with specific practice.

Motors Ability

Traditionally, motor ability has been viewed as a combination of factors that are basic to all movement. According to this theory, all or most of the factors discussed in the preceding paragraphs become a part of the motor ability mosaic.

Motor ability has been defined as the present acquired and innate ability to perform motor skills of a general or fundamental nature, exclusive of highly specialized sports and gymnastic technique. This definition implies that motor ability is a result of innate capacity and diverse training and experience. It further implies that a valid measure of it must avoid highly specialized skills as revealed in dance or sports.

Since motor ability is looked upon as a mosaic comprised of many components, then each of these components must contribute independently in a successful performance of a movement skill. However, there is no common agreement on what these components are. Test items are generally used in a battery to measure as many of these components are.

Test items are generally used in a battery to measure as many of these components as possible. Test administrative feasibility, however, discourages measurement of each the factors independently.

Some scientists and theoreticians believe that there is no such quality as general motor ability and that all abilities are specific to the task. An inevitable controversy exists between the traditionalist, who believes that some abilities are general in nature, and the researcher, who views all abilities as highly specific

Some present-day research tends to support the specificity of motor skill. It is theorized that performance from one skill to another is independent provided that these skill patterns are unrelated.

The "skill is specific" group headed by Henry and Slater-Hammel go so far, as to deny that there can be any transfer between skills. In Henry's so-called "memory drum" theory, an action pattern, once learned, is stored in the nervous system much as a program in a computer for recall. Only specific skill patterns can be stored, and they are recalled much as in the digital computer.

Proponents of generality and specificity of motor skills generally tend to take an extreme point of view. The generalist would deny the specificity theory first on the grounds that in the past well-validated tests of motor ability have served well the purpose for which they were designed and used, which simply was to classify students into ability groups.

They further would question reliability and hence the validity of the claim of the task specificity proponents that there can be no transfer from one task to another and that all tasks stored on a "memory drum" as specifics, those who recognize the generality of abilities claim that general motor ability is a combination of the acquired and the innate in fundamental skills are universal in nature.

Although they do furnish the basis for specialized play and work skills, they are the simple basic skills that are acquired in childhood and early youth through incessant play and movement. Within the limits of heredity through maturation, these basic skills become generalized and consequently can be used automatically under varying conditions.

When these movement patterns are present in gross form, they can be adapted rapidly through transfer if similar elements are present. The claim that a soccer-style kick is highly specific to the task place kicking is to deny that it is unrelated to all other kicking skills which themselves are based on the simple skill of kicking employed throughout the formative years of childhood.

Some researchers now, however, are taking a middle-of-the-road position. They would not deny the specific nature of many task, but they do recognize the importance of some general abilities that have been acquire out of past experience. Cratty has presented a conceptual framework of motor behaviour that provides for both general and specific elements.

The hierarchy of perceptual motor behaviour present 3 levels with general elements at the base, perceptual motor abilities at the middle, and specific tasks at the top. The base middle elements are perhaps more important during childhood, whereas the apex become some influential in adolescence.

Since the controversy has nots been resolved, much sophisticated research is needed. In the meantime, well-validated tests of general motor ability have been devised and are still in use. In general, such tests have been used for purpose of classification of students into homogeneous groups. These tests are not designed to disclose small difference in abilities, nor they employed to predict potential skill levels.

Fitness

The term "fitness" is perhaps one of the most nebulous in the area of measurement in physical education. It is an elusive quality until delineated and frequently has been defined in rather abstract terms.

In this definition, the reference is to "total fitness" and refers to the individual's capacity to survive and live effectively in his environment. Much has been said concerning total fitness where the total person or whole person is involved: the spirituals, mental, emotional, social and cultural, as well as the physical aspects.

When viewed in this light, physical fitness is a limited phase of total fitness. However, it is one which is basic to other forms of fitness. Physical fitness, as one aspect of total fitness, is a means to amend; the end of the good of the whole individual.

Physical education has long accepted its obligation with regard to this principle of the human entity. This does not imply that physical fitness is not a significant aspect of total fitness and a highly desirable means. As a means directed toward the whole individual, it should become an important objective of the overall physical education program.

Physical fitness, while it is not so broad in its meaning as total fitness, includes adequate degrees of health, posture, physique, proper functioning of vital organs, nutritions, and good health habits, along with an adequate amount of endurance, strength, stamina, and flexibility.

A more limited phase of physical fitness is "motor fitness." Since it is limited in its scope, it becomes a less elusive quality and can be defined more easily than total fitness or physical fitness. Motor fitness may be defined as a readiness or preparedness for performance with special regard for big muscle activity without undue fatigue.

It concerns the capacity to more the body efficiently with force over a reasonable length of time. Motor fitness, as a limited phase of physical fitness, would seem to be the aspect that most fitness tests actually measure. Motor fitness does not assess the factors of physical fitness directly, but does reflect them to a degree. Furthermore, it is highly related to total fitness in the same manner. This interpretation is in keeping with the principle that the individual is an integer and cannot be divided into divisible units for education and training.

Motor fitness is gauged by performance and this

performance is based on a composite of many factors. The most commonly mentioned fitness factors are strength, endurance, power, speed, agility, balance, flexibility, and stamina. Some of these factors evidently are more dominant than others and thus have a higher relationship with motor fitness.

It factors resemble the list experts have used to analyse motor ability. Furthermore, although experts have assigned to motor ability and motor fitness definitions that seem to distinguish one from these other, the same factors have been used to described them and, in many cases, the same test items have been used to measure the same factors in each.

In contrast to motor ability whose dominant factors are relatively static and enduring, motor fitness is made up of factors that seem more dynamic and changeable, such as strength and endurance.

Improvement in some of the more dominant ones might be quite rapid as exhibited by the results achieved in an accelerated physical training program during World War II. Minimum standards of motor fitness may be achieved over a short period of time. By the same token, fitness is lost unless it becomes a product of day-to-day living.

Numerous tests are designed to measure fitness. Most of these are similar in design and measure similar factors. The AAHPER Fitness Test has been the most widely used.

Specialized Physical Abilities

One of the most fundamental aspects of physical education is the teaching and acquisition of specialized skill. Most of the "education through the physical" takes place by means of those skills that include sports or athletic activities as well as dance and gymnastics.

Development of these skills in sports and dance has long been recognized as one of the major objectives of physical education.

These specialized skills may be defined as those physical activities constituting each sport that are distinctive to that sport. They are unique in this respect. Skills vary according to the sport, and measurement must be made on a specific basic.

The particular skill techniques involved are not common to all people as the fundamental skills, but vary according to the customs, mores, nationally, and geography of a people. They result from training and experience and are acquired through specialized practice.

A sport skill is a unit and, when compounded with other units into a group, along with certain rules, a sport or athletic game results. These units are based on the fundamental skills such as running, jumping, or throwing. Proficiency in these skills depends upon the basic factors that underlie them, such as agility, speed, power, or coordination.

Thus, specific skills are the effect of both the fundamental skills and the basic factors that have been previously described. Combinations of these fundamental skills in various sequences along with the functioning of the basic factors results in skills in various sequences along with the functioning of the basic factors results in skills that are specific for each sport or activity.

Sport skills are the heart of these physical education program and the key to future participation. Most of the objectives of physical education remote and immediate, are dependent on the development of skills. Without skill there can be little, if any, satisfying participation in physical activities, and without participation, the lasting values—organic, neuromuscular, mental, and social—sought through a comprehensive physical education programme are impossible to achieve. In the final analysis, skill provides the medium through which all the objectives of physical education can more nearly be attained.

Naturally, a measurement program for sport skills is specifically related to the activity of which it is a part. Sport skills may be evaluated in 2 ways. First, subjective methods may be used. Where the skills involved are complex and present problems in accurate measurement, these techniques may be employed. In this case, rating scales are used and judgments of the ratters are indicative of the level of the student's ability.

Second, objective skills tests may be used. Most skill tests have been devised by analysing the sport into its major component parts, identifying each fundamental separately, and devising a test item to measure each.

Sometimes the skill itself becomes the best measure and it is standardized as a test item in the overall battery. All test items used to measure skill should meet certain requirements with respect to test criteria, including validity either on a logical basis or a statistical basis or both. There are ski tests for practically all sports. A classic example is the Dyer Tennis Test.

Perceptual-Motor Learning and Performance

Perceptual-motor refers to the ability of the individual to receive, interpret, and react properly to a multitude of stimuli that are impinging on him not only from outside himself but also from within. This linking of perceptual abilities to movement and motor learning has become a new dimension in learning theory.

Only recently has physical education become

involved with its processes. Psychologists, optometrists, special education people, and others have pioneered in this work.

Perception has been defined as "the total pattern arising from many sensations and resulting in a meaning which is more than the sum of its parts." Motor learning is the integration of movement into a pattern for a purpose as a result of training procedures or environmental conditions. Proponents in this area maintain that perception and environment are but 2 sides of the same coin and that they cannot be separated in the learning and performance processes.

The impinging stimuli are called input and are made up of sensations from the senses of sight, hearing, touch, teste, and smell from outside and from the kinaesthetic or proprioceptor senses from within. The uniqueness of perceptual-motor performance is that emphasis is now placed on sensations that influence performance and the interpretation of these sensations along with the motor activities which succeed and precede them, called output.

Thus, in perceptual-motor learning there is input and output along with a control system to integrate the input and a storage system for memory. Modern theory holds the view that input-output cannot be separated and are inexorably related as they occur in a closed-loop system controlled by feedback.

The current ideas surrounding perceptual-motor behaviour are primarily based on the new information theory which views the mind and human behaviour as a computer. This computer analogy for the mind is sometimes called the cybernetic theory of the feedback theory.

One of the major obstacles in studying perceptual-motor behaviour has been the lack of instruments to evaluate status and progress. Not only are standards lacking in what is considered normal, but the area is so complex that the many aspects of perceptual-motor behaviour have not yet ben identified. Most evaluation schemes are highly subjective, lack validation, and do not have established rehabilitates. Some surveys and check lists are currently in use.

Structural Factors

Posture

The body, with its approximately 200 bones and 700 muscles, is subjected repeatedly to the forces of the universe. Man's environment is filled with stress as gravity is incessantly pulling the body downward. In addition to the forces of gravity itself, the human body also has to overcome strains growing out of its own movement, tensions, and inertia.

Even the body at rest in a sitting position is vulnerable to these intrinsic and extrinsic forces. There also appears to be a relationship between the position of the body and certain psychologic factors.

The study of posture and its evaluation comes within the province of physical education since it concern a knowledge of body mechanics and a maintenance of muscle tone. Although it has not been proven objectively, most authorities concedes there is probably a relationship between posture and health.

Posture is concerned with the position of the whole body and its segments. It may run the gamut from good to bad with all shades in between. Good posture is the proper alignment of the important segments of the body so they are balanced over the base of support to produce the most mechanical efficiency, the least interference with organic functioning, and the greatest freedom from body strain. Two facts concerning posture should be clearly understood at this point. First, there is no one, single, ideal posture, but many postures.

The human body is not a static organism. It is dynamic as action produces change. This action results in such postures as standing, sitting, reclining, walking, and exercising. Second, posture as a basis for evaluation. Yet in daily normal activities, standing posture is used relatively little by the average person. In regard to the second part, there are individual differences in anatomic parts, body builds, and body types, and these relate to posture. Yet posture standards have not been devised in accordance with these differences.

It fact, there are no universal posture standards of a functional nature. Present posture tests are chiefly of standing posture. Most measures have been largely subjective, although many objective devices are employed, they are based to a great extent on subjective judgment. This is true because objective devices must be based on certain standards which in turn are based on criteria. In the final analysis these criteria revert to subjective judgment as do all criteria since they are based on expert opinion.

It is obvious that precise techniques for posture measurement does not preclude posture evaluation, however. If evaluation is to occur, it must start with a norm or standard. Present posture standards are not universally agreed upon by experts, but most of the recognized posture standards reflect the consensus of experts regarding the make-up of good standing posture.

This ideal has come to be recognized as an erect straight-line position with all main segments of the body balanced over their bases of support. Certainly the ability to stand in the designed position does reflect how well the above ideal can be met.

Many objective methods are available to evaluate this position, but perhaps the best approach for the average teacher is through use of a simple inspection type of measurement. Much progress has been made the last few years in the use of such subjective devices.

Much progress has been made the last few years in the use of such subjective devices might be more valuable in motivating the student, but the subjective devices probably yield results that have far more value to the teacher. The objective devices can record posture only 1 time, whereas the subjective devices may be projected and the subject rated more than 1 time and in terms of several postures. In any event, the results of such observation should be interpreted in terms of the student's age, sex, skeletal structure, body type, and nutritional status.

Nutrition

Another area that seems to come within the sphere of the physical educators is the evaluation of the nutritional status of students. This is true because nutrition plays an unimportant role in physical fitness and health. Nutrition is related to the body's intake and consumption of food.

It also affects growth and development. It is related, through its various processes, to posture, and resistance to disease. There is an indirect relationship with ability in general, and resistance to disease. There is an indirect relationship with ability in motor learning and performance, and even some evidence of a relationship with personality development.

Nutrition maybe defined as the sum of the processes

by which the body takes in, assimilates, and utilizes food substances. It is directly related to growth, development, maintenance, and repair of the body and its parts. Nutrition, like health, may be good or bad.

Good nutritional status implies that all the processes mentioned above are operating efficiently and that each part of the cycle is performing its function. Poor nutrition or malnutrition inefficiency interrupts normal growth and development cycles, especially in children and youth. This breakdown may be caused by a shortage in the total food intake itself, or malnutrition may be present because the body is not able to assimilate and use the essential nutrients due to some failure in the physiologic processes.

Physical educators are in an excellent position to observe nutritional status of their students and have a special opportunity and a compelling obligation to detect cases of malnutrition. Because they work in close intimacy with their students, they can watch for the revealing symptoms.

They should have a knowledge of the characteristics of both good and poor nutrition and should know how measurement techniques can be employed to identify those students in need of help. The primary purpose of such screening is to recognize the malnourished. The next step after identification is referral of the cases of possible malnutrition to the health specialist.

Measurement of nutritional status has been done for many years. The original methods of appraisal were anthropometric and consisted chiefly of age, height, and weight measurements. These techniques were not valid chiefly because they failed to take into consideration of the same sex, age, and height in the same mould regardless of size and proportion of the skeleton, muscles, and fat. More recent techniques acknowledge the difference in body type and provide norms for them.

At present there are 2 approaches to the appraisal of nutritional status. One approach involves subjective opinion and is made in terms of the signs and symptoms of good or poor nutrition.

The inspection techniques is used with a inspection can take place in the locker room, shower room, gymnasia, or playground. The second approach is through objective measurement where special devices and forms are used.

Body Type

The belief that body is related to health and personality as well as physical performance dates back to ancient times. Since 1860 the physical educator in America has always been interested in this subject. Body type is no doubt a result of hereditary factors, but what is commonly recognized as physique is partly a product of environmental influences and comes about as a by-product of exercise, diet, and good health habits.

It is also true that occupation and climate have played a role in long-term modification of body types tend to fall along a curve of normal distribution. Thus, it seems that body type, like other human traits, follows along a continuum rather than into readily quantified and well-defined categories. However, in the past body types have been categorized into dichotomies and trichotomies for the sake of convenience.

The physical educator should be concerned with body types for several reasons. First, since objective evidence now indicates a relationship between body type and success in physical education activities, the curriculum must be adapted to meet the different needs that are presented because of the great variation in body types.

It has been further shown that there is a low positive correlation between physical structure and both mental and social traits. Probably the most important reason for the physical educators to comprehend this area is so they may help students to understand and appreciate the nature of their body type, to accept it as a part of their heritage, and to learn to live happily with it.

Appraisal for body type has been highly subjective, but little used in physical education. There are several techniques or methods of classification but the concept of somatotype by Sheldon is the best known. Somatotyping divides individuals into 3 types: endomorph rated as 7-1-1, mesomorph rated as 1-7-1, and ectomorph rated as 1-7-1. Somatotype rating involves categorizing subjects according to the numbers listed above.

Cognitive Domain

A physical educated person is more than one educated in movement. The intellectual abilities and skills are present also. In traditional education the acquiring of these has become the most important and common objective in American education. Learnings in the cognitive area in physical education about sports, dance, other movement activities, and the self may either be directly a part of the school curriculum or they may be projected as outcomes of the activities themselves as associated learning.

However, the cognitive domain generally has become an important facet of the physical education curriculum and is evaluated along with the psychomotor domain, they also learn particulars in the cognitive domain.

In the taxonomy of educational objectives. Bloom et al. have classified this cognitive domain into the following 6 levels: knowledge, comprehension, application, analysis, synthesis, and evaluation. Knowledge and comprehension are the bases for cognition and beyond these parameters are the higher intellectual abilities and skills.

(i) Knowledge is defined as an awareness of specific facts, universal, and information and involves remembering and the ability to recall. The most common knowledges in the cognitive domain of sports, exercise, dance, and related activities are: (a) rules governing the activity; (ii) terminology; (iii) techniques involved in performing the activity; (iv) historical background; (v) strategy; (vi) equipment and facilities ; (vii) game courtesies and etiquette; and (viii) values inherent in the activity for the participant.

Satisfying and effective participation in an activity cannot be experienced until the student has learned much of this information. However, learning in physical education does not stop here. Certain other areas seem essential if physical education is to achieve its goal of continuing and intelligent participation.

In addition to learning motor skills, the learner, to be physically educated, must also have knowledge and understanding regarding such aspects as: (i) the importance of fitness; (ii) how fitness may be achieved; (iii) the need for systematic activity; (iv) the values derived from systematic activity; (v) how to achieve neuromuscular relaxation; and (vi) the technique of using the fundamental skills.

(ii) Comprehension is the lower level of understanding and implies the abilities to interpret knowledge and to determine its implications, consequences, and effects. An example would be knowing the facts and principles concerning the effect of exercise for survival.

(iii) Application is a higher level cognitive structure that enables the learner to use his knowledge and understanding in a particular concrete situation. It is possible to know and understand the facts, but still not apply them.

In this case there is the inescapable close relationship between the affective and cognitive domains. For this reason it has been said that every cognitive behaviour has its affective counterpart. Cognitive skills are essential for affective adjustment.

Knowing and understanding in physical education have much more significance if they enable the student to participate more effectively in his motor skills and movement activities. This involves one's value system.

(iv) Analysis involves a higher level cognitive process than application. It is based on knowledge and understanding, but implies the ability to identify the elements or parts of the whole, to see their relationships, and to structure them into some systematic arrangement or organization.

(v) Synthesis involves a level similar to that of analysis, but is a reverse procedure. As a process it moves from the specific elements or parts to form the whole. Once again knowing and understanding become the basis out of which facts and information are combined into wholes or some patterns that are different and larger than any part.

(vi) Evaluation is the highest level of the cognitive domain because it is used to form judgements with respect to the value of information made available through the other cognitive processes. Again it is obvious that the cognitive cannot be separated from the affective domain at this point since values and adaptive behaviour are involved.

Some cognitive learning may be looked upon in physical education as psychomotor learning extended. For example, once the facts and ideas are known and understood by the learner, they may influence skill learnings and enhance further efficiency in performance of these skills. For example, in learning to play a sport the athlete is given directions by the coach on training procedures.

This knowledge has value for the conditioning and fitness of the athlete, but also reverts to the skills of the spot that are themselves improved as a result of the knowledges.

Since these knowledges and understanding of the cognitive domain comprise one of the major objective of physical education, they must be planned for in the educational process. The physical education curriculum should include the cognitive domain involving these knowledges and understanding of man and human movements as they are concerned with sports, dance, gymnastics, and exercise.

It should also include the ideas that are necessary for a better understanding of relationships and significance in the conduct of the activities so the student will not only become a better participant but also will have greater intellectual appreciation of the world of movement. The first textbook concerning this cognitive domain was made available by the AAHPER and should serve as a springboard for more work in this area.

If the cognitive domain is to be included in the curriculum as an important objective, it must be evaluated in the same manner as all other objectives and for the same reasons. The most valid method for appraising achievement in these areas is through observation to determine whether knowledges and understandings have become functional.

A student's application of knowledge and understanding through performance in an activity is the best test of his achievement. Another method is through oral response as the student answers questions asked by the teacher. As a "steady diet" for evaluation both of these methods are impractical, chiefly because of the time element involved and the lack of an adequate sampling of the material for all the students.

The generally accepted way of evaluating cognitive learnings is by the more formal approach of written tests. These take many forms, but in the final analysis they may be classified in 2 ways. First, from the standpoint of test format, the test may be either essay or objective.

The essay test enables the student to discuss the questions involved and is probably best to appraise understanding and higher levels of learning. The objective test makes use of short answers that can be graded objectively and makes use of simple recall and recognition questions.

It is weak in measuring higher level learning, but can measure knowledges quite adequately. Second, from the standpoint of construction, test may be classified as teacher-made or standardized. The standardized test is constructed by a test expert who presents the reliability and validity coefficients as supporting evidence and may -present norms.

The teacher-made tests, while they may be similar in their construction to the standardized tests, do not provide validity and reliability coefficients. However, they are constructed by teachers according to some systematic procedure so the test measures the knowledge and understandings taught in the activity.

11

EVALUATION — AN INTRODUCTION

Evaluation is systematic determination of merit, worth, and significance of something or someone using criteria against a set of standards. Evaluation often is used to characterize and appraise subjects of interest in a wide range of human enterprises, including the arts, criminal justice, foundations and non-profit organizations, government, health care, and other human services.

Evaluation is a methodological area that is closely related to, but distinguishable from more traditional social research. Evaluation utilizes many of the same methodologies used in traditional social research, but because evaluation takes place within a political and organizational context, it requires group skills, management ability, political dexterity, sensitivity to multiple stakeholders and other skills that social research in general does not rely on as much. Here we introduce the idea of evaluation and some of the major terms and issues in the field.

There is a new word in value education or moral science. It has a wide meaning. It is very important in education because education cannot progress without the help of value education. In physical education it is not possible to succeed without the help of value education.

The decision about the usefulness of any subject thing

can be done only with the process of evaluation. This evaluation is always done according to the aims.

Meaning of Evaluation

In the process of assessment some signs are fixed for the different results of any events or phenomenon, so that a firm decision regarding that event or phenomenon can be taken whereas in evaluation the value of that incident or phenomenon is judged.

For example if we test a computer educated student with other students regarding computer education and the result is this, that he can compose 40 words per minute and there are only 5 mistakes in it, we call this a form of assessment.

In this the main phenomenon has to be composed. Speed and accuracy are those results which are being assessed. 40 words and 5 errors are those symbols by which the compulsory ability of the student was brought to the other students or if the general assessment by which the other student gained marks is kept in front and assessed on that basis. The composing student is given 'B' grade such a thing is called as evaluation.

To find out the symbol for this, the marks obtained in general assessment or the ability of other students is taken as the measuring rod.

Definitions of Evaluation

Evaluation is the systematic assessment of the worth or merit of some object.

This definition is hardly perfect. There are many types of evaluations that do not necessarily result in an assessment of worth or merit -- descriptive studies, implementation analyses, and formative evaluations, to name a few. Better perhaps is a definition that emphasizes the information-processing and feedback functions of evaluation. For instance, one might say:

Evaluation is the systematic acquisition and assessment of information to provide useful feedback about some object

Both definitions agree that evaluation is a systematic endeavour and both use the deliberately ambiguous term 'object' which could refer to a program, policy, technology, person, need, activity, and so on. The latter definition emphasizes acquiring and assessing information rather than assessing worth or merit because all evaluation work involves collecting and sifting through data, making judgements about the validity of the information and of inferences we derive from it, whether or not an assessment of worth or merit results.

1. According to James M. Bredfield :- "The work of evaluation is to fix symbols for events. That gives or fixes the goals of the usefulness of different events and their importance. In general this work is done to assess some special social, cultural or scientific levels"

2. According to J. W. Rightstone "in a statistical form evaluation is a new formed post whose use is done for assessment of traditional thoughts and in place of examination it is described in a vast manner."

3. Quelan and Hanna says that :- "The progress of the school with the help of children and the behavioural changes that take place in them, information gathered about them and the method of its description is called evaluation."

4. Bredfield and Gardok have written :- "Symbols are fixed for the different results of events and phenomenon in the procedure of assessment so that a firm decision can be taken regarding that event of phenomenon whereas in evaluation the value of that event or phenomenon is known."

5. According to E. B. Vigil :- "Evaluation is a

collection of thoughts that points towards described results in quality, importance and the decision of effectiveness for every type of means and efforts. This is an assimilation of material characteristics and the observation of spirit. This is the complete and final estimate. This is a change of form of policies and important for future work and also essential animators.

The definition of evaluation is often problematic and it can be argued that evaluation does not need a definition. Practical problems are not due to a lack of a definition but rather are a result of attempting to define evaluation.

Within the last three decades there have been tremendous theoretical and methodological developments within the field of evaluation. Despite its progress there are still many fundamental problems faced by this field as Davidson (2005) argues 'unlike medicine, evaluation is not a discipline that has been developed by practicing professionals over thousands of years, so we are not yet at the stage where we have huge encyclopaedias that will walk us through any evaluation step-by-step', or provide a clear definition of what evaluation entails. Using Davidson's argument one can argue that a key problem that evaluators face is the lack of a clear definition of evaluation. Hurteau, Houle and Mongiat (2009) observe that the lack of a clear definition may "underline why program evaluation is periodically called into question as an original process, whose primary function is the production of legitimate and justified judgments which serve as the bases for relevant recommendations." However, Potter (2006) postulates that the strict adherence to a set of methodological assumptions may make the field of evaluation more acceptable to a mainstream audience but this adherence will work towards preventing evaluators from developing new strategies for dealing with the myriad of problems that programs face.

Datta (2006) states that "from an often huge body of relevant evaluations and reports, only about 10% of these reports" or less, are used by the evaluand's (clients) (cited in, Hurteau, Houle, & Mongiat, 2009). Fournier and Smith (1993) comment that, "when evaluation findings are challenged or utilization has failed, it was because stakeholders and clients found the inferences weak or the warrants unconvincing". Some reasons for this situation, may be the failure of the evaluator to establish a set of shared aims with the evaluand, or creating overly ambitious aims, as well as failing to compromise and incorporate the cultural differences of individuals and programs within the evaluation aims and process.

None of these problems are due to a lack of a definition of evaluation but are rather due to evaluators attempting to impose predisposed notions and definitions of evaluations on clients. The central reason for the poor utilization of evaluations is arguably due to the lack of tailoring of evaluations to suit the needs of the client, due to a predefined idea (or definition) of what an evaluation is rather than what the client needs are. As House (1980) explains "unless an evaluation provides an explanation for a particular audience, and enhances the understanding of that audience by the content and form of the arguments it presents, it is not an adequate evaluation for that audience, even though the facts on which it is based are verifiable by other procedures".

If one were to page through many well reviewed books on the topic of evaluation one would be sure to come across a definition similar to these. An evaluation is a systematic, rigorous, and meticulous application of scientific methods to assess the design, implementation, improvement or outcomes of a program. It is a resource-intensive process, frequently requiring resources, such as, evaluator expertise, labour, time and a sizeable budget.

St. Leger and Walsworth-Bell have defined evaluation as 'the critical assessment, in as objective a manner as possible, of the degree to which a service or its component parts fulfils stated goals'. The focus of this definition is on attaining objective knowledge, and scientifically or quantitatively measuring predetermined and external concepts.

Stufflebeam defines evaluation as 'a study designed to assist some audience to assess an object's merit and worth'. In this definition the focus is on facts as well as value laden judgements of the programs outcomes and worth.

Stake and Schwandt (2006) argue that "the main purpose of a program evaluation is to determine the quality of a program by formulating a judgment". This definition is contested by Reeve, and Peerbhoy who argue that " projects, evaluators and other stakeholders (including funders) will all have potentially different ideas about how best to evaluate a project since each may have a different definition of 'merit'. The core of the problem is thus about defining what is of value."

Reeve and Peerbhoy (2007) argue that evaluation "is a contested term", as 'evaluators' use the term evaluation to describe an assessment, or investigation of a program whilst others simply understand evaluation as being synonymous with applied research. The above definitions outline some facets of evaluation whilst excluding other functions and goals of an evaluation. Not all evaluations serve the same purpose some evaluations serve a monitoring function rather than focusing solely on measurable program outcomes or evaluation findings, and it would be a tremendous feat to define the numerous types of evaluations that can be conducted. As Alkin and Ellett eloquently state that "evaluation is a large, but not unified theoretical area. No single theory specific to evaluation is available to describe, explain and predict all types of evaluation activities".

Potter contends that "evaluation is an eclectic and diverse field". He argues that this diversity is reflected in the body of literature around evaluation, as the literature, "draws on a number of disciplines, which include management and organisational theory, policy analysis, education, sociology, social anthropology, and social change". These arguments capture an important facet of evaluation, namely, that evaluation is a theoretically informed approach, and consequently a definition of evaluation would have be tailored to the theory, approach, needs, purpose and methodology of the evaluation itself. Therefore, the problem of defining evaluation is not that the field of evaluation does not permit a definition but rather that a definition of evaluation would depict evaluation as a static concept rather than the fluid approach it is.

The following things are clear by these definition:

1. Evaluation is a vast post in which assessment and test both are included.

2. The field of evaluation is vast within which every aspect of a child is included such as physical, mental, moral etc.

3. Evaluation is a method that keeps on going continuously by which the behavioural changes of a child is tested.

4. The aim of evaluation is not only to assess impartiality of study or director but also to rectify it.

Standards and Meta-evaluation

Depending on the topic of interest, there are professional groups which look to the quality and rigor of the evaluation process.

The Joint Committee on Standards for Educational Evaluation has developed standards for educational programmes, personnel, and student evaluation. The Joint Committee standards are broken into four sections: Utility, Feasibility, Propriety, and Accuracy. Various European institutions have also prepared their own standards, more or less related to those produced by the Joint Committee. They provide guidelines about basing value judgments on systematic inquiry, evaluator competence and integrity, respect for people, and regard for the general and public welfare.

The American Evaluation Association has created a set of Guiding Principles for evaluators. The order of these principles does not imply priority among them; priority will vary by situation and evaluator role. The principles run as follows:

Systematic Inquiry: Evaluators conduct systematic, data-based inquiries about whatever is being evaluated.

Competence: Evaluators provide competent performance to stakeholders.

Integrity / Honesty: Evaluators ensure the honesty and integrity of the entire evaluation process.

Respect for People: Evaluators respect the security, dignity and self-worth of the respondents, program participants, clients, and other stakeholders with whom they interact.

Responsibilities for General and Public Welfare: Evaluators articulate and take into account the diversity of interests and values that may be related to the general and public welfare.

Furthermore, the international organizations such as the I.M.F. and the World Bank have independent evaluation functions. The various funds, programmes, and agencies of the United Nations has a mix of independent, semi-independent and self-evaluation functions, which have organized themselves as a system-wide UN Evaluation Group (UNEG), that works together to strengthen the function, and to establish UN norms and standards for evaluation. There is also an evaluation group within the OECD-DAC, which endeavours to improve development evaluation standards.

Approaches

Evaluation Approaches

Evaluation approaches are conceptually distinct ways of thinking about, designing and conducting evaluation efforts. Many of the evaluation approaches in use today make truly unique contributions to solving important problems, while others refine existing approaches in some way.

Classification of approaches

Two classifications of evaluation approaches by House and Stufflebeam & Webster can be combined into a manageable number of approaches in terms of their unique and important underlying principles.

House considers all major evaluation approaches to be based on a common ideology, liberal democracy. Important principles of this ideology include freedom of choice, the uniqueness of the individual, and empirical inquiry grounded in objectivity. He also contends they are all based on subjectivist ethics, in which ethical conduct is based on the subjective or intuitive experience of an individual or group. One form of subjectivist ethics is utilitarian, in which "the good" is determined by what maximizes some single, explicit interpretation of happiness for society as a whole. Another form of subjectivist ethics is intuitionist/ pluralist, in which no single interpretation of "the good" is assumed and these interpretations need not be explicitly stated nor justified.

These ethical positions have corresponding epistemologies—philosophies of obtaining knowledge. The objectivist epistemology is associated with the utilitarian ethic. In general, it is used to acquire knowledge capable of external verification (intersubjective agreement) through publicly inspectable methods and data. The subjectivist epistemology is associated with the intuitionist/pluralist ethic. It is used to acquire new knowledge based on existing personal knowledge and experiences that are (explicit) or are not (tacit) available for public inspection.

House further divides each epistemological approach by two main political perspectives. Approaches can take an elite perspective, focusing on the interests of managers and professionals. They also can take a mass perspective, focusing on consumers and participatory approaches.

Stufflebeam and Webster place approaches into one of three groups according to their orientation toward the role of values, an ethical consideration. The political orientation promotes a positive or negative view of an object regardless of what its value actually and might be. They call this pseudo-evaluation. The questions orientation includes approaches that might or might not provide answers specifically related to the value of an object. They call this quasi-evaluation. The values orientation includes approaches primarily intended to determine the value of some object. They call this true evaluation.

When the above concepts are considered simultaneously, fifteen evaluation approaches can be identified in terms of epistemology, major perspective (from House), and orientation (from Stufflebeam & Webster). Two pseudo-evaluation approaches, politically controlled and public relations studies, are represented. They are based on an objectivist epistemology from an elite perspective. Six quasi-evaluation approaches use an objectivist epistemology. Five of them—experimental research, management information systems, testing programs, objectives-based studies, and content analysis—take an elite perspective. Accountability takes a mass perspective. Seven true evaluation approaches are included. Two approaches, decision-oriented and policy studies, are based on an objectivist epistemology from an elite perspective. Consumer-oriented studies are based on an objectivist epistemology from a mass perspective. Two approaches—accreditation/ certification and connoisseur studies—are based on a subjectivist epistemology from an elite perspective. Finally, adversary and client-centered studies are based on a subjectivist epistemology from a mass perspective.

Pseudo-evaluation

Politically controlled and public relations studies are based on an objectivist epistemology from an elite perspective. Although both of these approaches seek to misrepresent value interpretations about some object, they go about it a bit differently. Information obtained through politically controlled studies is released or withheld to meet the special interests of the holder.

Public relations information is used to paint a positive image of an object regardless of the actual situation. Neither of these approaches is acceptable evaluation practice, although the seasoned reader can surely think of a few examples where they have been used.

Objectivist, Elite, Quasi-Evaluation

As a group these five approaches represent a highly respected collection of disciplined inquiry approaches. They are considered quasi-evaluation approaches because particular studies legitimately can focus only on questions of knowledge without addressing any questions of value. Such studies are, by definition, not evaluations. These approaches can produce characterizations without producing appraisals, although specific studies can produce both. Each of these approaches serves its intended purpose well. They are discussed roughly in order of the extent to which they approach the objectivist ideal.

Experimental research is the best approach for determining causal relationships between variables. The potential problem with using this as an evaluation approach is that its highly controlled and stylized methodology may not be sufficiently responsive to the dynamically changing needs of most human service programs.

Management information systems (MISs) can give detailed information about the dynamic operations of complex programs. However, this information is restricted to readily quantifiable data usually available at regular intervals.

Testing programs are familiar to just about anyone who has attended school, served in the military, or worked for a large company. These programs are good at comparing individuals or groups to selected norms in a number of subject areas or to a set of standards of performance. However, they only focus on testee performance and they might not adequately sample what is taught or expected.

Objectives-based approaches relate outcomes to prespecified objectives, allowing judgments to be made about their level of attainment. Unfortunately, the objectives are often not proven to be important or they focus on outcomes too narrow to provide the basis for determining the value of an object.

Content analysis is a quasi-evaluation approach because content analysis judgments need not be based on value statements. Instead, they can be based on knowledge. Such content analyses are not evaluations. On the other hand, when content analysis judgments are based on values, such studies are evaluations.

Objectivist, Mass, Quasi-Evaluation

Accountability is popular with constituents because it is intended to provide an accurate accounting of results that can improve the quality of products and services. However, this approach quickly can turn practitioners and consumers into adversaries when implemented in a heavy-handed fashion.

Objectivist, Elite, True Evaluation

Decision-oriented studies are designed to provide a knowledge base for making and defending decisions. This approach usually requires the close collaboration between an evaluator and decision-maker, allowing it to be susceptible to corruption and bias.

Policy studies provide general guidance and direction on broad issues by identifying and assessing potential costs and benefits of competing policies. The drawback is these studies can be corrupted or subverted by the politically motivated actions of the participants.

Objectivist, Mass, True Evaluation

Consumer-oriented studies are used to judge the relative merits of goods and services based on generalized needs and values, along with a comprehensive range of effects. However, this approach does not necessarily help practitioners improve their work, and it requires a very good and credible evaluator to do it well.

Subjectivist, Elite, True Evaluation

Accreditation / certification programs are based on self-study and peer review of organizations, programs, and personnel. They draw on the insights, experience, and expertise of qualified individuals who use estabiished guidelines to determine if the applicant should be approved to perform specified functions. However, unless performance-based standards are used, attributes of applicants and the processes they perform often are overemphasized in relation to measures of outcomes or effects.

Connoisseur studies use the highly refined skills of individuals intimately familiar with the subject of the evaluation to critically characterize and appraise it. This approach can help others see programs in a new light, but it is difficult to find a qualified and unbiased connoisseur.

Subjectivist, Mass, True Evaluation

The adversary approach focuses on drawing out the pros and cons of controversial issues through quasi-legal proceedings. This helps ensure a balanced presentation of different perspectives on the issues, but it is also likely to discourage later cooperation and heighten animosities between contesting parties if "winners" and "losers" emerge.

Client-centered studies address specific concerns and issues of practitioners and other clients of the study in a particular setting. These studies help people understand the activities and values involved from a variety of perspectives. However, this responsive approach can lead to low external credibility and a favourable bias toward those who participated in the study.

Principles of Evaluation

The principles of Evaluation can be described in the following manner:-

1. The selection of equipments should be done after seeing to the objectives of the work.

2. The selection of equipments should be according to the aims and objectives of evaluation.

3. Different means and methods should be used for the evaluation of individual and groups.

4. The evaluator should have complete knowledge of the usefulness of the means and equipments.

5. The moral values should be kept in mind by the evaluator while carrying out the evaluation.

6. The evaluation should reach the achievement of high goals.

7. Evaluation should use the equipments according to the fixed aims.

8. Evaluation never ends.

Importance of Evaluation

Evaluation consists of measuring achievement in terms of accomplishing the goals, aims, and objectives established when planning the program. Because the objectives and goals include a number of kinds of development, many different skills, and various concomitant learnings, the methods of appraisal must also be diverse and comprehensive. Because many of the outcomes are intangible in nature, the methods of evaluation must of necessity be both subjective and objective.

1. Improvements are brought about in the method of education with the help of evaluation.

2. Improvements are brought about in the methods of

training with the help of evaluation.

3. There is clarity in the objectives with the help of evaluation.

4. The ways of learning becomes good with the help of evaluation.

5. Evaluation helps to bring about changes in the syllabus.

6. The classification of students become easy with the help of evaluation.

7. We get information regarding the players level of games with the help of evaluation.

8. The players talents are developed with the help of evaluation.

9. The list of training can be improved with the help of evaluation.

10. The weakness of the students are known.

11. The virtues of the students are known with the help of evaluation. Proper educational guidance can be given.

12. Professional guidance can be given to students with the help of evaluation.

13. The information regarding the performance of the games of players is done with the help of evaluation.

14. The assessment of the skill and success of the teaches is done with the help of evaluation.

Procedure of Evaluation

The following are the procedure of evaluation:- The steps of Evaluation process

1. Identifying and defining objectives :- The objectives should be fixed keeping in mind the students subjective process. Social condition and the level of education. It is essential to accept both the subjective and behavioural changes as equally very important, while defining the objectives.

2. Planning the learning experience:- With the help of learning experience such as situation can be created in which the student can perform separate activities. Once the objectives are identified and fixed then attention should be paid towards learning experience.

3. Providing evidence through various tools of evaluation :- After preparing the plans of objectives and learning,, experience the evaluator should pay attention towards the selection and development of useful equipments. After using the tools the characters should be collected.

4. Area of change in behaviour :- According to the results of evaluation the behavioural changes take place in a student. Evaluation is a means for behavioural changes. The behavioural changes can be divided mainly in three categories: a

a) Cognitive aspect :- According to this aspect the importance is given to the objective of knowledge. The following things are included in cognitive aspect:

1. The knowledge of special principles
2. Knowledge of assessment
3. Knowledge of special principles and processes
4. Knowledge of principles and simplifications
5. Knowledge of customs and traditions
6. Knowledge of process and methods
7. Knowledge of events

b) Affective aspect :-

1. To accept
2. To oppose
3. Meditate
4. Revaluation

5. Characterise
6. Arrangement

c) Creative aspect

1. Excitement.
2. Control
3. Activeness
4. Attitude
5. Skill
6. Adjustment

The Goals of Evaluation

The generic goal of most evaluations is to provide "useful feedback" to a variety of audiences including sponsors, donors, client-groups, administrators, staff, and other relevant constituencies. Most often, feedback is perceived as "useful" if it aids in decision-making. But the relationship between an evaluation and its impact is not a simple one -- studies that seem critical sometimes fail to influence short-term decisions, and studies that initially seem to have no influence can have a delayed impact when more congenial conditions arise. Despite this, there is broad consensus that the major goal of evaluation should be to influence decision-making or policy formulation through the provision of empirically-driven feedback.

Evaluation Strategies

'Evaluation strategies' means broad, overarching perspectives on evaluation. They encompass the most general groups or "camps" of evaluators; although, at its best, evaluation work borrows eclectically from the perspectives of all these camps. Four major groups of evaluation strategies are discussed here.

Scientific-experimental models are probably the most historically dominant evaluation strategies. Taking their values and methods from the sciences -- especially the social sciences -- they prioritize on the desirability of impartiality, accuracy, objectivity and the validity of the information generated. Included under scientific-experimental models would be: the tradition of experimental and quasi-experimental designs; objectives-based research that comes from education; econometrically-oriented perspectives including cost-effectiveness and cost-benefit analysis; and the recent articulation of theory-driven evaluation.

The second class of strategies are management-oriented systems models. Two of the most common of these are PERT, the Program Evaluation and Review Technique, and CPM, the Critical Path Method. Both have been widely used in business and government in this country. It would also be legitimate to include the Logical Framework or "Logframe" model developed at U.S. Agency for International Development and general systems theory and operations research approaches in this category. Two management-oriented systems models were originated by evaluators: the UTOS model where U stands for Units, T for Treatments, O for Observing Observations and S for Settings; and the CIPP model where the C stands for Context, the I for Input, the first P for Process and the second P for Product. These management-oriented systems models emphasize comprehensiveness in evaluation, placing evaluation within a larger framework of organizational activities.

The third class of strategies are the qualitative/anthropological models. They emphasize the importance of observation, the need to retain the phenomenological quality of the evaluation context, and the value of subjective human interpretation in the evaluation process. Included in this category are the approaches known in evaluation as naturalistic or 'Fourth Generation' evaluation; the various qualitative schools;

critical theory and art criticism approaches; and, the 'grounded theory' approach of Gläser and Strauss among others.

Finally, a fourth class of strategies is termed participant-oriented models. As the term suggests, they emphasize the central importance of the evaluation participants, especially clients and users of the program or technology. Client-centered and stakeholder approaches are examples of participant-oriented models, as are consumer-oriented evaluation systems.

With all of these strategies to choose from, how to decide? Debates that rage within the evaluation profession -- and they do rage -- are generally battles between these different strategists, with each claiming the superiority of their position. In reality, most good evaluators are familiar with all four categories and borrow from each as the need arises. There is no inherent incompatibility between these broad strategies -- each of them brings something valuable to the evaluation table. In fact, in recent years attention has increasingly turned to how one might integrate results from evaluations that use different strategies, carried out from different perspectives, and using different methods. Clearly, there are no simple answers here. The problems are complex and the methodologies needed will and should be varied.

Types of Evaluation

There are many different types of evaluations depending on the object being evaluated and the purpose of the evaluation. Perhaps the most important basic distinction in evaluation types is that between formative and summative evaluation. Formative evaluations strengthen or improve the object being evaluated -- they help form it by examining the delivery of the program or technology, the quality of its implementation, and the assessment of the organizational context, personnel, procedures, inputs, and so on. Summative evaluations, in contrast, examine the effects or outcomes of some object -- they summarize it by describing what happens subsequent to delivery of the program or technology; assessing whether the object can be said to have caused the outcome; determining the overall impact of the causal factor beyond only the immediate target outcomes; and, estimating the relative costs associated with the object.

Formative Evaluation includes several evaluation types:

- needs assessment determines who needs the program, how great the need is, and what might work to meet the need
- evaluability assessment determines whether an evaluation is feasible and how stakeholders can help shape its usefulness
- structured conceptualization helps stakeholders define the program or technology, the target population, and the possible outcomes
- implementation evaluation monitors the fidelity of the program or technology delivery
- process evaluation investigates the process of delivering the program or technology, including alternative delivery procedures

Summative Evaluation can also be subdivided:

- outcome evaluations investigate whether the program or technology caused demonstrable effects on specifically defined target outcomes.
- impact evaluation is broader and assesses the overall or net effects — intended or unintended—of the program or technology as a whole.

• cost-effectiveness and cost-benefit analysis address questions of efficiency by standardizing outcomes in terms of their dollar costs and values.

• secondary analysis reexamines existing data to address new questions or use methods not previously employed.

• meta-analysis integrates the outcome estimates from multiple studies to arrive at an overall or summary judgement on an evaluation question.

Evaluation Questions and Methods

Evaluators ask many different kinds of questions and use a variety of methods to address them. These are considered within the framework of formative and summative evaluation as presented above.

In formative research the major questions and methodologies are:

What is the definition and scope of the problem or issue, or what's the question?

Formulating and conceptualizing methods might be used including brainstorming, focus groups, nominal group techniques, Delphi methods, brain-writing, stakeholder analysis, synectics, lateral thinking, input-output analysis, and concept mapping.

Where is the problem and how big or serious is it?

The most common method used here is "needs assessment" which can include: analysis of existing data sources, and the use of sample surveys, interviews of constituent populations, qualitative research, expert testimony, and focus groups.

12

EVALUATION PROCESSES AND TECHNIQUES

Physical Education Tests

It is not within the scope of this chapter to outline test procedures for every test in physical education. The following list of tests includes examples of those being used successfully to assess the various aspects of physical education.

Rogers Strength Test

This test includes seven items—right and left grip strength, back lift, leg lift, push-ups, pull-ups, and lung capacity. The gross score is a measure of overall strength called the strength index. The physical Fitness Index is obtained by dividing the strength index by the norm.

Kraus-Waber Test

This is a test of minimum muscular fitness and consists of six items each testing the strength of a specific muscle group; or the flexibility of the body.

Cable-Tension Strength Tests

A tensiometer that measures the tension on a cable is the principal instrument. Tests have been devised to measure the strength of approximately forty different muscle groups throughout the body.

Larson Strength Test

The items consist of chins, dips, and the vertical jump. It is useful for classifying and grouping students.

New York State Physical Fitness Test

Posture, throwing accuracy, strength, agility, speed, balance, and endurance are measured. The test is designed to provide an instrument with which to evaluate the status and progress in fitness of boys and girls grades four to twelve.

Army Physical Efficiency Test

The items are pull-ups, squat jumps, push-ups, sit-ups, and 300-yard shuttle run. It is used to test the physical condition of members of the armed forces.

Tuttle Pulse-Ratio Test

Subjects step up and down on a 13-inch stool. A formula using the resting pulse rate and the pulse rate after exercise has been devised. The test score is based on the ability of the heart to compensate for exercise.

Harvard Step Test

Subjects step up and down on a 20-inch bench the rate of 30 steps per minute for five minutes. The duration of the exercise in seconds × 100, divided by 2 × the sum of pulse counts in recovery gives the score. It is one of the best of the tests measuring cardiovascular endurance.

Wetzel Grid

This is a chart that depicts the growth and development of the individual based on measures of age, height, and weight. It provides a cumulative growth record during the child's school years and in most cases detects serious deviations from accepted norms.

General Motor Capacity

This test, developed by McCloy, is intended to measure an individual's innate potential. The score is obtained by combining the results of the Classification Index, the Sergeant Jump, the low Brace Text, and the Burpee Test.

The Johnson Test

Classified as a test of motor educability, the Johanson Test consists of a number of balancing and hopping stunts performed on a mat.

The Sargent Jump

This consists of leaping vertically as high as possible. There are a number of adaptations. Basically, it measures the ability of the extensor muscles to "explode" and generate force and velocity.

Aerobic Capacity

Most physiologists accept the measurement of maximal oxygen consumption as the most valid test of cardiorespiratory fitness. There are three general methods of measurement—treadmill running, riding the bicycle radiometer, and stepping up and down on a bench. There are carefully prescribed directions that must be followed for accurate measurement.

Scott Motor Ability Battery

The three items contained in this test are the obstacle course, the basketball throw for distance, and the standing broad jump. It was designed to be used for testing high school and college women but has also been modified by Kilday and Latchaw to measure motor ability in ninth-grade boys.

Achievement Tests

These are tests to measure the performance of students in skills taught in physical education classes. There are now available achievement tests for most of the skills commonly taught. By administering tests at various time intervals, the improvement of the students can be assessed. Teachers may use previously validated and scientifically constructed tests, or they may devise tests of their own. The use of achievement tests as a basis for determining grades is quite common and is certainly one of the important techniques of appraisal.

Tests of Knowledge and Understanding

Written tests of knowledge and understanding in physical education are similar in format to those in other subjects. All teachers and supervisors will be familiar with their preparation and grading.

OTHER EVALUATIVE PROCESSES

While the assessment of changes in pupils is the ultimate criterion by which the success of a program should be measured, there are many other evaluation devices that will assist in Keeping the administration informed. Some of these are :

Medical and Health Records

These should be kept meticulously. Form time to time, they should be studied scientifically be qualified research specialists and the findings interpreted for practical application.

Student Checklists

Students set goals for themselves, write them down in a notebook, and check them off as they are achieved. Checklists of stunts to perform, records to attain, teams to make, mountains to climb, weights to lift, or deeds to do can be helpful and inspiring. They also reveal students' progress.

Critical Incidents

Teachers and supervisors may employ the critical incident technique to evaluate the behaviour of pupils. A record of incidents will reveal good and bad behaviour and progress toward a higher level.

Questionnaires and Surveys

These may be utilized to assess attitudes toward physical education, interests, and suggestions for future programs. Successive questionnaires a year or more apart may reveal changes in attitudes and accomplishments.

Cumulative Records

Cumulative personnel records will reveal a child's adjustment to school, physical condition, test scores, grades in school, absences due to illness, intelligence scores, and many other useful bits of information indicating progress or lack of it.

Autobiographies

Some teachers find an autobiography or a statement of the student's philosophy of life very helpful in understanding his/her motivation, ambitions, and problems.

Sociometric Techniques

Sociograms, social Distance Scales, and similar techniques are helpful in determining the student's relationship with others, status with peers, and how he/she behaves in a group.

Daily Schedules

Students who keep diaries or other personal inventories can learn much about themselves through this practice. If the diaries are kept with the understanding that they may be reviewed periodically be the teacher, they will probably not reveal much of the students' inner thinking, but they can still include a great deal of information about their habits, friends, recreation, and social life.

Anecdotal Records

The pupil, the teacher, or both they keep anecdotal records. If these are carefully kept and not cluttered up with too many trivial note, they can be a valuable source of information.

Rating Scales

Rating scales are widely used to evaluate individuals, courses, and programs. They identify judgments about the degree to which qualities and characteristics are present. They make possible the combining of the judgment of many pecple in assessing the quality of facilities, teaching, administering, and performing. They are a necessary adjunct to evaluation at all levels.

THE ADMINISTRATOR AND EVALUATION

While pupil growth and progress are the basic criteria upon which to judge the success of any educational enterprise, administrators need to be kept informed about many other phases of the operation for which they are responsible. Evaluation of the teaching, the environment, the staff work, the facilities, the supervision, the fiscal procedures, the coaching, and the administration itself are important. Some of the means of being kept informed are:

PERSONNEL AUDITS

These are usually written evaluations of teachers, secretaries, custodians, and other personnel. They may be in the form of written memorandums or standardized rating sheets. Any individual who has supervisory responsibilities should be required to turn in periodically a completed evaluation form describing the competence with which those under his or her jurisdiction have performed. While these are always requested at the time recommendations for salary increments and promotions are being considered, they may also be submitted more frequently.

Such personnel audits should provide the superior with as many specifics as possible. Too often they take the form of vague generalities that are not very meaningful and do little to substantiate the recommendations for tenure, promotion, salary increases, and the like.

EQUIPMENT AND FACILITY CHECKS

Custodians, teachers, and other personnel should be required to submit reports of safety hazards of every description. Unsafe playground equipment, fire hazards, slippery floors, broken bleacher seats, open manholes, worn-out bolts or chains, unguarded trenches or ditches, traffic hazards, or reckless behaviour—all should be reported. There should be immediate follow-up to see that remedial action is taken.

OBSERVATION

Regardless of the formal and scheduled evaluation processes, which are part of the normal operation, careful attention should be paid to what is seen, heard, and sensed. An experienced and sensitive administrator does not need to move about in the department very long or converse with very many staff members before being able to assess the climate. The warmth or lack of it as the department head enters the offices of staff members, the spirit of buoyancy or of depression, the exhibition of anxiety or of relaxation, and the openness or restraint that characterizes the conversation—all these are easily discernable and quite informative.

An administrator is constantly evaluating. Whether talking to a pupil reading the school paper, attending a basketball game, or walking through a crowded hallway, one is listening, observing, sensing. In meetings with staff members, either individually or in groups, in reviewing budget requests, signing requisitions, reading memorandums, participating in coffee breaks, or playing a game of golf, the administrator is assimilating and evaluating.

REPORTS

Annual, quarterly, special, and other types of reports may be required by various administrative officers. These constitute one way of keeping informed but should not be the only means employed. Even such written reports must be carefully interpreted. There are many instances where a written report represents a program in glowing terms—yet a deeper investigation reveals weaknesses and flaws.

SUPERVISION AND EVALUATION

These two processes bear a very close relationship. Both serve the same basic purpose—as efforts to make the outcomes coincide with the aims and objectives. Both processes proceed continuously; both employ informal and formal procedures; both are applied to all aspects of the operation. Supervision, however, is more concerned with remedial action while evaluation is concerned principally with assessment and appraisal.

Physical Education Evaluation—Appraisals

The determination and appraisal of what has happened or what is happening to boys and girls as a result of school experiences is known as evaluation. Evaluation is important in the modern school as a means of discovering the points at which individual pupils need assistance. It is also important as a means of discovering the effectiveness of the physical education programme as a whole. Unfortunately, we think of testing as a basis for grading pupils, as a means of determining promotion or failure. These are not the significant purposes of an adequate testing programme. Evaluation seeks to determine the quality and amount of student development. It has a broader connotation than measurement in appraising the consequences of one's teaching efforts.

Evaluation is a qualitative process dealing with a wide range of human activity, such as achievements, attitudes and interests. It is the process of stock-taking. Appraisal of all outcomes of learning, both quantitative and qualitative, is included in the concept of evaluation. The evaluation of physical education practices must be in terms of their effects. As Lockhart would put it, "Results must be planned for; to be convincing, they must be shown". If we really heeded the five requirements for a successful physical education programme, we would lessen our present trend toward confusion and more in the direction of more consistency of action by insisting upon the following:

i. A sound philosophy and measurable objectives.

ii. A realistic curriculum which translates the philosophy into experiences to achieve the objectives.

iii. Good class organization and teaching methods to implement the curriculum.

iv. An evaluation programme to appraise achievement.

v. An interpretation and reporting programme to inform the public.

Parents, pupils, taxpayers and school administrators should insist upon results from a physical education programme. To indicate results, some means of measuring the change in the status of pupils is imperative. Sometimes physical education programmes are difficult to sell because the claims for them are difficult to prove. While evaluation seeks to determine the quality and amount of student development and is the more inclusive determination of amount, which quantity, with the focus. How much does the child know? How far or how high can he jump? What is his grip strength? Although measurements are the raw data for evaluation, the two terms are not synonymous.

For evaluation, tools, techniques or instruments are needed. These range from standardized tests to observational judgements. The first step in evaluation is to formulate in clear and understandable fashion the major purposes of the physical education programme. We must indicate the changes in pupils we expect to facilitate. We must ask, "What do we expect to result from this activity?" Unless objectives really make a difference in what we do as teachers, their formulation is simply a waste of time. We should think of objectives as the directions in which we are trying to change pupils. Each physical education department must clarify its own objectives and formulate its underlying philosophy in clear and consistent terms. It must critically examine its own practices, determine the foundations upon which they are based and commit itself with respect to fundamental issues, of which today there are many. Some rather specific purposes of evaluation are:

i. To help teachers, parents, and pupils examine the values they want to achieve from the physical education programme.

ii. To give strong encouragement to administrators, teachers, parents, and students to evolve certain policies, blueprints of goals and direction, as basic agreements of educational purposes against which to validate their educational procedures.

iii. To provide a periodic check on the degree to which specified objectives are attained for an individual or group of individuals.

iv. To improve counselling methods by providing basic information and new insight into the needs of individual students.

v. To encourage teachers to adjust and improve the teaching process and methods to aid in the achievement of objectives.

vi. To give administrators, teachers, parents and students certain psychological security and a feeling of accomplishment.

vii. To form the basis for sound public relations by helping the taxpayer to realize that his money is contributing toward healthy and happier children today and better citizens tomorrow.

viii. To stimulate greater professional growth in teachers.

The Use of Tests and Other Devices

A test is a systematic procedure for comparing the behaviour of two or more people. It is also the task that is performed as well as the method of appraising or defining an ability. We deal with proficiency tests, achievement tests and aptitude tests. Such factors as muscular strength, agility, flexibility, speed, endurance, balance, depth perception, kinesthetic memory, co-ordination, insight, and a host of other psycho-physical and psycho-social traits or individual attributes are involved. A proficiency or achievement test measures ability to perform some task which is significant in its own right, such as swimming, general motor ability, the dance, or gymnastics.

Principally, the tests are used to evaluate the performance of people who have received special training in the activities tested, hence the term achievement test. An aptitude test in physical education is one used to predict success in some future physical education activity. While an achievement test examines a person's success as a result of past physical education experience, an aptitude test is used to forecast his success in future physical education experience. A test of athletic aptitude, for example, represents present motor traits or attributes as predictors of future athletic achievement. In using the term aptitude, specific inherited aptitude is not implied. A good achievement test of strength is a predictor of future achievement in physical education performance since it measures one important aspect of physical education performance since it measures one important aspect of physical education aptitude, just as pitch discrimination is one aspect of musical ability. We deal with such outcomes as development as physical fitness, motor fitness and motor ability.

Uniformly acceptable definitions of these terms are

still to be determined and in some cases will have to await further factor analysis research studies to stabilize the definitions. Motor fitness is a state of general physical efficiency. It is a state of adaptability or possession of traits which enable one to be efficient in muscular movement. The chief criterion of motor fitness is the ability to perform motor activities with physical efficiency, skill, and competence. Motor fitness and motor ability are rather difficult to isolate separately in terms of definition. Fitness implies the state of adaptability or possession of attributes or traits. Ability represents the power to perform.

Physical fitness is best defined in terms of work capacity, and this is what we test either directly or indirectly by the several variables we employ in a battery of test items.

As educators, we are not interested merely in physical education skills and organic power but in what happens to human personality as a result of these, evaluation must include appraisal of personality development, interests, attitudes and other aspects of pupil behaviour. If we accept education as the social process of change in the behaviour of the human organism, we agree that these changes include many phases in the life of the learner and that, to be comprehensive, an evaluation programme cannot be limited to the use of tests alone. Instruments such as rating scales, anecdotal records, interest inventories, and check lists are needed. What we cannot measure, we will have to judge. We can see that, since the primary purpose of evaluation is to improve learning, evaluation must be as wide and diversified as the instructional programme.

We need not only the formal testing programme concerned with such factors as knowledge, skills, strength and endurance, but, also the informal evaluation of social development based on sociometric friendship tests and personal distance scales. Attitude scales and appraisal of character traits by rating scales and guess who techniques provide additional means of informal evaluation of important non-intellectual determiners of success. The ultimate purpose of evaluation is to establish, as objectively as possible, a comprehensive picture of each pupil's developmental growth. Evaluation should aid us in finding answers about the progress pupils are making toward the objectives, first, of the physical education programme, and secondly, toward the general objectives of the school as a whole.

Data in an evaluation programme will have value for individual guidance and curriculum revision only if thoughtful interpretations are made. Furthermore, it is difficult to draw valid conclusions from one test or disregarded in the light of evidence drawn from other sources. No one item in a record should be taken at its face value alone but always considered in relation to all other information about a pupil before an accurate picture of his various attributes can be obtained. For this reason, a graphic record of developmental growth is exceedingly helpful. Let us ask ourselves frankly, "What does an A or a D as a single mark in physical education actually mean to the teacher, the pupil, and his parents?" Surely a single mark can neither indicate the point at which the pupil needs improvements nor guide him in planning his next steps. Progress can be determined only if we have at least two evaluations, the first being the base line for reference. The pupil's present status becomes important in relation to his past performance records. The all-round growth of the pupil rather than his present status alone should be the focus of attention in any good evaluation and guidance programme.

The Relation of Physical Education to Guidance

The guidance programme in a school provides that body of services organized specifically to help pupils identify and solve their problems and improve their planning. It is not concerned with telling the student what to do or with making decisions for him, but with assisting him through component counselling, to direct his own life, develop his own point of view, and make his own decisions. The goal for the student is self-realization, self-direction and self-determination. One cannot go through life with a chairperson. Guidance has many aspects such as educational guidance, health guidance, vocational guidance, and personality guidance. In the broad sense, guidance has to do with the understanding and development of a human personality.

Guidance cannot be rendered effectively without the co-operation of all members of the school staff. They must have a clear understanding of the purposes to be achieved, the activities to be performed, the methods to be used, and the particular responsibilities of all concerned. The physical education teacher and athletic coaches are in key position to make valuable contributions.

13

EVALUATION OF PERFORMANCE TESTS

The Need for Selecting Appropriate Tests

Selection of appropriate tests is necessary if wise application oı results is to be realized. The little time allotted for measurement activities should be spent wisely. The choice of tests should be made in light of the objectives sought. If the tester is a researcher, a detailed, technical measurement may be desired.

The teacher is just as concerned about the accuracy and honesty of the results, but needs to find a test that is easy to use and appropriate to the group situation present in most schools. The theme of this text is centred on helping the teacher get the best answers with the best tools.

The pressure of time probably should not be the deciding factors, but it must be considered. A test should serve the student directly and indirectly, but it must do so with efficiency.

Such questions as "Why give a test?" "What information is needed?" and "To what use will the result be put? " Help in making appropriate test selections. If these questions cannot be answered, the job of selection will, be difficult and the measurement program likely will be ineffective.

Further, an aimless program without direction and focus will be evident. With a good concept of what physical education is and what the teacher is hoping to accomplish, and with some definite objectives and plans in mind, the measurement program can be a positive force.

Criteria For Test Selection

(1) Practical Standards

The practical standards to be considered when selecting tests are more immediate than the technical ones. In fact, if they are not satisfactory, the test probably will not be selected regardless of its technical credibility in objectivity, reliability, and validity. These practical considerations are important when preparations are being made to give a test, when it is actually administered, and when the results are used.

Development Values

These values are nebulous and intangible, but nevertheless vital to the overall decision of test selection. Tests can influence the program, the instructor, and the student. But the effects on the student are most important, and these indirectly influence the program. The student reacts to tests in various ways that should be considered when selecting tests.

Mental

The attitude of the student is closely related to his/her physical performance. If a test is of appropriate difficulty and presented to the student in an educationally sound manner, the student should be motivated to perform well. The test should be interesting, sensible, and meaningful. A test is too complicated, too difficult, or unrelated to the skill area for which it is used will fail to provide a sound educational experience.

The student will lose respect for the measurement program in physical education. A poor performance could very well be the result of poor test selection. The student is penalized because the teacher has not made a competent test selection. Testing can be a worthwhile mental practice because, through it, students learn concepts about interpretations, comparisons, reasons for various kinds of performance, individual difference, growth, and personal reactions.

Physical

Scotland French relate various criteria for effective tests, especially in the are of skill measurements. They state that tests should be game-like, should encourage good form, should test important skills, should be of suitable difficulty, and should meet various statistical standards.

The instructor should be reluctant to use a test that will have negative aftereffects on students. Some fitness items are administered to the point of exhaustion and may cause nausea. All-out performance on some items causes muscle soreness and discomfort lasting 2 or 3 days.

Items inappropriate for a certain group might cause student to develop a mental block against all testing. Such traumatic experiences are unnecessary and uncalled for, and the teacher should be alert to prevent them.

Most test descriptions state that the tests are constructed for a specific sport and for a certain grade level. It would be unfair to the test constructors, and certainly to the students, to administer a college fitness test to junior high school boys and to except a comparable performance. A skills test should challenged the students to perform to the best of their ability. Tests that require no effort are meaningless to students and contribute little to their physical development.

Appropriateness should be the key word for selection. If the tests are geared to the skill area involved and designed for that age group, then the student should have a meaningful and satisfying physical experience. A student continues to practice and train in the fundamentals of basketball during a skills tests. Tests can be as much a part of the instructional plan as drills and games.

Social

Testing in a school situations is usually a group experience. Not often is it appropriate or feasible to administer tests in a solo fashion. Groupings, waiting turns, helping score and administer tests, tolerance, patience, cooperation, and competitiveness are some of the factors that are present.

The student has time for introspection about group roles, testing procedures, performance in relation to classmates, and interpretations of the entire process. If poorly used, testing opportunities and follow-up sessions can be negative social experience rather than vehicles for better interpersonal relationship. This must be structured, however, by the teacher and students.

There are many factors for the teacher to consider when selecting tests that, at firsts, it may seem to be a formidable job. Test selection is one way for the teacher to approach class objectives. When the test is over, the result should be a better student. With program objectives well understood and with the development of the students uppermost in mind, the teacher should be able to include appropriate measurement tools in the program.

Administrative Considerations

Time

The equipment, floor and wall markings, and all preliminary arrangements should be refined to such a degree that they can be efficiently readied with a minimum of extra preparations. A test that require many intricate markings calling for an excessive amount of the teacher's after-school time will seldom be the test selected.

The time required to administer the test is factor to consider. Group testing, partner testing, and station testing illustrate the efficient use of personnel to streamline the time requirements for administering tests. Not many test will be used that require an individual performance of several minutes while the remaining students wait their turns. Most test batteries can be administered to an entire class in 1 or 2 class period of the procedure are well-planned and organized.

Money

The cost of measurement equipment need not be prohibitive. Equipment can be collected from year to year in most school systems. The teacher should collected high quality and accurate measurement tools over period of time and refrain from making large investments for highly specialized and expensive equipment. A budget allotment should be designated for measurement equipment just as for sports equipment, supplies, uniforms, records, and first aid supplies.

Equipment

The equipment and supplies should be readily available and inexpensive. A test which requires an elaborate and expensive piece of equipment will not be used often in a school situation. Most tests require the use of some equipment, but it should be the kind that is either on hand or can be easily and economically constructed. Sports equipment such as balls, rackets, and the like should be of good quality to help the performance of the students.

Utility

The test results should be readily usable. If norms are available and appropriate, the raw scores should be convertible quickly. No complicated formula should be necessary for each step of the conversion. The quicker the results are available to the students in some meaningful form, the more educational application they will have. Profiles, graphs, and charts can be used by the instructor to help the students understand their performance.

Often a teacher finds a test that seems appropriate after some revisions and adaptations are made. Caution should be used in making revisions because they influence the validity and reliability of the tests and may make the norms inappropriate.

Adjustments can be made to make the test into a drill or practice test, but little leeway should be assumed by the teacher in making appreciable adjustments. Deviations from the prescribed directions may make the test a measure of something quite different from what was intended.

(2) Technical Standards

Standards for judging tests are of a technical nature are established during the developments of the tests, and certainly prior to the publication and general use of them by the teaching public. These standards involve the application of some technical and statistical steps which should accompany each test when published.

Validity

Logical Validity

Logical validity is a more precise terms for what has formerly been referred to as face validity or empirical judgement. The obviousness of what a test is measuring is supplemented by a stated, clear-cut definition of the skill to be measured. The, if the skills test satisfies that definition, a logical validity can be inferred.

The 50-yard dash is considered to be measure of runhing ability if speed in running also means excellence in running. He/she concludes this on the basis of logical, common sense, and judgement; one can see inherently what it is measuring.

For example, the basketball wall pass may be a measure of shoulder girdle strength, reaction time, ball handing ability, basketball playing ability, and height. It is perhaps related to each of these factors to some degree. On the other hand, the dash, while influenced by reaction time, weight, and the like, is basically a measure of running ability and there is very little controversy over that definition.

It is generally accepted to be such a measure and thus the dash is an example of a test that is said to have logical validity. Logical validity involves no statistical procedures, it is useful at times, and often recommended for use is conjunction with ways of establishing concurrent validity.

Construct Validity

Construct validity is used to establish validity of tests for complex ideas such as overall playing ability in some sport or fitness. The isolated, specific, and well-defined motor acts can be validated with concurrent validity. The more obscure, general, less easily defined motor acts can be validated by construct validity.

Occasionally a new test appears in the measurement literature which uses a combination of these approaches to establish validity. This procedure adds further credence to the validity or honesty of the new test. Concurrent validity usually involves the statistical technique of the correlation to measure the relationship of one measure to another. Construct validity, on the other hand, is determined by comparing the differences in performance of groups.

Comparison Over Time—Assuming that a test battery claims to measure validity of overall playing ability in tennis, the battery is administered to a group of players early in the unit, but not until a reliable measure of skills development can result. Toward the end of the unit, after considerable time has been provided for skill acquisition to occur, a second administration of the test battery is given.

The mean performance of the group of the 2 administrations is compared and, if statistically different, the group can be assumed to have gained something they did not have early in the unit: the ability to play tennis. Consequently, construct validity can be claimed for the test battery. This is comparison between groups essentially because the original group has changed, is different, by the time of the second administration of the test battery.

Comparison With Levels—Assuming that the same test battery is under study for validity purposes, it might be administered to a group completing a beginning class in tennis and to another group completing an intermediate course in tennis. If the comparison of mean scores revealed a statistically significant difference, then it would be assumed that the test was able to distinguish between those who could be expected to perform better and those who could be expected to perform with less skill.

Sometimes such validation procedures use varsity groups as one of the comparison groups to be sure those who should be "good" are clearly distinguishable from those who could not be expected to perform as well.

The inference is that some construct, in this case,

tennis playing ability, is present in one group which is not present to such a degree in the other group. Construct validity is more indirect than concurrent validity because it infers the presence of some, whereas the latter shows a direct relationship.

Current Validity

Concurrent validity measure the degree of relationship between 2 measures taken at approximately the same time. For example, if a group of tennis players took a new tennis serve test and also an established tennis serve test, the relationship between the 2 performances would be an indication of the concurrent of the new test. Did the new test. Did the new test measure about the same things as the old one at about the same time? There are several ways of ascertaining concurrent validity.

Each way involves the comparison of the new test with some external standard, called a criterion, which has already been established. This results in 2 sets of scores: 1 for the new test being developed, and 1 for the criterion measure. These sets of scores, 1 set for each student, are correlated.

If the relationship is close, the test is considered valid. If the standard chosen for making the comparison is poor, then the validity reported is often misleading. The standard or criterion used as the comparison factor must be the best possible.

Several have been used to establish the validity of various motor tests and each will be discussed. They may be used in combination as well as separately. For example, a new test may be compared with tournaments standing as well as with subjective ratings. This multiple use of criterion measures is an attempt by researchers to make doubly sure that the new test is valid.

Subjective Rating—Subjective ratings are given by the teacher sometimes to use in grading. When used for establishing validity, however, they are given by at least 3 judges and often 5 or 7. Rating generally involve judgments on the form of a performance.

The tennis serve provides an example. The technique of the serve, its execution, force, form, accuracy, and the like are noted for each student by 3 judges. They evaluate on the basis of a rating scale that defines carefully the distinguishing points between a performance worth 5 points and one worth only 2 points, for instance. As a second step, these same students are given a service placement test. Then the composite or average of the 3 judges ratings is compared with the objective service placement test score fore each student.

Two assessments are available for each student. They are correlated, and the resultant coefficient is used as the basis for interpreting the validity of the service placement test. If the scores on the test rank the students in approximately the same order that the judges evaluate them, the coefficient is relatively high and the service test said to be valid on the basis of the criterion of judge ratings.

The opinion of experts is often a more accurate measure than a poor test. No apologies need be made for the use of subjective ratings. Care should be taken, however, that the skill is well-defined, that the rating scale is refined, and the rates are competent. Rating can be poor criteria, but if carefully done they may be relied upon to yield dependable results.

Many of the motor tests reported in the professional literature have been validated on the basis of subjective ratings. Many others have been validated on the basis of other objective measures. The teacher needs to realize that the objective test used as a criterion was probably itself validate by subjective rating.

It is possible that some of the early subjective ratings were poorly executed and this emphasizes the need for constant re-evaluation of the objective tests that are available in the measurement literature.

There is one other controversial point about the use of subjective ratings: they make a judgment on the process of the skill when the product or result of the skill is what counts in the game. Some would argue that good performance is highly related to good form. Others would argue that it does not matter how the performer looks when executing the skill as long as the results are effective.

This might imply that the proper use of subjective ratings would be reserved for establishing tests for gymnastics routines or diving, where a highly objective score is not available. It is not possible to settle the argument here, but only to alert the user of tests about this reservation regarding subjective ratings as a criterion for establishing concurrent validity.

Previously Validated Tests—Some skills tests are created as refinements of other tests already available. The test may be simplified, shortened, or revised in some way. The old form of the test is administered to a group and then the new form is given to the same group.

If the standings of the people in the group remain similar, then the new test may be said to measure appreciably what the old test measured. And, if the old test was reputed to be a measure of the badminton clear, for example, then the new test may assume validity for the same measure.

Researchers seem to favour the use of previously validated tests as criteria for establishing concurrent validity because the tests yield objective scores as opposed to subjective ones. Care should be taken that the previously validated test was itself carefully and accurately validated before it is accepted as a standard for measuring the validity of a new test.

Composite Scores—Composite scores have been used as a criterion when tests for a broad type of ability such as fitness or motor ability have been developed. Validity for such measures, however, should probably be established by construct validity, a concept to be discussed subsequently. Composite scores might be used wisely as the criterion when the development of a test battery is anticipated instead of a single test item.

The researchers may realize that 1 skill test will not give an ample measure of football playing ability, for example, but that several tests sampling the essential skills of football will be needed.

A composite scores is achieved by administering a gamut of tests, each supposedly related to the measurement are in question. The scores are put into some type of comparable form, such as T-Scores, and are added to get 1 total or composite score.

Other tests or perhaps even some that were in the composite list are then correlated with the composite score, each in turn, and in various combinations. The composite score is then used to help select the battery of tests that comes closest to measuring whatever all the individual tests collectively were attempting to measure.

The composite score used the "buck shots" theory which implies that if enough related tests are given, some of them will be measures of the skill in question. This particular standard for establishing validity is somewhat in question for this reason. It may encompass too broad a base of skills to identify anything but very general kinds of ability. If, on the other hand, the test items are carefully selected, the composite score theory has merit.

Tournament Standings—Tournament standings serve as adequate standards for establishing concurrent validity when a high level of skill is anticipated. Some tests are designed for beginning players, others for advanced players, some for young players, and others for more developed players. This is taken into account when planning a test.

Tournament standings for advanced players are rather stable and serve as good indications of playing ability. There are less dependable when the tournaments players are beginners or when the sport involved a team sport instead of an individual one.

A round robin tournament is a good style to use, as some type of ladder tournament. These longer tournaments require more contests and may be counted on to put the players in their proper order of playing excellence. Once this standing is set and assigned some numerical value, it can be compared with various tests that measure the fundamental skills in a game.

For example, tennis tests for the service, and forehand and backhand drives could be validated against tournament standings, if these strokes are considered important to overall tennis playing abilities.

The correlation coefficients could be expected to be fairly low, yet significant and acceptable, because only one aspect of the sport would be correlated with total game performance.

Definition

Validity is the most important of the technical standard because it tests the honesty of a test. The teacher wants to have confidence that a test selected to use a measure of the tennis serve, for example, is indeed just that and not a test of shoulder girdle strength or of generals motor abilities. It must be a measure of a rather specific skill—namely, the tennis serve.

It would be unfair to use a fitness test as one basis for assigning grades if the test were so complicated that an intelligence factor weighed heavily in the performance score of each student. If a test is presented as a measure of the volleyball volley, then, to be valid, it must measure volleying ability and, ideally, it must measure it to such a degree that other influencing factors such as height and weight are incidental to the final results.

A test may be considered valid if it is measuring, as accurately as possible, what it is described as measuring. Validity is inherent in the purpose of the test. Validity can be ascertain either empirically or statistically. Logical validity usually comes first and is sometimes considered sufficient without the follow-up of either concurrent or construct validity using statistical technique.

Objectivity

Objectivity is the first of the technical standards to be considered. Objectivity is the degree of uniformity with which various persons score the same test. It refers to the lack of any personal influence of the scorer on the test results.

If the test is well-standardized and is administered properly, the role of the scorer should not have a noticeable influence on the results. Objectivity is measure of the worth of the scores and is inherent in the test. If a test is scored by 2 instructors, concurrently and independently, the results should be similar.

The correlation coefficient product from the 2 sets of scores should be high. This standard, which is similar to reliability, changes only 1 condition in the testing procedure and that is the scorer.

The statistical technique employed for ascertaining objectivity is a correlation. The agreement of 2 judges rating a gymnastics routine will be less stable. This is one reason rating scales have been devised to objectify, as much as possible, subjective observations.

The motivation, clarity of directions, organization, and scoring accuracy provided by one instructor should be so different from that given by another as to influence the scores appreciably. If such is the case, however, the test is said to be lacking in objectivity. Objectivity is enhanced by clear test directions, precise scoring methods, and adherence to these factors.

Reliability

Methods of Establishing Reliability

Reliability is also interpreted by using the statistical technique called a correlation coefficient. The reliability coefficient is obtained by correlating one measure of type test with another measure of the same test and thus is judged by an internal and dependent measure.

Consequently, reliability coefficients are generally higher than validity coefficients. Reliability coefficients may be derived either by the interclass method suggested by the product-moment correlation or by the intra class approach employed in analysis of variance.

Test Re-test—One method of establishing reliability is to administer the test completely on time and then to given it another time. Usually the second administration is on the next day or two under very similar conditions and certainly before forgetting, practising, and hearing factors become to influential in the results.

This method is time-consuming and sacrifices some of the interest factor of the students during the second administration. The scores of the first and second administrations are correlated to determine the coefficient.

Split Halves—An alternative time-saving method is to administer the test only once and then correlate the total of the even-numbered trails with the total of the odd-numbered trails. In a 10-trail test, the 1st, 3rd, 5th, 7th, and 9th trails totalled provide 1 score and the 2nd, 4th, 6th, 8th, and 10th trials totalled provide the second score for the correlation problem.

This method requires the subsequent use of the Spearman-Brown Prophecy Formula to predict what the reliability would be had the test-re-test method been used instead.

The Prophecy Formula predicts the reliability of the whole test on the basis of only half of it. This formula is also useful to predict what effect additional trials or longer trials or even reduced trials would do to the reliability of a test. The resultant coefficient is usually referred to as "Stepped-up."

Analysis of Variance—The analysis of variance technique of establishing reliability has been recommended in the research literature and has some merit over the other 2 methods. This intra-class method permits the identification of source of variability in performance that are used in estimating reliability.

These sources of variability are usually day-by-day differences in performance and trial-by-trial differences in performance. The Spearman-Brown Prophecy Formula permits the manipulation of the number of trials to arrive at an acceptable coefficient of reliability.

The analysis of variance technique permits the additional manipulation of the number of days to determine adequacy of the coefficient. For example, the researcher could report several reliability coefficients representing various combinations of days and trials of test performance.

The subsequent user of the test were given 4 days with 5 trials on each day. This same test might give a reliability coefficient of .90 if given 2 days with 1 trial on each day. The research report might show the matrix of possible reliability coefficients and the teacher would select the plan most appropriate to a particular teaching situation. Baumgartner states that the intra-class correlation method is the most preferable method of established reliability, the test-re-test is the second best, and the split-halves method is least desirable.

For the student of measurement, it is sufficient to recognize the method used just as the method of establishing validity is important. The coefficient alone is not nearly as meaningful as the coefficient accompanied by the method of attaining it.

Parallel Forms—This type of reliability is used generally with written tests. The object is to construct 2 tests of similar difficulty and content. The student take both test and the 2 sets of scores are correlated. If the students perform similarly on the 2 forms and if the 2 forms of the test are really parallel, then the test may be considered reliable.

Some authors make a distinction between reliability coefficient required for tests used in groups measurement and for tests administered on an individual basis. Group measurement reliabilities can be lowered because so many uncontrollable factors are present in mass administrations which adversely influence reliability indices.

Definition

Reliability is the second technical standards that the teacher can use when selecting tests. A test is said to be reliable if it is dependable: if similar results occur when the test is repeated by the same group under like conditions. Reliability is related to the test performance the itself.

The tester is the same, the students are the same, and the test is the same. Assume that the test is administered and then re-administered. If the students scores fall in the same position, the test is reliable.

The student who performed best the first time is still best, the poorest performer is still poorest, and all in between are approximately in the same order. A test is given to position students on a ladder, so to speak. If their positions are true indications of their skill, then the test is said to be valid; if their positions are dependable and consistent, then the test is considered to be reliable.

Countless factors influence reliability. The equipment used in the test may not be of sufficient quality to produce consistent results. The instrument recording the measurement may be too gross, such as a 100-pound spring scale to measure flexion of the wrist.

The number and length of the trials needed to get a stable measure are important. Usually the best of 3 board jumps is needed to get a stable measure are important. Usually the best of 3 board jumps is considered adequate, whereas most accuracy test require about 20 trials. Generally, the longer the test, the more reliable it is.

The test may be so long, however, as to introduce a fatigue factor. Averaging scores usually produce more reliable results than taking only the best score because averaging has a levelling influence on the scores.

14

CURRICULUM EVALUATION

Introduction

Curriculum evaluation is an essential phase of curriculum development. Through evaluation a faculty discovers whether a curriculum is fulfilling its purpose and whether students are actually learning. Curriculum evaluation, at the provincial level, involves making judgments about the effectiveness of provincially authorized curricula. It involves gathering information (the assessment phase) and making judgments or decisions based on the information collected (the evaluation phase), to determine how well the curriculum is performing. The principal reason for curriculum evaluation is to plan improvements to the curriculum. Such improvements might involve changes to the curriculum document and/or the provision of resources or inservice to teachers. It is intended that curriculum evaluation be a shared, collaborative effort involving all of the major education partners in the province.

In the assessment phase, information will be gathered from students, teachers, and administrators. The information obtained from educators will indicate the degree to which the curriculum is being implemented, the strengths and weaknesses of the curriculum, and the problems encountered in teaching it. The

information from students will indicate how well they are achieving the intended objectives and will provide indications about their attitudes toward the area of study. Student information will be gathered through the use of a variety of strategies including paper-and-pencil tests (objective and open-response), performance (hands-on) tests, interviews, surveys, and observation.

Curriculum is frequently defined by educational theorists as the link between society and the schools, the major source of stimuli found in instructional settings, or as pupil behaviour pertinent to the goals of the school. According to these definitions curriculum could include everything that happens to a child in school from learning how to accept last Friday's football game loss to the complete sequence of experiences that produced his 800 SAT score. Abramson (1966) described the use of broad, general definitions in a Review issue on curriculum development and planning: "Clarification of the specific role of curriculum research and evaluation is a continuing problem in the field because of lack of agreement as to the distinctions to be made among curriculum, instructional organization, teaching, and learning."

Curriculum evaluation involves gathering information in order to determine how well the curriculum is performing. The principal reasons for curriculum evaluation are to make improvements such as changes to the curriculum document to provide resources or inservice to teachers.

It is intended that curriculum evaluation be a shared, collaborative effort involving all of the major education partners in the province. Teachers contribute in the development of instruments, validation, field testing, scoring and data interpretation.

In the assessment phase, information is gathered from students, teachers and administrators. The information obtained from educators indicates the degree to which the curriculum is being implemented, as well as the strengths and weaknesses of the curriculum. The information from students will indicate how well they are achieving the intended learning outcomes and will provide indications about their attitudes toward the curriculum.

All provincial curricula are included within the scope of curriculum evaluation. Evaluations are conducted during the implementation phase for new curricula and regularly on a rotating basis thereafter.

Curriculum evaluation is described in greater detail in the document Saskatchewan Education (1990) Curriculum Evaluation in Saskatchewan.

Using Curriculum Evaluation as a Basis for Clinical Faculty Development

Professional development is the phrase that many professions use to describe the continuous learning that professionals may need to maintain, enhance, or broaden their competence. Professional development in physical therapy is essential to update physical therapists (PTs) and physical therapist assistants (PTAs) regarding new developments in knowledge, skills, and technology to ensure continued competence within the profession. Clinical faculty members provide a vital role in the education of physical therapy students. This role necessitates that faculty development plans include input from student evaluations that reflect how well the program prepared them for clinical practice. This study completed a survey investigation to identify the professional development needs of 50 clinical faculty and 25 graduates affiliated with an established physical therapist assistant program. It also examined the professional development needs of clinical faculty as identified through PTA students' evaluation at the time of graduation and through the programs' overall curriculum evaluation. Graduates reported that overall they were well prepared as entry level PTAs and rated the effectiveness of the program favourably. Curriculum content areas identified by graduates as needing improvement included wound care and leadership skills. Clinical instructors concurred with the graduates by identifying wound care as an area of need for their professional development. Recommendations from this study would be to: perform similar studies encompassing more than one program, follow-up with future curriculum evaluations to verified if the identified weaknesses were addressed through curriculum changes, and for allied health programs to offer education methodology courses for their clinical instructors.

Professional development is defined as the continuous learning that professionals need to pursue throughout their careers to maintain, enhance, and broaden their professional competence (Physiotherapy, 1994). It is the phrase that many professions use for continuing education and development, which in college and university settings, may be called faculty development (Mathis, 1982; Millis, 1990). Professional development activities may encompass research and teaching activities, personal health and growth, and the management of a professional career over time.

Professional development in the physical therapy profession is important to update physical therapists (PTs) and physical therapist assistants (PTAs) in new developments in terms of knowledge, skills, and technology to ensure continuing competence within the profession. Traditionally, professional development has been viewed as short training courses; however, professional development can be formal or informal. Physical therapy clinicians are often recruited to serve as clinical instructors for physical therapy education programs, with many clinicians assuming this role within one to two years of entry into the profession. Success in the role of clinical instructor requires attention to aspects of teaching that may not have been included in the clinical instructor's professional training.

Teacher Self-Evaluation

An important aspect of good teaching practice is that of teacher self-evaluation. Teachers can use the table entitled Where are you in all of this? that appears later in this section to assess their strengths and weaknesses.

Clarification of Terms

To enhance understanding of the evaluation process, it is useful to distinguish between the terms assessment and evaluation.

Assessment is a preliminary phase in the evaluation process. In this phase, various techniques are used to gather information about student progress.

Evaluation is the weighing of assessment information against some standard, such as the Foundational objectives of the physical education curriculum, in order to make a judgment or decision. This may then lead to other decisions and action by the teacher, student or parent.

There are three main types of student evaluation: formative, summative and diagnostic. Assessment techniques are used to gather information for each type of evaluation.

Formative evaluation is a continuous classroom process that keeps students and educators informed of students' progress toward program learning objectives.

The main purpose of formative evaluation is to improve

instruction and student learning. It provides teachers with valuable information upon which instructional modifications can be made. This type of evaluation helps teachers understand the degree to which students are learning the course material and the extent to which their skills, fitness levels, knowledge, understanding and attitudes are developing. Students are given direction for future learning and are encouraged to take responsibility for their own progress.

Summative evaluation occurs most often at the end of a unit of study. Its primary purpose is to determine what has been learned over a period of time, to summarize student progress and to report to students, parents and educators on progress relative to curriculum objectives.

Seldom are evaluations strictly formative or strictly summative. For example, summative evaluation can be used formatively to assist teachers in making decisions about changes to instructional strategies or other aspects of students' learning programs. Similarly, formative evaluation may be used to assist teachers in making summative judgments about student progress. It is important that teachers make clear to students the purpose of assessments and whether they will later be used summatively.

Diagnostic evaluation usually occurs at the beginning of the school year or before a unit of instruction. It identifies students who lack prerequisite skills, fitness, knowledge or understanding so that remedial help can be arranged. It also serves to identify gifted learners to ensure they are being sufficiently challenged. Diagnostic testing also identifies student interests. Diagnostic evaluation provides information essential to teachers in designing appropriate programs for all students.

Teachers conduct all three types of evaluation during

the course of the school year.

Guiding Principles

Recognizing the importance of evaluation as an integral part of the curriculum, Saskatchewan Education has developed five general guiding principles to provide a framework to assist teachers in planning for student evaluation:

- Evaluation is an essential part of the teaching-learning process. It should be a planned, continuous activity that is closely linked to both curriculum and instruction.

- Evaluation should be guided by the intended learning outcomes of the curriculum and a variety of assessment strategies should be used.

- Evaluation plans should be communicated in advance. Students should have opportunities for input regarding the evaluation process. The weighting of criteria and in some instances the establishment of criteria can be negotiated among teacher and students.

- Evaluation must be fair and equitable. It should be sensitive to family, classroom, school and community situations. It should be free of bias. Students should be given opportunities to demonstrate the extent of their skills, fitness levels, knowledge, understanding and attitudes.

- Evaluation should help students. It should provide positive feedback and encourage students to participate actively in their own learning.

Phases of the Evaluation Process

Although evaluation is not strictly sequential, it can be viewed as a cyclical process made up of four phases: preparation, assessment, evaluation and reflection. This process involves the teacher as a decision-maker throughout all four phases.

During the preparation phase, decisions are made that identify what is to be evaluated, the type of evaluation to be used (i.e. formative, summative or diagnostic), the criteria against which student learning outcomes will be judged and the most appropriate assessment techniques with which to gather information on student progress. The teacher's decisions in this phase form the basis for the remaining phases.

During the assessment phase, the teacher identifies information-gathering strategies, constructs or selects instruments, administers them to the students, and collects and organizes the information on student learning progress. The teacher continues to make decisions in this phase. The identification and elimination of bias (e.g., gender and culture bias) from the assessment techniques and instruments, and determining where, when and how assessments will be conducted are examples of important considerations for the teacher.

During the evaluation phase, the teacher interprets the assessment information and makes judgments about student progress. Based on the judgments or evaluation, teachers make decisions about student learning programs and report on progress to students, parents and appropriate school personnel.

The reflection phase allows the teacher to consider the extent to which the previous phases in the evaluation process have been successful. Specifically, the teacher evaluates the utility and appropriateness of the assessment techniques used. Such reflection assists the teacher in making decisions concerning improvements or modifications to subsequent teaching and evaluation.

Information Gathering and Record Keeping

Reporting to students and parents must be based upon real evidence. In order to build up a record of growth, teachers will have to rely to a great extent upon accurate observation and adequate record keeping.

Evaluation in physical education should focus on both process and content. Many of the objectives in the elementary physical education curriculum are best assessed through ongoing observation.

Assessment Techniques

Methods of Organization

These methods refer to the broad organizational structure of the assessment techniques a teacher may decide to use.

- Assessment Stations
- Individual Assessments
- Peer and Group Assessments
- Learning Contracts
- Self-Assessment
- Portfolios

Methods of Data Recording

These methods may be used within the structure of any of the methods of organization and with any of the ongoing student activities, as well as quizzes and tests.

- Anecdotal Records
- Observation Checklists
- Rating Scales

Ongoing Student Activities

These techniques are those a teacher would use

throughout the course of a regular school day when students are engaged in their usual learning activities.

- Performance Assessment
- Written Assignments
- Presentations
- Discussions
- Journal Writing
- Problem Solving
- Projects
- Homework
- Conferences
- Interviews

Quizzes and Tests

- Oral Assessments
- Performance Tests
- Extended Open-Response
- Short-Answer Items

Student Assessment Ideas

Conferences and Interviews

The teacher confers with groups as they work, recording responses on an anecdotal observation grid. Conferences and interviews with individuals are a means of measuring understanding, satisfaction, setting of goals and ongoing planning. Teachers can confer with the class as a whole to get a sense of students' likes and dislikes and to give direction for planning units.

Contracts

Contracts can be used for students doing projects and independent work.

Peer and Group Assessment

In this assessment, either each member of the group or the group as a whole provides an assessment of its effort in the assigned task. A list of descriptors can be provided and marks or a rating scale can be provided for the assessment.

At times, where a project has been the task, each member of the group may provide a rating for other group members. If presentations involve all members of the class, peer assessments of each presentation may be done.

Performance Assessments

These can be part of contracts or station work and include some peer and self-assessments. Usually, materials are provided for an activity and the student must go through a series of steps to complete the task. The student may then record the results, or orally tell what he or she did and the resulting conclusion. Besides the visible product, if one is required, the process of completing the task, and the written or oral response become part of the assessment. This may be rated on a numerical or a poor-to-excellent rating scale.

Portfolios

Portfolios are useful as an ongoing measure of student work. They are the "evidence" for reporting purposes and can include student work, reports, reflections, self-assessments, peer assessments, photographs and videotapes of performances (e.g., individual movement skills, skill combinations, sequences, routines, application of game strategies). They can be used at all grade levels.

Use portfolios and records of conferences to validate students' marks when reporting to parents. The portfolio provides samples of the quality of students work and their own and peers' ratings. Together with the teacher's assessment and observational notes these become a cohesive collection tracking student progress. There should be no surprises!

Recording Anecdotal Comments

• Anecdotal comments can be recorded on post-it (sticky) notes and affixed to a chart that lists the students and the days of the week. At the end of the week, the recorded information is transferred to each student's file and the chart is used again the following week.

• Create a grid on 11.5 × 17 size paper to handle the class size. For example:

4 × 6 if 24 students in the class

4 × 7 if 28 students in the class

5 × 6 if 30 students in the class

Arrange student names alphabetically in the corner of each rectangle. At the end of the week or observation period, cut up the grid and paste the notes into individual student folders. The sheets in individual folders can be color-coded for each reporting period for easy access.

• Laminate a piece of bristol board large enough to hold a sticky note for each student.

Using a permanent marker, write every student's name. (Names can be erased with alcohol and the board can be used over and over again from year to year.

Place a stack of 3 to 4 notes under each name.

Write observations on sticky notes and periodically remove the notes and stick them into individual student folders.

Self-Assessment

Happy Face

A happy face self-assessment can be used by students to rate their own performance on such things as:

- respect for the rights and feelings of others
- participation and effort
- self-direction
- caring about and helping others
- (cooperation, sharing, taking turns, encouraging, helping, asking for help, etc.)

Task Assessment

Forms are used to ask the student to evaluate the resulting product and learning that occurred. Each of the areas can be assigned different weight depending on the objectives and type of task. Some descriptors might include:

- Task completion (this could include work assigned, final product presentation.)
- Cooperative participation (this may be within the group or class and would cover use of time, helpfulness, sharing, etc.)
- Content, creative solutions, ideas and approaches
- Suggestions, extensions and rating (Task assessment might be in the form of a rating scale or include assignment of marks.)

FOCUSES OF EVALUATION

Evaluations may focus on progress in student learning (student evaluation), the effectiveness of school programs (program evaluation), and the effectiveness of the curriculum (curriculum evaluation). Teachers also reflect on the effectiveness of their instruction (teacher self-evaluation).

Student Evaluation

Sample assessment and evaluation strategies are provided in Part Two of this document for each grade level for each perspective (Active Living, Movement, Personal-Social-Cultural), and for each Activity Area-Alternative Environment Activities, Educational Rhythmic and Dance, Educational Games, Educational Gymnastics and Individual and Dual Activities. Sample templates for recording data are provided in the sample units and in this section of the document. The assessment techniques are not prescribed. Rather, they are meant to serve as suggestions only, as the teacher must exercise professional judgment in determining which techniques suit the unique circumstances and purposes.

Assessment techniques are selected or designed to gather information related to how well students are achieving the learning objectives of the curriculum. The specific assessment technique used at any given time will depend on several factors, including the type of learning outcomes (i.e. movement skill development, fitness development, conceptual understandings, personal and social skills, attitudes and values), the subject area content, the instructional strategies used, the student's level of development and the specific purposes of the evaluation.

For further information on the various assessment techniques and types of instruments that can be used to collect and record information about student learning, refer to Saskatchewan Education (1991)

Student Evaluation: A Teacher Handbook.

Program Evaluation

Program evaluation is a systematic method for collecting, analyzing, and using information to answer basic questions about projects, policies and programs. Program evaluation is used in the public and private sector and is taught in numerous universities. Evaluation became particularly relevant in the U.S. in the 1960s during the period of the Great Society social programs associated with the Kennedy and Johnson administrations. Extraordinary sums were invested in social programs, but the impacts of these investments were largely unknown.

Program evaluations can involve quantitative methods of social research or qualitative methods or both. People who do program evaluation come from many different backgrounds: sociology, psychology, economics, social work. Some graduate schools also have specific training programs for program evaluation.

Program evaluation is a systematic process of gathering and analyzing information about some aspect of a school program in order to make a decision or to communicate to others involved in the decision-making process.

Program evaluation can be conducted at two levels: relatively informally at the classroom level or more formally at the classroom, school or school division levels.

At the classroom level, program evaluation is used to determine whether the program being presented to the students is meeting their needs and the objectives prescribed by the province. Program evaluation is not necessarily conducted at the end of the program but is an ongoing process. For example, if particular lessons appear to be poorly received by students or if they do not seem to demonstrate the intended learnings from a unit of study, the problem should be investigated and changes made.

By evaluating their programs at the classroom level, teachers become reflective practitioners. The information gathered through program evaluation will assist teachers in program planning and in making decisions for improvement.

Most program evaluations at the classroom level are relatively informal, but they should be done systematically. Such evaluations should include identification of the area of concern, collection and analysis of information and judgment or decision-making.

The table, entitled Where are you in all of this?, which appears later in the section can be used for evaluation of the program.

To support formal school-based program evaluation activities, Saskatchewan Education has developed the Saskatchewan School-Based Program Evaluation Resource Book (1989) to be used in conjunction with an inservice package. Further information on these support services is available from the Evaluation and Student Services Division, Saskatchewan Education.

Paradigms in Program Evaluation

Potter (2006) identifies and describes three broad paradigms within program evaluation . The first, and probably most common, is the positivist approach, in which evaluation can only occur where there are "objective", observable and measurable aspects of a program, requiring predominantly quantitative evidence. The positivist approach includes evaluation dimensions such as needs assessment, assessment of program theory, assessment of program process, impact assessment and efficiency assessment (Rossi, Lipsey and Freeman. 2004).

The second paradigm identified by Potter (2006) is that of interpretive approaches, where it is argued that it is essential that the evaluator develops an understanding of the perspective, experiences and expectations of all stakeholders. This would lead to a better understanding of the various meanings and needs held by stakeholders, which is crucial before one is able to make judgments about the merit or value of a program. The evaluator's contact with the program is often over an extended period of time and, although there is no standardized method, observation, interviews and focus groups are commonly used.

Potter (2006) also identifies critical-emancipatory approaches to program evaluation, which are largely based on action research for the purposes of social transformation. This type of approach is much more ideological and often includes a greater degree of social activism on the part of the evaluator. Because of its critical focus on societal power structures and its emphasis on participation and empowerment, Potter argues this type of evaluation can be particularly useful in developing countries.

Despite the paradigm which is used in any program evaluation, whether it be positivist, interpretive or critical-emancipatory, it is essential to acknowledge that evaluation takes place in specific socio-political contexts. Evaluation does not exist in a vacuum and all evaluations, whether they are aware of it or not, are influenced by socio-political factors. It is important to recognize the evaluations and the findings which result from this kind of evaluation process can be used in favour or against particular ideological, social and political agendas (Weiss, 1999) [6]. This is especially true in an age when resources are limited and there is competition between organizations for certain projects to be prioritised over others (Louw, 1999).

Dimensions of Program Evaluation

Program evaluators may assess programs on several dimensions to determine whether the program works. Rossi et al. (2004) divide these dimensions into 5 main categories: needs assessment, program theory, process analysis, impact analysis, and cost-benefit & cost-effectiveness analysis.

A needs assessment examines the nature of the problem that the program is meant to address. This includes evaluating who is affected by the problem, how wide-spread the problem is, and what effects stem from the problem. For example, for a housing program aimed at mitigating homelessness, a program evaluator may want to find out how many people are homeless in a given geographic area and what their demographics are.

The program theory is the formal description of the program's concept and design. This is also called a logic model or impact pathways. The program theory breaks down the components of the program and shows anticipated short- and long-term effects. An analysis of the program theory examines how the program is organized and how that organization will lead to desired outcomes. It will also reveal unintended or unforeseen consequences of a program, both positive and negative. The program theory drives the hypotheses to test for impact evaluation. Developing a logic model can also build common understanding amongst program staff and stakeholders.

Process analysis looks beyond the theory of what the program is supposed to do and instead evaluates how the program is being implemented. The evaluation determines whether target populations are being reached, people are receiving the intended services, staff are adequately qualified, etc.

The impact evaluation determines the causal effects of the program. More information about impact evaluation is found under the heading 'Determining Causation'.

Finally, cost-benefit or cost-effectiveness analysis assesses the efficiency of a program. Evaluators outline the benefits and cost of the program for comparison. An efficient program has a lower cost-benefit ratio.

Determining Causation

Perhaps the most difficult part of evaluation is determining whether the program itself is causing observed impacts. Events or processes outside of the program may be the real cause of the observed outcome (or the real prevention of the anticipated outcome).

Causation is difficult to determine. One main reason for this is self selection bias. People select themselves to participate in a program. For example, in a job training program, some people decide to participate and others do not. Those who do participate may differ from those who do not in important ways. They may be more determined to find a job or have better support resources. These characteristics may actually be causing the observed outcome of increased employment, not the job training program.

If programs could use random assignment, then they could find a strong correlation or association. Causation is not something that can be proved through correlation.

A program could randomly assign people to participate or to not participate in the program, eliminating self-selection bias. Thus, the group of people who participate would be the same as the group who did not participate, and this would be helpful in

However, since most programs cannot use random assignment, causation cannot be determined. Impact analysis can still provide useful information. For example, the outcomes of the program can be described. Thus the evaluation can describe that people who participated in the program were more likely to experience a given outcome than people who did not participate.

If the program is fairly large, and there is enough data, statistical analysis can be used to make a reasonable case for the program by showing, for example, that other causes are unlikely.

Types of Program Evaluation

Program evaluation is often divided into types of evaluation.

Evaluation can be performed at any time in the program. The results are used to decide how the program is delivered, what form the program will take or to examine outcomes. For example, an exercise program for elderly adults would seek to learn what activities are motivating and interesting to this group. These activities would then be included in the program.

Process Evaluation (Formative Evaluation) is concerned with how the program is delivered. It deals with things such as when the program activities occur, where they occur, and who delivers them. In other words, it asks the question: Is the program being delivered as intended? An effective program may not yield desired results if it is not delivered properly.

Outcome Evaluation (Summative Evaluation) addresses the question of what are the results. It is common to speak of short-term outcomes and long-term outcomes. For example, in an exercise program, a short-term outcome could be a change knowledge about the health effects of exercise, or it could be a change in exercise behavior. A long-term outcome could be less likelihood of dying from heart disease.